"WILDCATS"
OVER CASABLANCA

To Those Who Did Not Come Back

Library of Congress Cataloging-in-Publication Data
Wordell, M. T. (Malcolm Taber), 1911–1996.
"Wildcats" over Casablanca: U.S. Navy fighters in Operation Torch / by M. T. Wordell and E. N. Seiler; as told to Keith Ayling; foreword by Peter B. Mersky.
      p. cm. – (Aviation classics series)
  Originally published: Boston: Little, Brown and Company, 1943.
  ISBN 1-57488-722-X (alk. paper)
1. Wordell, M. T. (Malcolm Taber), 1911–1996. 2. Seiler, E. N. (Edwin Norton),
1918-1945. 3. World War, 1939–1945—Aerial operations, American. 4. United States. Navy—History—World War, 1939–1945. 5. World War, 1939–1945—Personal narratives, American. 6. Operation Torch. I. Seiler, E. N. (Edwin Norton), 1918–1945. II. Ayling, Keith, b. 1898. III.Title. IV. Aviation classics series (Washington, D.C.)

D790.W6 2004
940.54'23438—dc22

          2004045148
ISBN 978-1-57488-722-8
(alk. paper)

Potomac Books, Inc.
22841 Quicksilver Drive
Dulles, Virginia 20166

First Edition

10 9 8 7 6 5 4 3 2 1

"WILDCATS" OVER CASABLANCA

U.S. NAVY FIGHTERS IN OPERATION TORCH

LIEUTENANT M. T. WORDELL, U.S.N.
AND
LIEUTENANT E. N. SEILER, U.S.N.R.

As told to Keith Ayling

FOREWORD BY PETER MERSKY

Potomac Books, Inc.
Washington, D.C.

Series Editors
WALTER J. BOYNE AND PETER B. MERSKY

Aviation Classics are inspired nonfiction and fictional accounts that reveal the human drama of flight. The series covers every era of military and civil aviation, is international in scope, and encompasses flying in all of its diversity. Some of the books are well known best-sellers and others are superb but unheralded titles that deserve a wider audience.

OTHER TITLES IN THE AVIATION CLASSICS SERIES

Ploesti: The Great Ground-Air Battle of 1 August 1943
by James Dugan and Carroll Stewart

Operation Overflight: A Memoir of the U-2 Incident
by Francis Gary Powers with Curt Gentry

Thirty Seconds Over Tokyo
by Capt. Ted W. Lawson

*New Heavens: My Life as a Fighter Pilot
and Founder of the Israel Air Force*
by Boris Senior

Contents

Foreword

PETER B. MERSKY, *Series Editor*

AS A child I must have checked out this book from the public library more than a dozen times. The librarian had to replace the lending slip because the previous one had my name all over it. In the intervening forty-five years, I saw *"Wildcats"* only once, appropriately enough at a Navy lending library in Washington, D.C. In 1992, author and publisher John W. Lambert used the title for his own book on Operation Torch. He worked closely with Mac Wordell, a VF-41 Wildcat pilot flying from USS *Ranger* (CV-4) and coauthor of the original 1943 book. Jack Lambert's monograph sheds new, more organized light on the often-confusing events and orders of battle of Operation Torch.

Still, there's nothing like having the original. After considerable effort, I was thrilled to find Ruth Wordell Packard, Mac's widow. Mac had died in 1996, and Ruth had remarried. After tracking her whereabouts, I was delighted to find that she was living only a few miles from me. Ruth proved to be informed and knowledgeable, and anxious to see her first husband's book once more in print in an updated edition. Without her interest and consent, we could not offer this classic wartime memoir to several new generations of readers.

As for the campaign itself, it began because of British concern over German influence in occupied France and its territories, particularly North Africa. Vichy French government controls in Morocco and along the northwest coast of the continent were merely window dressing for the reality of German mastery. The British had been fighting the fearsome Afrika Corps for more than two years. Under Gen. Erwin Rommel, nicknamed "the Desert Fox," the Germans had pushed the King's forces right to the wall, and although the Brits returned the fight in kind with typical British stoicism and resourcefulness, the Germans were still in control.

Four months before Pearl Harbor, President Franklin D. Roosevelt had met with British Prime Minister Winston Churchill to discuss a joint operation against French North Africa, something that appealed to the British because they feared having Germany gain the large French fleet and associated installations. However, recent British actions against French naval units to keep them from falling into German hands had stirred up tension with their traditional French antagonists, and London felt that to go into North Africa alone would only exacerbate the touchy situation. A campaign that included the United States in a starring role promised little resistance and eventual French cooperation. Reality was somewhere in the middle.

Although the French loathed their German occupiers, they accepted their new subservient role as long as the Germans kept their hands-on policy very low-key. The Allies would have to fight the Germans on their own, occasionally supported by the French underground resistance. Furthermore, whereas many French military men, along with refugees from countries previously conquered in the initial Blitzkrieg, had escaped to England to man special Free French units in the Royal Air Force and other services, many experienced pilots chose to remain in France and fly for the Armee de l'Air, even if it meant outwardly supporting the Nazis and fighting longtime friends such as the Americans. Indeed, among the Curtiss and Dewoitine fighter pilots that rose to intercept American and Royal Navy strike forces on 8 November 1942 were a number of seasoned aces with more than five kills to their individual credits, all against German Luftwaffe crews flying what were among the world's most advanced aircraft.

The Germans had made significant gains by June 1942, and a desperate Churchill flew to Washington to drum up support for an Allied invasion of North Africa. He found a ready ally in President Roosevelt, who lent his considerable influence to persuade congressional leaders that the time was now, not later. Planning continued through the summer, and the overall operation was handed over to Lt. Gen. Dwight D. Eisenhower, a protégé of Gen. George C. Marshall. In a rehearsal for the eventual invasion of Europe two years later, Eisenhower amassed a huge number of people, supplies, vehicles, ships, and aircraft for the campaign, which was called Operation Torch.

Finally, on 8 November 1942, the first of some thirty-four thousand troops came ashore at Casablanca. Another eventual thirty-nine thousand men landed at Oran, and another thirty-three thousand at Algiers. This last group included twenty-three thousand British troops. French ground resistance was sporadic, and although several naval units did manage to clear their harbor and sortie against the Allied task forces, the most determined resistance came from the various French fighter squadrons distributed along the coast. The Frenchmen in the Hawks and Dewoitines couldn't believe their predicament and wondered how the Americans could think of fighting them. After all, hadn't they been waiting for them for two years, and didn't they fly American-built aircraft? And didn't their aircraft carry the same American Indian headdress insignia as the Escadrille Lafayette? (The Lafayette Escadrille was a famous American-manned French fighter squadron in World War I.)

With Allied aircraft launching from twelve carriers (seven British, five American), supported by long-range aircraft from Gibraltar, the outcome was never seriously in doubt. However, nearly one thousand British and American soldiers were killed, along with seven hundred French defenders. Vichy commander Adm. Jean Francois Darlan signed the surrender on 13 November.

"Wildcats" Over Casablanca was one of a group of battle memoirs written right after the action. (Other such books included Ted Lawson and Bob Considine's *Thirty Seconds Over Tokyo*, which is the

classic account of the Doolittle raid on Tokyo in 1942, and Stanley Johnston's *The Grim Reapers*, which tells the story of VF-10, a Navy fighter squadron that had seen action in the Solomons.) The two authors, Mac Wordell and Ed Seiler, collaborated with a British-born writer to dash off the manuscript before they had to deploy once more. In Wordell's case, his career took him to the Pacific where he became an ace. Mac sailed without a chance to see the proofs for his book, and he was always concerned about occasional errors that had crept into the book. He took command of VF-44, recruiting several members of his squadron from *Ranger*, including coauthor Ed Seiler. Unfortunately, Lieutenant Seiler was killed in action on 22 January 1945, during a strafing attack on Japanese targets on Okinawa. Recommended for the Medal of Honor, he received a posthumous Silver Star. His friend and skipper, Mac Wordell, had to sign Lieutenant Seiler's final series of administrative and biographical papers.

Collaborating with youthful enthusiasm on *"Wildcats" Over Casablanca*, the two young naval aviators, recently returned from the North African campaign, tell their story—the plans; the breathless anticipation of first action; the surprise of combat and loss of friends; and in Wordell's case, of being taken prisoner after being shot down. Wartime security concerns required naming squadrons "Blue" or "Red," and holding references to ships to nondescript generalities. And no pictures. However, in this new edition, we have included a collection of photos that will complement the original text.

The Allied landing paved the way for the more expansive campaign into the African interior in pursuit of the Afrika Corps, and the eventual disruption of German control in northwest Africa. Torch was the first Allied offensive in the European theater and it allowed the commanders and rank-and-file servicemen to gain experience that would prove invaluable for the larger invasion that was to come, again on French shores.

The Fly on the Wall
Foreword to the First Edition

KEITH AYLING

WHEN I was invited to collaborate with Lts. "Mac" Wordell and Ed Seiler on the story of the experiences of the Red Ripper and its companion Navy fighting and scouting squadrons operating from a U.S. carrier during the opening of the second front in Africa, I jumped at the opportunity. For many months I had been looking for an opportunity of telling a simple, straightforward story of American fliers in battle. Here it was, a successful carrier action under unprecedented circumstances that passed with hardly a notice in the press, because the war correspondents and rewrite men had little conception of the history-making story that was behind the Navy communiques. For the first time, carrier-based aircraft had supported invading troops, and gained control of the air over hostile territory to enable military forces to take over airfields and prepare them for the occupation by land-based aircraft flown in from carriers, which had brought them from America.

These Navy fliers did their job in the face of severe, sharp, and increasing opposition by the Vichy forces. They were opposed by American-manufactured planes, as well as French aircraft. They themselves had

never been in action before, but they had been carefully trained for this action. They did their job with
swift and deadly efficiency, but not without losses in
men and planes.

After three days of hard fighting during which their
courage, doggedness, and efficiency were a shining
example to the American Navy's conception of modern amphibious warfare, the carrier returned to its
American base, a comparatively short time after leaving. Few people, not even the fliers' wives, knew what
had happened. The fliers themselves said nothing except that they had been "cooking with gas," and that
they hoped they would be in a bigger show soon.

The writing of this book has been a headache for
an author. Mac and Ed were just two members of a
squadron, which in itself was but a part of a Navy team
of squadrons, on an astonishingly well-handled carrier
commanded by Captain (now Admiral) Durgin, who
took his ship in and out of action in submarine-infested
waters with the sincere belief that the ship could fight
to its fullest efficiency if every crew member was kept
acquainted with what was going on, every day, and
every *hour* of every day.

How well Captain Durgin succeeded in his action
you will see in these pages. How much his command
and personality meant to the ship I learned when I sat
talking with him in his cabin after the action. The Captain knew what every man had done during the battle.
"I believe 'Popeye' kept a diary of what went on in the
ship," he said . "You should see it." I concluded Popeye
was a member of the wardroom. But Popeye was just a
seaman and the one man who could have had time to
write down these impressions, which helped so much

in the construction of this narrative, thanks to Captain Durgin's intimate knowledge of every man who served under him.

Wordell, Seiler, and I talked for many hours over the difficulty presented by the narration of this story, in which so many men were involved. Lieutenant Wordell naturally could only tell a small part because the geography of his position limited him to a few minutes of action. Lt. Edward Seiler was similarly plated because of the limitations of his pilot's cockpit.

Other pilots and other squadrons had played an equal part: in the story. Eventually we decided to use what Ed Seiler termed the viewpoint of the fly on the wall, who sees everything, hears everything, and is hardly seen himself. I have the honor of being that fly on the wall, but with the definite purpose of recording everything that happened on the ship, in the air, and back at the base where these typical American youngsters told their stories in their own varied American language. Occasionally you will find in the narrative the use of what is sometimes termed the editorial "we." This is not really an editorial "we" but the fly-on-the-wall "we," because the fly on the wall became to all intents and purposes a member of the squadron and of the ship's personnel. Without the use of this "we" the story would lose some of its dimension and would not convey an accurate impression of the team spirit of the Navy that unites fliers and the men who work the carriers from which they fly so closely together, in training as well as in action. This team spirit, bred on the football fields of America and developed to a high degree in Navy flying, has the quality of victory.

North Africa

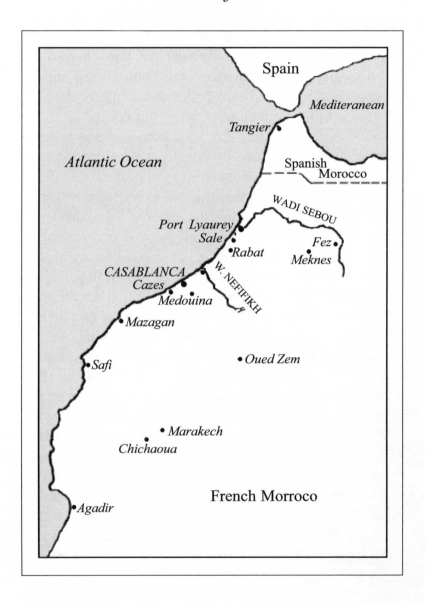

Spain

Mediteranean

Tangier

Atlantic Ocean

Spanish
Morocco

WADI SEBOU

Port Lyaurey
Sale

Rabat

Fez
Meknes

CASABLANCA
Cazes

W. NEFIFIKH

Medouina

Mazagan

Oued Zem

Safi

Marakech
Chichaoua

Agadir

French Morroco

Chapter 1

"WE KNEW we were really cooking with gas when the carrier got under way from the advanced base," said Lt. Mac Wordell, executive officer of the Red Rippers. "It seemed as if it were the real thing this time. Where we were going was where everybody could guess and nobody knew. It was to be action at last, that was my bet."

We had flown our planes on board and everything was ready for anything . . . so was everyone on the ship. It seemed as if everything about the carrier had changed too; as if she had taken on extra importance, plowing and plunging eastwards through the Atlantic swells. That we were heading east was something. We pilots of the Red Ripper squadron had been fretting for action ever since the outbreak of war. Before sailing from the advanced base we had been rehearing for something very definite. We had been trained to suppose ground troops in Texas months before, while at the island we had been doing strafing practice over beaches and gun emplacements. How we had strafed that "island"!

1

"It's funny how everybody gets wise to the same thing at the same time," said Ed Seiler. "The day we flew aboard, someone had said this was it, the Second Front, but somehow it seemed like scuttlebutt[1] then. And now we were really under way." The planes of the air group were in the hangar deck, stubby, dark gray–painted Grumman Wildcat fighters with their square-cut wings folded back. Half of them belonged to our companion squadron, which we shall have to call "Blue" squadron, and then there were the Douglas Dauntless dive bombers belonging to Lt. Cmdr. Pete Carver's scout-bombing outfit known as the "High Hat" squadron.

These Grummans are some planes—"exceedingly salubrious," as Lt.(j.g.) Hubie Houston would put it in squadron jargon. Hubie is the squadron "round man." With the rest of the pilots, he is most anxious to get into fighting and finish this war, which he figures is hindering his education and curtailing a great many of his other personal pursuits. All the men in the squadron call each other by nicknames—Hubie got his because he is surely the roundest man who ever sat in a fighter plane. He is a fighting man, too, quite a character, with a single ambition to try his Wildcat and its .50-caliber guns against the Germans or the Japs. Hubie would rather have the Germans; it's nothing but the best for him.

To get an idea of the squadron's spirit, new members are encouraged to read the story of our coat of

---

[1] Scuttlebutt—Navy slang for "rumor."

arms. The boar's head on our shield is taken directly from the one that graces a well-known gin bottle. The scroll under the head is a string of sausages, a good line of Bologna, which all members of the squadron should be adept at shooting. The balls on the shield might be termed balls of fire. The bolt of lightning is the bar sinister—a sign of bastardy. The whole group has been worked into a toast or creed with which the squadron members begin and end their gatherings. The squadron toast is, "Here's to the Red Rippers, a bunch of hell-raising, Bologna-slinging, two-fisted, he-man bastards."

That was how it was in 1927 when the squadron was formed and that's how it still is.

"That's how we are always," explained Mac Wordell, who is a solid, even-tempered New Englander, just half an inch off six feet in height. "The morale on this trip was wonderful—always has been. The boys put zest into everything. At the advanced base we had the gustiest, noisiest beer-party picnics that ever lighted up that respectable spot, even in the Golden Era when the cruise liners ran in. Now we were on the way to action and we were praying it would be action—this thing called morale was angels high.

"There was tension naturally. It grew with every mile we put behind us, but it was as exhilarating as hot coffee in a sub-zero temperature."

"At least," said Ed Seiler, who is cut on serious lines, quiet, dry of speech, and pinkly seraphic about the face, "we knew if this trip was really something, we shouldn't go through the war without firing a shot."

Ed is one of the boys in the Naval Reserve. He left Princeton to come into the Navy to fly and fight, but not for a career, like the Annapolis men.

"There are twenty-eight of us in all, who fly, all sizes and shapes and ages," went on Mac. "Quite a good bunch as men go. For months, some of us for years, we have flown together, trained, flown uneventful Atlantic convoy patrols. We have shot each other up in training combats, scared the life out of each other in dogfights, eaten and bunked together, and kidded each other all along the line. Each senior pilot has a wingman who flies with him and we each know pretty well what the other fellow is going to do. You can't be with men all that time and not know."

"Except that we hadn't been in the show then," remarked "Spanky" Carter. Spanky, a lieutenant, came into the Navy because he was crazy about flying. Now he likes the Navy so much he is going to stay. Spanky is squadron flight officer. Every squadron officer is assigned to one of the six major departments within the squadron, each officer usually having a specific job. This, incidentally, removes any idea that a pilot is in the Navy simply to fly. Flying may be his first love, but he has certain other responsibilities that require his attention.

"You have to meet the boys to appreciate them," said Ed. "Of course they are like other squadron types, but we feel there's a difference.

There's got to be that somewhere—everywhere, I suppose. It's that difference which definitely gives a squadron individuality and zest. Lt. Cmdr. Tommy Booth, for instance, the Red Ripper squadron leader, is one hell of a fine man. Tommy has got the good old U.S. Navy stamped on him. Lean and genial, he's a good straight shooter with just that touch of dignity that makes you respect him. Tommy would look like a Navy officer in his birthday suit. We pilots call the squadron leader 'Captain' by way of courtesy. Mac Wordell's a swell guy—just as Tommy is. A definite leader, a driver with a lot of laughs, a thorough, sincere man. He and Tommy Booth don't talk very much, but when they have something to say it's usually very much to the point."

There was naturally a lot of chatter on the first day at sea—and tension, as Lieutenant O'Callahan, the Padre, put it. It was the kind of tension you find in a football team before a big game, only this was an aircraft carrier and every man aboard was going to play in this game—there are no sidelines in carrier action.

The tension grew in the wardroom when scuttlebutt reported with considerable authority that Captain Durgin, the captain of the ship, was going to talk to the pilots. Everyone immediately began to give his idea of where we were going. Scuttlebutt flew here and there like a badminton bird. It was banged from the wardroom to the ready room and to the library and came back again cheerfully with a few more feathers of suggestion

tacked on to the first rumor. Even though we knew
it was only scuttlebutt, all of us were exceedingly
braced.

The most unforgettable day on the voyage out
was when we met over eighty ships that represented the main force of the first convoy. Nothing had ever been seen like this since the days of
the Spanish Armada. It gave a strong impression
of invincibility and, something more, it demon-
strated the efficiency of the Navy in that the rendezvous took place within five minutes of its announced time.

"The sight of that fleet in rendezvous in mid-
Atlantic was awesome," recalled Ed. "My first
thought was that I regretted I didn't have a good
seat at the bow. Being on the flight deck wasn't
high enough to see everything. You could see only
sixty-seven ships around the horizon—and there
were about two dozen more out of sight, but not
out of mind. Those flyers who were scheduled that
morning for anti-sub patrol were the lucky ones
because they could see the whole business at once.
The sky was clear blue; the sea was bluer, with
occasional whitecaps formed by the brisk sou'east
wind. Old Navy men with all their years of experience had never seen a show like this. There is a
time lag at sea that you don't experience ashore.
The ship proceeds on its regularly assigned course
. . . you hardly notice any relative movement of
the other ships. There is the queer silence of the
flight deck when the planes aren't in operation;
nothing seems to happen, but it's happening right

before your eyes. One hundred ships are meeting in the mid-Atlantic—and there isn't a bit of noise."

Activity on board the ship zoomed and there was plenty of noise. The crew was busy chipping off the paint on the hangar deck and making a hell of a din about it. Everything inflammable had to go. The constant banging of hammers and chisel on the ship sides was enough to drive you crazy. The banging on the lofty hangar deck echoed all over the ship. It sounded as if a thousand crazy Gremlins were battering on a cracked church bell with crowbars.

"The noise that ship was making was worse than anything I ever heard," went on Ed, "but it was a good noise to us, because it meant action. Aircraft carriers don't shed their pretty paint for nothing. The din began to get on our nerves a bit, though. It never stopped. You couldn't escape it even in the wardroom where the usual bridge and poker were going on. The romantic souls were writing letters to their wives and sweethearts, and the politicians and armchair generals were on their favorite topics. We could see that Mac was bubbling underneath that Navy calm he is at such pains to cultivate."

There was some other cultivation going on in the squadron. Chuck August, who is about six foot tall and on the handsome side, was cultivating the social side—writing letters. Chuck has never let on how many girls he writes to, but from the mail he turns out, even if each gets only two a week, they must be legion. Chuck had something else on his mind, or rather on his face. He was raising a bit of hair on his top lip and calling it a mustache. The general consensus is that Chuck wants to make himself a bit ferocious, or else he has seen too many Clark Gable pictures. He couldn't be content with an ordinary mustache. His had to be turned up at the ends: To get the desired effect he used to go secretly around the ship and swipe some goo from a pipe or plane to bolster up the sprouts when no one was looking. There was something significant about Chuck's mustache. I think he wasn't growing it only to increase his value as a fighting man, but that he had made a secret vow not to shave it until he shot down an enemy plane.

"If an enemy pilot sees that blowing in the wind," said Windy Shields of New Orleans, "the poor bastard will surrender without a fight before he gets it wound around his prop." Windy and Chuck are humorists above all. Both can give and take a lot of ribbing. The squadron would miss them.

Hubie is quite the opposite of Chuck. Hubie is on the short side, round—that's why he's called the round man—and tough. He's a fighting man and always eager to get on with the job. If there's any new gag word to be passed around, Hubie gets it and passes it on. You wouldn't suspect it, but underneath all his exuberance he is a thinker and quite a bit of a poet. Hubie loves music. It was he who presented the ready room with that invaluable jukebox which played incessantly through the action whenever we had time to listen. When he wasn't listening to that, or wisecracking, you would find him writing in a little black book.

We were a day out when the ship's executive officer called us to attention in the wardroom after dinner. Conversation snapped, and left a distinct and brittle hush as we stood up. Captain Durgin came in with a big smile on his face. The Captain is one of our veterans of Navy flying. The feeling you get about him is that the man who wouldn't go to hell with the Captain, or for him, wouldn't be a man. When you look at the Captain, it is easy to forget four stripes and remember only the man that wears them, as he puts some of his own spirit into you while you prepare for your task, and when he revives the atmosphere of the days of Paul Jones in expressing the Navy's appreciation of what you've done. The Captain was an athlete when he was younger. He still doesn't carry an inch too much flesh on him anywhere, and he walks as springily as the college athlete that he was.

He seemed as eager as we were as he looked around the room with a kind of "here it is" expression.

"Please be seated." There was a kind of ominous pause. We were bristling inside. We sat and stayed rigid. The Captain cleared his throat and began:

Gentlemen, I have a message that is of vital interest to you all and I would like to have you listen carefully. If you cannot hear don't hesitate to let me know. I am sure that it comes to you as no surprise that an operation against the enemy in which we are to participate is contemplated in the very near future; in fact, we are now headed for this battle area and will make no more stops between here and that point. I am sorry that the details as they were received during the past month or so could not have been made available to you. You, of course, realize the reason why such action on my part was not possible.

There are many of you whom I would have particularly liked to have had helping with the rather large task of analyzing and correlating the material furnished. This was not done for I felt that you could not be spared from your regular duties and stations especially now when there is so much to do in preparation for battle. Those to whom I have given the job of assembling, sorting out, and analyzing the enormous amount of information, orders and instructions received have had a full-time task even though they have had no watches or other collateral duty. This work will continue, requiring day-and-night study for the eight or nine officers detailed to handle this. The rest of you will have plenty to do in preparing your men and the material for which you are responsible.

Now to tell you something about our mission: The scene of our action, as you may have guessed, will be along the African coast, specifically French Morocco. The A Air Group will attack airfields, gun batteries, enemy ships, and airplanes, and will furnish air protection to our landing force in and around Casablanca. The B Air Group will do much the same in the area in and around Port Lyautey to the north of us, and the C Air Group will do the same at Safi some distance to the south of us. The D Air Group is to provide air coverage for the D and ourselves and also assist in the attack on enemy harbor installations at Casablanca. All this action will take place at dawn.

Just before dawn on the day of the attack a large amphibious force will land on a beach not far from us with the idea of capturing and holding all enemy installations and forces in the western part of French Morocco.

While the above operations are going on other operations of even greater size are to take place simultaneously or almost simultaneously along the Mediterranean shores of Algeria. I will tell you more of this operation at a later date.

This is the start of the real second front of which there has been so much talk. You may wonder why we start against the Vichy French in Morocco. The answer to that is easy. The Vichy French, ever since Laval has had control, have positively and definitely shown themselves to be friendly toward the Germans and unfriendly toward the United Nations. We know that they have permitted German and Italian submarines to use their ports, they have forced French civilians to go to Germany to work in war munition factories, they have harbored enemy forces in their ports and in many other ways have given aid to our enemies. Our attack on French Morocco is not with the object of gaining and holding territory from the French Government but to stop its being used by enemy forces. If the Vichy French do not attack us, we will not in any way harm them. We will, however, put an end to all Axis activities in French African territory.

The advantage of hitting the Germans and Italians in Africa are many-fold:

1. It is the most accessible and vulnerable flank of the Germans.

2. It will place us to the rear of Marshal Rommel's forces in North Africa and will make possible complete liquidation of his forces. This would relieve the British and ourselves of a long and costly supply line to this area via the Cape of Good Hope, and thus free much shipping and large military forces for use elsewhere.

3. It will give the Allies several locations through which to invade Europe, thus complicating Hitler's position on the continent.

4. It is by no means impossible that Italy will be forced to withdraw from the war.

5. The threat of a union of German and Japanese forces in the East or Near East will be eliminated.

6. The Axis will be deprived of its most important and most potentially dangerous bases for operation in the South Atlantic.

7. Dakar could be taken, or at least eliminated, as a base for German submarines and raiders

A second front at any point will raise the morale of the subjugated peoples in Europe and lower the morale of the Axis countries. Pressure on Russia will be relieved and the personnel in their armed forces will be vastly encouraged.

These are by no means all of the benefits to be gained but are enough to show you that if our operations, together with the similar operations along the Mediterranean coast of Algeria, are successful, and we are able to hold what we gain, a second front will then be definitely established and the war will be materially shortened.

You may remember I said when I first took command that we would have to work days and weeks and maybe many months getting ready for one big moment, and that if we worked hard and prepared ourselves well, we would be successful. I have been on this ship long enough to see what a hardworking, smooth-running organization and efficient group of officers and men I have under me. I have no doubt at all that when we do strike we will be successful and will return to our homes filled with satisfaction in knowing that we have accomplished our mission in a manner that is a credit to our country, our Navy, and ourselves.

There are, of course, many things still to be done and I want you to turn to these last few days to put the finishing touches on your training programs. Make sure you and your gun crews, lookouts, and all watch standers are always on the alert, that all of you know the various silhouettes of airplanes and ships so that you can readily and definitely identify our own and enemy aircraft, and that you learn and teach all of your men all you possibly can about fire fighting, damage control, and abandoning ship.

Do not forget that if any of you should be so unfortunate as to fall in the hands of the enemy, you are only required to tell your name and rank. Don't try to outsmart your captors because six or seven specially trained Gestapo agents can outsmart any one of us. Just remember all you need tell is your name and rank.

From time to time I shall let you know the progress we are making towards our objectives and give you all the information that I am permitted to tell. In the meantime I wish you would not discuss this matter in the presence of the men as I do not feel that we should let the whole ship's company know exactly where we are going to hit. I shall tell the men over the general announcing system as much of this information as it is wise to do at this time.

Last but not least, I want to tell you from the bottom of my heart that I am proud of you all. I expect great things because you have shown that you can do great things. Good luck and God bless you all.

A brief acknowledgment to us all and he had gone. So this *was it*. The Red Rippers were to have a leading part in the second front. "Cagey" Hammond, our squadron communications officer, strolled over to the notice board and came back a bit moody. "The British are licking Rommel headlong," he announced with considerable gloom. "Looks as if the whole of North Africa is going to be subdued before we get there."

"And the French won't fight," said one of the ship's officers, "the whole thing will be just a walkover."

A lot of us felt that way but we didn't want to say so. Later, the Captain sent for the squadron leaders. They were soon back.

"Fellows, you're in for a busy time," announced Tommy Booth briskly. "We're starting intelligence school after general quarters tomorrow. It will last all day." He spoke in his squadron-leader tone. "The Captain is relying on you fellows, that's why he's let you in on the show before anybody else on the ship. There will be no time for slacking. From what I can judge there is a hell of a lot to do."

Several huge packets of "paper" had been brought aboard at the advanced base, two tons in all. Immediately the news was broken; the Captain delivered them to the squadron intelligence officers and gave over his cabin to them. Out on the table they laid stacks of paper, guidebooks, and photographs. They plastered the hallowed walls with maps and notice boards. Lt. Fred Akers

and Lt. Bob Johnston, our squadron intelligence
officers, got themselves deep into the job of com-
piling information for our use. They were soon
wallowing in papers. Their job was to make out a
combat intelligence report for each pilot so he
would know the geographical aspects of the target over which he was to fly. He would have to
know the opposition he was likely to meet in the
way of aircraft and anti-aircraft fire. Their reports
were to show gun emplacements, aircraft hangars,
barracks, and spots we should avoid touching,
such as civilian areas, radio stations, rail tracks,
and bridges.

A ready room is an important part of a carrier. It is smallish and packed with comfortable
armchairs, of the type you get in private projec-
tion rooms of motion-picture companies. There
are usually a screen and a blackboard, and of
course the inevitable loud-speaker of the ship's
talker system. Ours had a jukebox, too, the one
Hubie had brought aboard. It was the squadron's
most treasured possession and it had become part
and parcel of the squadron life. The pilots assemble in the ready room before going into battle
and get their briefings and their pep talks. It's the
last room we see in our ship before we man our
planes. For many of us it becomes a kind of club.
We yarn there, sleep a bit, tell stories, and crack
the most atrocious jokes. "The funny thing about
a ready room is that you get attached to the hole,"
contributed Tommy Booth. "As much as you are
attached to the ship. It's more than sentiment. It's

an urge for protection. The loneliest feeling in the whole of a carrier pilot's world is when he's at sea with the gas running low, and he can't see his carrier. You think of the ready room then, and the noisy guys who make it the most desirable place in the world. It's your office, you live in it, it is the big thing in your life. It is in mine, and I know the other fellow feels the same about it. You sweat and worry in it, and grouse and argue, and you get mad at it when you can't hear yourself speak because everyone is yelling at once, but you're deeply attached to the place."

"Prof" Dowling, the squadron materiél officer, has a particular affection for the ready room. "The daily struggle of being still half-conscious and half-starved at 0550,[2] and having to stumble from one's sack to the ready room through a blacked-out pitching hangar deck, where every plane seems to look like a dinosaur's skeleton in Harvard's Museum of Comparative Zoology, is one of the most wearing moments of the engagement," he said. "But it surely is most satisfying to arrive at last in the lighted and air-cooled ready room, where one can resume one's sleep to the tune of somebody's reading of the ship's news or to the jukebox rendition of Harry James's 'You Made Me Love You.'"

This paperwork was colossal. There began to

---

[2] Navy time is based on the 24-hour clock. Thus 0550 is 5:50 a.m., 1400 is 2 o'clock, 2100 is 9 o'clock, and so forth.

flow from the intelligence officers a steady stream of material as well as the stuff they were getting out of those two tons of packages. The Captain's table was littered with a bewildering array. There were encyclopedias, Baedekers, French tourist guides, copies of the *National Geographic* magazine, and piles of photographs. The intelligence officers were working long after the pilots turned in and they kept it up most nights.

Classes started in the ready rooms, which are in the island on the flight deck. Tommy presided over one; Jack Raby, in command of the Blue fighter squadron, had another; Mac Wordell had a third; and the High Hat bombing squadron, skippered by Pete Carver, had the fourth.

"It certainly was rough on the boys," said Fred Akers. "At first they didn't seem interested, so we gave them hell. We had been waiting to jerk them up for some time. They weren't so keen to go back to school, as you can well imagine, but once we hammered into their heads the importance of getting this information right, they toed the line and did a good job. That's one of the things you notice about a squadron; men who have been living and working together and horsing around generally in their spare time suddenly get hep to an idea all at once. In three days those pilots' ability to observe and memorize increased 300 percent."

"We were hungry, that's why," contributed Ed. "I don't think any of us had ever engaged in such a concentrated study of geography; besides, those gedunks were very good."

"Well, we had to get you boys working, even if the only way to do it was filling your stomachs," retorted Fred. "One man not up to scratch could have ruined the operations."

"The gedunks," explained Ed, "started first as a penalty. The man with lowest score in the quiz had to buy gedunks all around. Gedunks, as you may know, are ice cream covered with syrup or chocolate sauce. We got them from the ship's service. We had to drop the penalty system very soon because everyone was eating too much, so we went on the prize system. Top man got the gedunk and the others had to watch him eat."

"Which sharpened the competition considerably," said Fred Akers, "but altogether the fellows did a good job. We made each man a map of his target and beat it the hell into him until he remembered every detail from trees to anti-aircraft guns. We put in everything except the blondes."

"I'll say you did," broke in Boyd Mayhew, nicknamed "Brat" and "Queenie"—leave it to him to say why. "When I got there I knew the place better than my home town. Quite a salubrious job for one so young, Fred."

After geography lessons came plane recognition. The intelligence officers gave us each a book of cards. "They're not for bridge or poker," said Mac, "just to help you guys save your lives." Each card contained a picture, a silhouette and armament details of the enemy aircraft we were likely to meet.

"Soak 'em in well, fellows," said Mac. "There'll

be no time for mistakes. If you don't know an H-75 from an ME-109 it will be just too bad."

Some of us must have gasped a bit inwardly. We were going to be up against American planes, the Curtiss Hawks, delivered to the French before the fall of France, and Douglas bombers. There was also a slick and sinister-looking French single-engine fighter, the Dewoitine 520, a useful-looking ship, armed with four small-caliber machine guns.

After dinner we got together for our plane-quizzing class. The pictures were shown on the screen by a reflecting projector, at first for as long as seventy-five seconds so as to identify them. Then time was stepped down. The boys were pretty good at that. We were soon getting down to recognition with a one-second flash.

Ship-recognition class followed. A Navy intelligence officer undertook this. There were more quizzes, more pictures on the screen, and more notes. No gedunks any more—everyone was getting extremely ardent for knowledge.

"Doc" Bell, the flight surgeon, contributed his part, an instructional lecture on the sanitary and hygienic aspects of Morocco. It seemed it was a very unhealthy place, with most of the water likely to induce dysentery. The food the Arabs would provide was to be avoided if we could do so without offending them. There would be lots of fleas, scorpions, spiders, malarial mosquitoes, and worms.

Outside, things were buzzing all over the ship.

At frequent intervals four-alarm fires would sound over the loud-speaker system. Crewmen in the areas dashed to their emergency posts. Everybody else carried on. Some of the men were gleefully practicing with machine-guns that had been set up at intervals along the catwalks. They were blazing away contentedly, as men will when authorized to handle these lethal weapons. They might serve us well, if we were attacked. The paint chipping was proceeding furiously, and all the linoleum had been taken up except that in the officers' country. The old carrier was beginning to look like a skinned cat. The weather was getting rough—the ship was pitching mightily and taking water over the flight deck. She came up from under the big combers like a submarine surfacing, making a lush, slashing noise. There wasn't much time to worry about rough weather—our studies went on all the time. School classes finished up with the code and visual signals to be used between the ground troops and the ships and the airplanes. We pilots had to commit these to memory and carry them in our heads, in case we were shot down. Two code terms were simple; no one could forget them: "Batter up" and "Play ball." Each had its own particular and vital significance in this bit of history we were going to make.

"The beginning of our little job of giving Hitler a body blow in Africa caught me in the bath," related Max Eaton of the High Hat scout bombers. Max is a short, spare, and sandy Bostonian. "I was in the shower when an unexpected call came to flight quarters," he said. "I was all covered with soap, and in no condition to go on a hop. But I was scheduled, and my plane was in number one spot on deck, so I took off with soap in my ears and with buttons undone. We went scouting for trailing subs some twenty-five miles astern, but there was nothing doing. We got back to the ship, jettisoned our depth charges, and landed aboard. The next day we were out again, challenging neutral ships. I encountered one about thirty miles on the beam. I challenged her, and this is how our conversation worked out:

Me : *Who are you?*

Ship: No answer.

Me: *Who are you?*

The ship had a light working and started sending, but she could only direct her light to starboard, and I kept getting out of range as I circled.

Me : *Who are you? Who are you?*

Ship: *Who are you?*

"Now there they had me. I certainly couldn't tell them who I was. So I challenged them again: *Who are you?*

Ship: *I have received your challenge saying "Who are you?" . . . Who are you?*

"I flew off in disgust. Who was I anyhow!"

One day we undertook the ticklish job of refueling. It was good to see the old tanker, plumply squat and maternal, come wallowing through the swell. Refueling in that kind of weather is a tough operation, but it went off according to schedule, with Wildcats from another carrier droning in wide circles overhead, keeping a lookout for subs. One of the ship's officers told us that the sea was lousy with them. Later, a destroyer came alongside. The word went round the ship—"Mail!" Everybody was rushing round, taking a look at the precious bags swinging aboard. The officer in charge of the transfer wanted something from us. The destroyer boys had run out of ice cream, which is pretty tough. Could we do anything? Our executive officer must have a touch of Scotch in him— descent—and finally he arranged a barter. We were to get copies of *Time* and *Life* in exchange for ten gallons of ice cream. These were the last magazines we were to see until some of us got back to America.

Every day now war news was appearing on the notice board and Commander Hoskins was reading the daily war communique over the ship's loud-speaker system, which shouts at you at any odd minute, in any odd place. The crewmen as yet did not know where we were going. The destination was being withheld from them just in case a sub got us and one of them might be captured. There seemed a good chance of this, too. The convoy would be a pretty good target for attack of U-boats. A communique told us that it was the biggest that had ever sailed, covering an area equal to that of the state of Rhode Island. Planes from another carrier were doing anti-submarine patrol. When the executive officer came on the loud-speaker system and read a message from the Captain to the crew, telling them pretty much what he told us, they were raised no end. The idea of the Captain taking all of the crew in on the show was something new. Even the mess boys were a little more alert.

With "Dog-day," the beginning of the operation, two days off, our squadron began combat patrols. General quarters was set at 0458, a bit early for those who like to stay in bed. It was rather eerie having to stumble across the blacked-out hangar deck to the ready rooms, but good practice for the real thing.

"The experience of going through a darkened ship at night is interesting, because it is contrary to all human laws," remarked Ed reflectively. "You have eyes, but you cannot use them—they're no good to you. There is absolutely no light whatsoever, except the dim overhead blue light at the center of the hangar deck, which isn't light at all—it's a blue shadow throwing a circle of pale blue on the hangar deck about twenty feet in diameter. To move through the hangar deck when it has planes requires four times the normal length of time, because you actually have to feel your way along. Old hands get used to memorizing the relative positions of all the planes the afternoon before, the next morning, which helps. It's dangerous, too, because if you're not careful, you may fall into one of the elevator pits or hit your face against a propeller or wing.

"They say a ship is human, but few people have brought out the fact that it's human because it has a definite human smell to it. If you took a ship's officer blindfolded from land and put him aboard ship, he would be able to tell you where he was, not because of the smell of sea air, or the particular kinds of noise, but because of the ship's individual smell. It's warm, musty—but not too musty; pleasant, clean, but a little oily; a combination of paint, grease, coffee, and sea air—all rolled into one, and the balance is one individual smell."

On Dog-day we would be up before sunrise. We had been dished out with dark glasses to wear in the ready rooms so that our eyes would be accustomed to taking off before daylight.

We hadn't been sitting very long before a report came that a strange plane had been snooping us. Fighter planes were ordered up to investigate. Mac went up with three others. He came back two hours later to say the strange plane had been identified. Later we heard that some fishing vessels had been trailing us to the northwest. A destroyer went after them and ordered them to proceed to Gibraltar. Then came an order: any plane in the vicinity of the convoy not belonging to a friendly belligerent was to be shot down.

That morning the pilots of each squadron were assembled in their flying gear on deck for photographs. Someone objected that Torpedo Eight, the squadron that did such a good job in the Pacific and lost so many planes, had had their picture taken—and only one man came through.

During the day the plane captains, crewmen who are responsible for looking after individual planes, got our Wildcats on deck. We settled in the cockpits and test-fired the guns. Then we took turns at combat patrols. Later photographic planes went up to test their gear and just before sunset the crewmen began loading clusters of incendiary bombs on the planes.

Tommy Booth gave us a final run over the operation. The Red Ripper squadron was to be divided into two parts for the action—one under himself and the other under Mac Wordell.

"The overriding principle of all this is that we are to take no action against the French unless they take offensive action against us first," said Tommy; "and bear in mind, all of you, that action contrary to this instruction might have repercussions far reaching in their effect."

"In other words, you can start a war just like that," echoed Hubie, *sotto voce.*

"And keep your hands off the gals, you Romeos," suggested someone in the background.

Tommy went on, "And don't use the radio until it's a case of 'batter up.' Then plain language, and no funny business."

"Batter up" meant hostile action and "Play ball" was a signal for us to take vigorous offensive action.

Our objectives were any French or German or Italian planes in flight, any on the ground with their engines running, or in formation ready to take off. All French vessels were to be counted as hostile, including any which attempted to get under way, either naval or merchant, or any at anchor which made an attempt to move. All submarines, except

those moored to piers, were to be considered like-
wise. We were to give as much support to the
ground attack as possible. Communication officers with equipment for ground-to-plane communication had been attached to the military landing
forces. We were to look for and attack columns of
troops moving towards their own forces, tanks, transports and light vehicles on the move, trains going
towards our beach heads, enemy supply and ammunition dumps, all troop concentrations and cavalry
movements. An enemy movement ten thousand
yards beyond the beach would be fair game until
our troops reached the point. We were warned to
take plentiful care to identify all tanks before
bombing them, as they might be our own outside
beach-head distances.

The squadron's priority defensive task was to
protect our own carrier and transports. At all costs
we were to avoid giving offense to the Moham-
medan population by avoiding damage to mosques
or to the Sultan's Palace. Even if Rommel or Adolf
himself got to such places they were still to be
avoided. Items not on the destruction list were
enemy fuel storage, and the radio stations at Rabat
and Casablanca. We were not to strafe bridges
over rails or highways, and we were to avoid destruction of the telegraph wires between Rabat and
Meknes and Rabat and Casablanca.

The ship's routine changed to battle order. At
supper a half-and-half seating arrangement was
introduced, so that if anything did happen, only
half the ship's officers would be in the wardroom

at the same time. The same thing went for the men. There were to be no mess lines on the hangar deck and never more than twenty-five mess tables set up at once. The men had been busy on aircraft identification as well as the pilots. The ship's orders stated, "There will be no more gedunk prizes for aircraft identification. Prizes will now be the safety of the ship. No mistakes allowed." The same old routine was going on though. Some guy had lost his pants at the laundry. Would whoever found them return them.

The pilots were served out with combat equipment; escape gear; medical supplies; fifty dollars in notes; and a passport, printed on white paper with explanations in French, Spanish, Portuguese, and Arabic, with the seal of the U.S. Government very prominently exposed on the cover and on every page. The Arabic said:

To EVERY NOBLE ARAB:

Greetings and peace of Allah be upon you. The bearer of this letter is an officer of the United States of America and a faithful friend of all Arab nations. We beg of you to treat him well, guard his life from every harm, and supply his needs of food and drink, and guide him to the nearest American encampment. You will be generously rewarded in money for all your services. Peace and Mercy of Allah be upon you.

Then there were instructions as to what we were to do on meeting an Arab in the desert.

"You note they say *desert*," remarked Tag Grell, our squadron engineering officer. "Personally I hope I don't have to meet an Arab in the desert. The air is good enough for me!"

The instructions said we were to ignore their women completely and to remove our footwear on entering their tents. Furthermore, we were not to expect breakfast if we stayed the night. The Arabs would offer a midday or evening meal and we were to drink the water they offered us, but not to fill our water bottles from their personal supply.

The fellows had to make a gag of the next information.

"Some of you will be in good company," remarked Prof Dowling. "Listen to this: 'The older Arabs cannot read, write, or tell the time—they measure distance by the number of days' journey'—just like Windy coming back from leave. '*Near* may mean ten minutes or ten hours. *Far* means over a day's journey. A day's journey is probably about thirty miles. The younger Arabs are more accurate.'"

Then we turned to like school kids trying out the useful words. "It's quite simple," said Bus Craig. "Water is *moyah,* you can't forget that; and near is *garceb*—it's simple; and far, which means you have to go a long way, is *baeed.* Just like *bad* only you *bah* it."

"So all you have to do, Buster, is to lie on your

back and make a noise like a sheep," retorted Hubie. "Seems to me it's a most pernickety and complicated language. Listen to this—'enemy . . . adoo-Ger-mani, Talini, and Sisiliani'—that's a hot one."

"That gives us four more names for these Nazi yokels—which is something," was Bus's contribution.

In addition to the passports and the escape kit, we were given a weapon that would turn a Boy Scout green with envy—a shark knife with a broad eight-inch blade, which we were to carry strapped to our legs under our pants.

That night we hung around with our minds pretty full. The orders were already on the board for Dog-day. They were headed "Battle Routine." General quarters was at 0400 with reveille at 0315. The Chaplain looked in. The Padre is a good type, a chunky, humorous-faced fellow who likes a smoke and a drink and the company of his fellow men, and is wonderful company himself. "Boys," he announced, "the Captain's going to allow me to give a blow-by-blow description of the show. We'll be able to keep everyone posted." He was excited, delighted with being allowed to serve, and a bit keyed up like the rest of us. He hung around for a while; then, at the door, he announced, "and there'll be Mass in the library at 0300 for anyone who likes to come." A big smile—everything about him is big—and then, "Needless to say, I'll be pleased to see *all* of you. I said, *all* of you!"

"There's one thing about the Padre," said one of the ship's officers—"He looks like a sailor. Somehow I can't imagine him anyhow else. They say the U.S. Navy has the best type of Padre of any service. I believe it."

"How could any man be anything but the best type if he has to go down to the sea in ships, with men like you?" his companion at table solemnly kidded him through the smoke haze.

The Padre is definitely a "character" in spite of that crack. There isn't a man on the ship that doesn't respect him, and recognize him as a real friend, which is as it should be.

Ship's orders were carrying a note for the anti-aircraft guns. "Lead that target and you will not be a target."

A new war communique said that Rommel's retreat was assuming the proportions of a rout and the Germans were leaving hundreds of planes behind. The British had been dropping pamphlets on Unoccupied France telling them that while we might invade their colonies we were doing so to liberate them and not to conquer.

Then came the news that Admiral Darlan, upon inspection, had found the shore defenses of Morocco satisfactory. (But the editor had facetiously noted, "Little does he know what's ahead of him.") For once, at least, we were in advance of war news instead of behind.

"Don't forget that Rommel has retreated before," warned the communique. "And remember we have been continually chased by and are now surrounded by enemy submarines."

This news was particularly cheering to the junior pilots who slept under the hangar deck in what is known as torpedo heaven—a nice, comfy little spot under the waterline. Somebody suggested that it wouldn't be a bad idea to sleep in the ready room so they could be ready for duty.

You can almost smell torpedo heaven from this good-humored poem someone extracted from Hubie's mysterious little black book.

ODE TO THE BUNKROOM

Deep down in a dark and dusky dungeon,
Who never take baths, not even a spongin',
With never fresh air in a foul-smelling room,
No music or pictures to lighten the gloom,
Five young rascals loggy and droopy-eyed stay
With beat of ole motor that runs night and day.
Now two were just married, the other three not,
And two of these known far and wide as a "sot,"
And all are as different as ever you've passed–
You'll ne'er find five people in such a contrast.

Now one of these men the circuses seek
To be in a sideshow featured as a freak;
From North Pole all down to the Antarctic frigid
You'll ne'er see a more remarkable midget.
To all he's the size of a grammar school child[3]
And to treat him as such he's considerably riled.

Old women are apt to pat him on the head
Late at night and say "Sonny, you'd better to
        bed."

_____
[3] Harris, the short man.

And give him a nickel because he's so cute.
Then he scowls and stamps and cusses to boot
And grows a mustache and smokes big black
    seegars,
And hangs round saloons, standing at bars,
And runs with bad women, if there are any that
    short—
So 'tis generally agreed he's quite a young sport.

Another is a foreigner you'd swear if you've
    heard,[4]
Cause I'm damned if at first you'll catch even
    one word.
His jargon is crossed 'tween a Chink and a
    Geech
'Bout fifty percent we attribute to each.
He too wails and gedaddles around all the night
And always makes of himself quite a sight.

Of the two married men there can little be said—
Just mooning and sighing around in their bed,
And half of their time spent in writing long
    letters
About ten to each one they receive from their
    betters.
But we're convinced they don't think
    nighttime's for sleepin'
For the profits of marriage they've been always
    a-reapin'.

---

[4] Pete Bolt, who comes from South Carolina.

The last is a saint when to them he's compared.
'Tis a misfortune with such a crew he is laired—
With a runt and a furriner 'n' two mournful
mutts,
'Twill be a wonder, I'm sure, if he doesn't go
nuts.

We settled in the wardroom for a cup of coffee and a game of cards, but tension was soon tiptoeing through the room. There was one thought in everybody's mind—would the French resist? The opinion that they would not was dominant. The argument became fierce in places. "I tell you," yelled someone, slapping the table, "the French will fight anyone, and anyone means us this time." Bus Craig and Hubie got into an argument on the subject that was quite a dog-fight. It ended with Hubie's siding down to the ship's service for cokes. Just another excuse for him to live up to his reputation as "round man." The cokes didn't come, so Hubie went down to investigate, and when he came back he got busy with the little black book. Hubie eats, talks, and sleeps, talks, eats, and argues and flies, but what does he think? Only the black book knows that, and we have a suspicion that his best thoughts are only committed to the little black book when he is mad at life, or Bus Craig, whose wingman he is.

Our poker game suddenly broke up for a quiz.

"But school's over," protested Ed in disgust. "What kind of a ship is this? Aren't we going to get any time for play?"

"Play?" said Tag Grell. "This is war."

"War, my foot," cracked back someone. "The French won't fight."

Tommy and Mac came in. "Boys, we're turning in. We've got to be up early in the morning."

Tommy, who isn't given to sentiment, managed to tack "good luck" onto his "good night."

Most of us turned in. Ed, on his way to torpedo heaven, heard a crew man scuttlebutting. "We've already made contact with sixteen submarines, I tell you. Big babies . . . they had swastikas on their conning towers too—but we dodged them. A tin fish missed us by inches."

"You get thirty days' leave if you get torpedoed," confirmed the other in a Texas drawl. "I haven't had leave for a hell of a time."

In torpedo heaven one of the pilots was sitting on his bunk contentedly playing with his shark knife.

Someone was snoring like a bull horn.

What morale!

Chapter 2

WE TUMBLED into the ready rooms early on Dog-day, 8 November—at 0400 to be precise. The morning was pitch black with cold pale pinpoints of stars overhead. The boys were pretty quiet, as they shook off their sleepiness. Getting up at that hour is uncomfortable. We sat blinking like owls in a searchlight for a while. With all our gear on, the Mae Wests and whatnot, the seats weren't any too large. Mac and Tommie were already up. Doc Bell was on hand to spray the nose of anyone who wanted such treatment. Some of us had colds, and you can't get to top efficiency if you have that kind of trouble.

Tommy called everyone to attention as the Captain came in. "Stay where you are, gentlemen," he said. "You'll be more comfortable. I've just come to wish you good luck and to say I've the greatest confidence in you pilots."

We began to cheer. Someone started singing, "He's a jolly good fellow." We felt that way. The Captain's cheery manner had a tremendously uplifting effect on us. When you can sing that so early in the morning you must be feeling good. The squadron was feeling extra—plus—come what might.

"Thank you," he said. "I feel that way about you, and if any of you think we're not going to have a show, we are—I have just had the news that the French are resisting strongly at Safi where our troops are landing."

The Padre, who is usually at the Captain's heels, was there too. He came in smiling. Ed says the Chaplain always reminds him of his football coach at school. Certainly the Padre is the kind of muscular Christian who you know could pull you through anything.

"What should a chaplain say to pilots who are gathered in the ready room getting their last-minute instructions before flying off to meet the enemy?" said the Padre, with a great deal of relish in his rich bass voice, as he recalled the scene. "A little banter, a serious word, and then a little more banter. A sort of sandwich seemed the ideal thing! I got the banter, of course. The Padre always does.

"Directly Mac spotted me he led his boys in a nifty little ditty they had improvised as a theme song specially for me. These lads began to sing, 'Happy Dog-day to Padre, happy Dog-day to you,' which was very flattering I'll admit.

"Of course I had to stand there patiently while Mac was doing his Tommy Dorsey stuff, but in a more robust style. At the end I took a bow, and someone at the back began another song. "Hey, not that one," warned Mac. "It's not fit for the Padre's ears."

"'The banter is still on, Mac,' I kidded, 'so you teach your squadron to sing that kind of song.' I was trying to be jocular and not to lay the Padre stuff on too strong, because the boys knew what I'd come for, and this banter stuff was their way of showing me that morale was good. 'That's just why I came here, to counteract such influence!' I said. I was getting along better and gaining confidence. In my mind was a picture of the others at Mass earlier. Jack, the leader of Blue squadron, and the fightingest, toughest of them all, had been there. Jack said he was coming every morning while it lasted. 'Now seriously, Mac,' I said, 'I came down here to suggest that we say a short prayer asking God's help for the work ahead. I mentioned this in last Sunday's service, which by the way a few of you didn't attend.' It was mighty few, but there was an excuse for the pilots because they were studying. 'As I said, our principal prayer should be not that we come out of the fracas unscathed, but rather that we do a good job.'

"'Hear, hear,' said someone at the back. I blessed him secretly for that and went on. 'To accomplish our task successfully is our object, so let that be our prayer to God. I'm going to say the Lord's Prayer and the Act of Contrition. Then I shall give General Absolution—this last principally for the Catholics among you, but we will let you non-Catholics in on it.' I delivered this one with the touch of the geniality they expect from the Padre. 'It won't do you any harm.'

"'We'll play ball, Padre,' said one of them, and I proceeded.

"The boys joined in the Lord's Prayer fervently and we stumbled through the Act of Contrition.

"I finished with the solemn words, *'Ego vos absolvo ab omnibus censuris et peccatis, in nomine Patris et Filii et Spiritus Sancti!'*—profoundly affected myself.

"I remembered that some of the boys, who had thought so little of religion in their lives, were going out to face battle and death for the first time. It was not that they were unbelievers, but youth is careless.

"The conclusion had been a trifle solemn, as I had wanted it to be. I saw that it had penetrated deeply into some, as it should, so it seemed appropriate to ease off in a lighter vein. There was a silence afterwards, which they were waiting for me to break. A padre is never quite sure whether his ministrations have touched his fellow officers and men, or just made them feel uncomfortable. 'Now Mac,' I advised, 'don't go and spoil my good influence by teaching them another not-fit-for-the-Padre song, or you'll be hearing from me.'

"'What they learn when I'm not there, Padre, is no one's business,' chuckled Mac, and that was that. They began yelling, 'Good luck, Padre,' and 'Thanks, Padre.' Their voices followed me back to the library. They were fine kids, the kind only Democracy can breed, and I'm not being sentimental in saying that. You can't live and work on ships with American boys without seeing that. It is the most salubrious thing about them. Yes, I said salubrious—even a padre catches the squadron's slang."

A bulletin came through. President Roosevelt had spoken in French to the French people. A task force supported by the R.A.F. was landing in North Africa. "There may be no resistance in our sector," reminded some pessimist. That meant that as our tasks were over Casablanca and Fedala we wouldn't see any action.

We didn't have long to wait. The news came through that the position of the carrier was about fifty miles off Casablanca and they were taking our planes to the flight deck.

Tommy looked in. "Boys, as I've said before, our primary mission is to cover the landing," he said. "I'm taking my formation to Cazes first. We'll take the first attacks. You are to make for Fedala and hang around till we need you." He finished with the good old squadron-leader tone. "Now I don't have to tell you fellows any more—keep in your sections, and stay in pairs. Good luck to all of you."

Mac took over then—a pep talk, direct as hell. "It is radio silence until we meet trouble. Get that. Remember the rendezvous, and for God's sake don't go straying all over the sky like a bunch of falling leaves. Got our rendezvous straight?"

"Saddle rock," we yelled. Saddle rock was a spot near Medouina airfield where we were to go if we got separated.

"Good, I guess that is everything. Good luck and good hunting."

The scouts, husky-looking Dauntless bombers, had taken off at 0645 before the fighting to attack any naval forces the Vichymen might dispatch against the transports. They assembled over their targets at Casablanca at ten thousand feet, circling like dark birds of prey. Until the defenders attacked they would not "play ball."

The Dauntless scout bomber is a two-place, single-motored airplane carrying a pilot and a rear-seat gunner and is designed for scouting and bombing. It is properly designed on rugged lines, to withstand the strain of steep, high dives and attacks by anti-aircraft guns. How sturdy these Dauntless bombers are is shown by the fact that one returned from a sortie in the Pacific with 214 bullet holes.

Back on the carrier fighter command officers waited tensely. The planes had not spoken yet. Only a few static crackles had come from the ship-to-plane radio.

Then, from the pillboxes along the Casablanca jetties there appeared orange stabs of fire, and the upper air was spattered with black blots of smoke. It was battle.

There was pride in the Padre's voice as he went on with his story.

"We heard it over the plane-to-ship radio," he said. "The news that Pete Carver of the scout-bomber squadron had encountered opposition was the signal we were in action.

"Carver called back, 'Batter up.' 'Play ball,' answered the ship. 'Good luck.' From that moment the air was becoming crowded with dramatic little messages of pilots talking to each other, giving orders and advice, and going down to do their jobs. We were living drama on the ship. There was no need for me to dramatize anything that happened."

"It was quite dark when we were ready to take off," said Max Eaton of the High Hats. "Going into action for the first time is something you're inclined to remember. Little things that are ordinarily unimportant stick in your mind. I spoke to Shackleford, my radioman, before getting into my plane. He's just a boy. I remember giving him a few conventional reminders about the oxygen or something, just as if it were nothing more than a hop back home. There was a pal of his standing beside the cockpit and talking conversationally, but excitedly. I heard him say, 'Do you want me to keep your ring for you?' Shackleford answered rather solemnly, 'No, I'll keep it.' I sensed that the guy who was kibitzing wasn't exactly boosting morale, so I interrupted the conversation, and young Shackleford smiled at me as if he knew why I was doing it. We took off in good style and headed towards Casablanca and there I got my first glimpse of the Old World. I had always planned to make the trip, and here it was, the shore between Casablanca and Fedala. Perhaps I didn't see it at its happiest moment. There was an oil tank afire somewhere and sheets of flame were stabbing the darkness as our ships let go. The thing that really jarred me with the stunning reality that it was war was, some little black dots on the field, lying motionless. I knew that was as far as some American kids ever got.

"We turned for Casablanca and, as we approached, black puffs of smoke blossomed out in front of us. That was flak, but it seemed unreal and entirely without menace. The skipper turned left and wheeled around the city in a wide semi-circle. Dawn came fairly quickly as if someone had turned up the lights on a stage setting, and there was Casablanca suddenly gleaming in the daylight. It made me excited to see it that way, and the harbor looked just exactly as our maps and photographs had indicated. It was like seeing a place where you think you've been before and finding it just as you imagined. We went around in a wide circle. There were no fighters yet, so we hugged in formation. The anti-aircraft puffs were getting closer and closer as the gunners found the range and deflection. Two of them jolted my plane, but I didn't worry them because we were straightening out for a dive. I could see the planes ahead starting down. The harbor beneath us was a mass of twinkling lights. That is what it seemed at first. It reminded me of Coney Island. Then as another shell burst near and jolted my wing, I realized it wasn't Coney Island. Those weren't lights, they were machine-guns, spitting at us.

"We had no trouble finding the submarines moored against the Jetée Delure. The *Jean Bart* began to throw up everything she had. The stuff was going wide. I took my aim at the sub formation, and held it all the way down. As I came near, red tracer was coming right for my nose and streaking by over the wings. You get a strange feeling of aloofness as the stuff goes by.

"I remember feeling that I couldn't miss. I couldn't, it didn't seem possible. I released and pulled sharply on the stick. Then followed some rather desperate moments that elongated themselves astonishingly. I shoved the throttle wide-open, jerked the prop into low pitch, and the plane suddenly lurched ahead as I closed the diving flaps. But it seemed centuries before I could get out of range. The Jetée underneath had burst out into a new rash of flickering gun flashes. I jerked as something burst very near, changed course violently and headed out to sea. Puffs of anti-aircraft were trailing behind me from astern and there was a lot of stuff hitting the water. Ahead of them I could see the others. A mighty fine sight. I noticed a few French fighters were waiting for us as we came out of the dive, but they didn't press their attack. Some of our radio gunners opened up at them.

"Directly we got back into formation, we raced for a blessed cumulus cloud cover. Then I saw anti-aircraft puffs bursting like black roses behind one of the guys ahead and to my left. Each successive burst was getting nearer and so we changed our direction and scooted off to starboard into more clouds. As I got nearer the ship, I remember that I hadn't looked back after the pull-out. I tried to, but it had been almost impossible to do it."

The Padre went on with his story.

"The pilots had been told to minimize their conversation but sometimes the human touch burst through the official parlance like a brightly colored light, and remained through the action, a dramatic high spot of a series of thrilling encounters. This is the kind of thing we heard when the dive-bombing squadron got a message from the ship to silence a heavy shore battery that was shelling the landing troops. 'O.K., we'll fix it,' said the squadron leader laconically. Some time would elapse, and then we would hear him over the target talking quickly to his pilots. 'I'll start you down in a minute. Don't mind that anti-aircraft fire. It hasn't been anywhere near us yet. Now remember to adjust your flaps. Ready? Let's go.'

"Radio silence again, then I was saying a silent prayer for those kids going down into that anti-aircraft fire. The officers with me who had time to listen to this strange drama of war looked at each other, but said nothing."

Just before 0700 the loud-speaker blared suddenly, "Red squadron pilots man your planes.

"We ran up to the windy flight deck, our chart boards and pistols clanging noisily against the ladder rails. Outside, we each went to our individual plane, ducking under wings and propellers, and scrambling into our cockpits.

"All you can hear at times like this," said Ed, "is the sound of running feet, the wind, and the clatter of the pilots climbing up. There is little talk except for intermittent commands. Those hinged steps in each plane to aid in climbing up make a definite snapping sound as your foot leaves the step. I'll always associate that snapping sound with the business of manning your plane.

"The flight deck isn't noisy, it isn't a madhouse or anything like that. There is a quiet urgency, efficient speed, hurry-hurry-hurry—but hurry efficiently. How many shots to prime this engine? The plane captain holds up two fingers. The bull horn blares: 'On the mark, the time will be 0700'—pause—'Ten seconds to go!' . . . 'Mark!' We synchronize our clocks. Then comes the bull horn again: 'Check all wing lines, wheel chocks, and propeller clearances. Stand by to start engines.'

"Hurry-hurry-hurry, but carefully! Give her two shots. O.K. Again the bull horn: 'Stand clear of propellers.' The handling crews winding the inertia starters for the scouts' bombers yank out their cranks and stand clear. Starting cartridges are inserted in the fighters, and we wait for 'Start engines.' Four dozen airplanes engage their engines, and the quiet of the deck is gone. As the engines break into a roar, smoke from the exhaust stacks whips back among the planes and disappears over the fan tail, carried by the twenty-five-knot wind across the deck. The engines settle down to moderate revolutions per minute, while each pilot checks all his instruments, pressures, fuel system, operation, flaps, and so forth. If you treat your

plane right and watch its pulse and temperature
before you make any demands on it, it will carry
you to hell and back. 'O.K., all set.' God, this is
exciting. You know you're set, you've got a good
plane, you've got a good job to do, you're working with a swell bunch of men. You're ready.

"Each pilot signals a thumbs-up O.K. to his
plane captain. Getting on the flight deck early in
the morning, as dawn is breaking, is like a scene
from a movie. Shadowy figures in silhouette seem
to dance round the planes. There are planes in
front of you and behind you, shadowy, sharply
silhouetted, and closely packed together. The dark
outline of the ship's 'island' is framed clearly
against the growing light of the dawn. You are
conscious of the black etched lines of the bridge
of the foretruck, and of the battle flag whipping
in the wind. In the dawn light, everything looks
much bigger than it actually is."

The crewmen were bristling with excitement.
"Good luck, sir!" "Give 'em hell." The plane captains tucked in their pilots as tenderly as mothers
putting their babies to bed. The propellers began
to turn in indecisive jerks. One by one the engines
began to purr, the exhaust manifolds spitting out
purple sparks which looked like pygmy gun
flashes in the gloaming. The noise of the motors
became suddenly deafening, concerted itself into
a roar, and then subsided into a steady moan. One
by one the planes began to creep forward to their
positions for the takeoff.

"As you go forward you are turned over to

the flight-deck officer," continued Ed. "He is the big man of the flight deck, who controls all the takeoffs, the intervals. He stands next to the island braced against the wind. He points to you with his left hand, wags his forefinger at you quickly to make you open up to full throttle as you test your oil and fuel pressures and check your magnetos. 'Everything O.K.?' 'Right,' you nod at him. He looks ahead to check the interval of the last plane that took off, holds his flag up and then quickly drops it. As you release the brakes, the plane leaps forward, its tail swishing to and fro as you adjust the rudder to take care of the increased torque. For a while the tail seems to dance, rather like a ballet dancer, and then settles as you get speed—more and more speed. You approach the bow, and the plane begins to feel lighter and lighter, becoming buoyant, and suddenly you are away from the frantic noise of the flight deck and alone in the humming silence of your own plane. It is the most terrific change of atmosphere a human can experience—as if an express train suddenly passed you, standing on the platform of a local station, leaving only silence—vibrant, electric, but almost peaceful."

One by one the Wildcats took off into the morning sky. Over the ship they circled noisily, gaining height, and then, forming into their sections, they flew southeast to their targets at high speed.

Squadron leader Booth led the formation of eighteen planes divided into two sections, which were each made up of four plane sections, pilots flying in pairs. Spanky Carter led the second division.

There's a mighty sweet charm about flying in formation, and beauty as well—that roaring mechanical beauty the pattern of which man has borrowed from nature. The basic formation of all air forces is the V pattern used by wild geese to protect themselves. The geese knew a thing or two when they started their long migrations in those great arrow-headed formations, spreading across the skies, each bird flying on the leader, and with sections of tough old honkers on the flanks and bringing up the rear. The squadron flew into battle, a convoy of flying guns on dark wings, the formation cutting a straight swift pattern through the morning sky. Each pilot in his closed cockpit was shut away in a vacuum of silence, seeing the outside, but hearing nothing of it.

The comfort of a formation is something that only a pilot can understand and appreciate. Men who have been in action many times against Jap and German have waxed ecstatic in their leisure hours on the great and mighty confidence they have extracted from the sight of another airplane constantly in view bobbing and sliding along the airways. To them the sight of that other pilot crouched over his controls, behind the slivering circle of his propeller, is the citadel of their strength in the air, the red meat to appease the hunger of loneliness that at one time or other assails the cerebral stomach of every flier. To have friends around you, to know they are as efficient as you yourself, that their machines can do what yours can, that they will follow you to hell, is as warmly comforting as a fleecy woolen blanket on a cold night in a freezing hunting lodge.

Some pilots become lyrical about their wingmates. You get on with a man in the air, and you make yourself like him on the ground. If he has flown in step with you on the vertical flank where your work is, where you are going to play the game of life or death for both of you, you can forgive his bad habits on the ground. You and he are a secret society, obligated to each other perpetually, closer than you can perhaps ever realize.

In the wardroom, on the way over, a half-finished letter was lying around. It began, "My darling Wing-mate." The subsequent expressions of masculine tenderness led even the most cynical of us to believe that it could not have been addressed to anyone aboard, so the obvious conclusion was that the writer was about to take himself a wife, or was writing to the wife he already had, because when a flier allows his imagination to cast such binding garlands of emotional blossoms round a female, it is a sign that he means business. In other words, though this may be secret information for men only, if a man calls a gal "wing-mate," he's probably going to take his course on her at whatever altitude she flies.

"It was just daylight when we got over the target," said Tommy. "The sky had cleared, and it was quite a fair day, with good visibility except for some cloud mist about two thousand feet above the ground. The sea was coloring up to a dark blue flecked with whitecaps."

"While we were about five miles from the coast," said Ed, "we came upon a beautiful sight— a gigantic U.S. battleship and her accompanying destroyers were whamming away with broadside after broadside at various Vichy ships which were standing out of the harbor, smoking heavily. You could see their wakes plainly sketched on the surface of the sea; at intervals their guns spit out orange plumes as the shells screeched across.

"We got over the coast at fifteen thousand feet. Beneath us the invasion was making good progress. I could see two of our big battleships turning in slow wide circles and blazing away at the French coastal batteries.

"Some ship threw up a pretty accurate A.A. barrage, as a warning to us to keep clear, so we changed course. The destroyers supporting the landing were snicking here, there and everywhere like disturbed water beetles. To the east our transports were plainly visible, formed up in rows protected by planes and surface ships. Every now and then clusters of little dark oblong shapes would shoot out from their sides and fan out, to join the rendezvous circle which turned around the mother ship until all landing barges had joined up. Once all the assault boats were together, they would start in to their objective, leav-ing their tiny feathery wakes.

"We crossed the coast heading towards our

target, which was Cazes airfield. Africa at least looked just as we had expected, thanks to the good intelligence work. The beaches showed up like bleached ribbons speckled here and there with dark rocks.

"Long, white combers were rolling onto the beaches. These combers were dangerous for landing barge operations, so they had to be avoided. The amount of cultivation was surprising—orchards, vineyards, fields of grain. The predominating color of the countryside was a warm brown, with the white houses standing out sharply, like cubes of sugar scattered everywhere. There were belts of sagebrush, roads lined with palm and eucalyptus trees, and little red-roofed farmhouses surrounded by lush green crops. To the northeast, the great city of Casablanca shone, like a giant white palace or super-hotel.

"Cazes airport, our target, has a green surface and runways, with rust-covered hangars. There was no sign of movement, but French aircraft could be observed on the ground. The fighters were dispersed to the north, with the bombers to the east. From below, the airfield anti-aircraft guns were beginning to blast at us. I noticed one of them blow out a huge smoke ring. The flak didn't seem to be anywhere near us. It was hostile action though. We were at war with Vichy!

"Tommy called back to the ship, trying not to sound excited; 'Batter up.' The reply came, 'Play ball.'

"'Here it is, boys,' Tommy told his group.

'We're going in. Keep together.'

"'O.K., Captain, O.K.'

"I told Lieutenant Carter to keep his section above the airfield to support our attack and drive off any enemy fighter opposition," said Tommy. "There wasn't anything in view but it might come at any moment. One quick look back at the upper sky behind us, and we went in. Our first objectives were the anti-aircraft gun pits, the positions of which we knew. As we came in low they sent up a tremendous fire. All at once merry hell came spurting out of that quiet green carpet. Everywhere were puffballs of smoke and lines of tracers stretching out toward us like red fingers. There seemed to be many kinds of flak, but it wasn't giving us any trouble. We blasted one gun emplacement though, and got away. I called back to the ship that I was sending the rest of the section down to attack. The guns we had attacked were out of action."

"That order didn't last long," remarked Spanky Carter dryly and with some contrition. "We ran into trouble—and plenty. We came in from the west to attack planes on the ground in drill order. As we got near, an anti-aircraft gun the French had installed behind a fuel dump opened up. They gave us all they had. The air ahead was sizzling lead and smoke. I heard something crack against my machine. I couldn't see where I was hit, but as a lot of the stuff was coming pretty near, it was more than probable I got away over the target and headed to the rendezvous. The rest of the boys weren't in view. I heard Windy calling to Bud Furney, his section leader, and gave him my position. Windy Shields, wingman of the last element of Lieutenant Carter's section, had taken the full blast of the anti-aircraft fire. As he came in close to the ground his windshield fogged and he was blinded temporarily. "I thought they were hitting me and I got mad," said Windy. "I'd get that gun if it was the last thing I ever did. I had been mildly scared at first with that funny feeling in my stomach, but it went just like that. I began to bawl at them, and gave her the gun as I came in with a sight dead on the gunners. I could see their faces. I gave them a long burst with all six guns. As I turned back I saw other Wildcats coming in. The gun wasn't firing any more. That made me feel kind of good, until I found I was lost.

"It's a hell of a feeling when you find yourself alone in the air, and your leader is nowhere to be seen. I could see fires starting on the airfield and shellfire over the front with big columns of smoke rolling up. I called Furney again. There was no answer. Then he came in view, giving me a thumbs-down on his radio. It had failed so when I got to the rendezvous for the next attack, I took the lead. We went down together going to get another gun position.

"As we dove on the field I spotted two French planes coming to attack us on the starboard side. There were two Dewoitines, with mottled camouflage and red-and-yellow striped noses. Cripes, I thought, this is it. They were near enough for us to see their insignia. 'Look at that,' someone said in my ear. 'The bastards. That used to be an American squadron. Tallyho.' Higher up two more P-36s were milling about the sky. I chose the Dewoitine, but I was going too fast, so fast that I overshot him. As I went past I saw he was coming round on my tail. I pulled up and came back over in a quick turn that brought me with my nose towards him. I was too far away and much too anxious. I gave him a burst for quite a long range. These .50-calibers got him. I could see him, standing still in the air as if something had jerked him up by the tail. He looked as though he was going to stall to take evasive action, and he fell over to starboard, his wing fluttering. The plane's nose went into a sharp dive. I followed him down too excited to think of doing anything else. He hit the ground, bounced, and with his motor still running ricocheted across the field till he came to a stop in a water hole. I circled round. There was no sign of the pilot.

"Then I remembered about our keeping together. I knew I was plumb crazy to be down there all alone. Presently I saw a Wildcat coming in across the airfield very fast with two P-36s on his tail. The French pilots were scissoring round behind him and giving him alternate bursts. He was only about ten feet from the ground. I could see it was our handsome boy Chuck August. Chuck called me over the radio. 'Windy. . . Windy, get those bastards off my tail—quick!' I went down then with my throttle wide open. One of the

French planes saw me and broke away. I got on his tail, but he slipped away. These P-36s are extremely maneuverable. Out of the corner of my eye I saw August going up in a steep *chandelle* and getting his plane with a beautiful shot. I think I cheered him. It was a wonderful piece of work. I got my man in the sights, lost him, got him again, and gave him a burst, then another. He went up into a climbing turn, a darn silly thing to do. I only had to pull up my nose and take a simple shot at him. He staggered and rolled, over, then righted himself. A streak of orange flame came from his starboard side, and he went down spinning and burning.

"I knew better than to go down to look this time. I looked round for the rest of the squadron but there were no Wildcats anywhere. My wing had caught some bullets, which gave me an uncomfortable feeling. Over the mike I heard Spanky Carter calling the boys to rendezvous, so I began to climb. I waggled my stick to see how I was. The machine was in good shape with all the controls working. At eight thousand feet I was still alone. I turned and weaved and looked everywhere. There wasn't a darned Wildcat in the sky.

"It looked at how I would have to go back to the carrier alone. I called the ship and then I heard Carter again, so I made for our rendezvous, like a bat in hell. Another pair of P-36s came in sight but they turned away. This gave me a kind of invincible feeling. They were scared of me even if I was alone. Then below my starboard wing tip

forward I saw a French P-36 coming in to land,
but I was too high to do anything. The air was
alive with them. Another appeared and made a
pass at me. I anticipated the attack, but he got on
my tail and began to give me a burst that hit my wing.
I threw the old Wildcat round, but I couldn't shake
that Frenchman off. He was much more maneuverable than I was and a swell flier. I got hot. Everything I did he did. I saw his wingmate coming in to
make a kill so I stuck down my nose and pulled up
sharply to the left and came round above and between them. Right underneath me was another P-
36. My monkey was up now. These Vichyites were
giving us everything they had. I got this P-36 in
my sights, and gave him a long burst. Then another got on my tail again and I knew I had gotten
myself into a darned fool position. Bullets were clattering on my wings. I could see the holes. I gave the
P-36 I had first attacked another burst. He wobbled
then fell down and his companion turned away. He
went so fast that pursuit seemed out of the question.

"We were right over the airfield at that moment, and I saw a Douglas bomber on the ground
hurrying to the runway. I decided to strafe him,
but again I went in too fast. I overshot badly and
that calmed me down a great deal, so I turned for
another run. This time I got him with several
bursts. He blew up just as my plane was overhead,
and the explosion rocked me. I realized then that
the incendiary bombs were still in my machine,
which was probably why I hadn't been able to
shake off those P-36s.

I decided to make a last attack and then go back to the carrier. I climbed, pulled up to the east, and put down my nose. Just as I pulled the bomb releases, a P-36 dived out of the sun. He gave me all he had. Some bullets ripped my fuel lines, and the cockpit filled with fumes. I knew what a fool I was to stay round such a hot spot alone. I was cold duck now. I prayed for a Wildcat somewhere. Three more Vichy planes were coming down to get at me. I would have to fight. I turned my nose to the man on my tail to get a shot at him, but my port guns went dry on me. He gave me a burst that ripped open the top of my wing. I called into the mike. 'This is Windy! Windy over Cazes! Attacked by four P-36s! Can't continue!' There was no answer. I called again. 'Hank . . . Chuck . . . Windy, four on my tail . . . .'

"The fumes were getting thick now, but the machine was still flying. Then an incendiary bullet started a fire. A great lick of flame came up at my face and I knew it was the end. I pushed back the hood and tried to turn the plane on her back, but she wouldn't have it. The tabes and aileron surfaces were not working. How the heck was I to get out? I decided to stall her, and at the moment when she lost flying speed I braced my knees and jumped for it. I got clear. The parachute opened, and I floated down feeling angry and frustrated. A French plane came at me. I thought he was going to shoot me up but he just flew past me, wagging his wing tips and waving his hands and laughing like hell. I waved back. Suddenly

several infantrymen on the ground opened fire on
me. A bullet wammed past my ear a few feet away.
What the heck was all this? I'd been shot down.
Weren't they taking prisoners? If I had to get shot,
I'd take a few of them with me. I spotted them
quickly, got out my automatic, and returned their
fire. They stopped shooting as I crashed on a
barbed-wire fence on the edge of the airfield.

"As I landed three German Heinkel bombers
and a Junkers transport were being wheeled into
the runway followed by a crowd of German officers who seemed to be in a scramble to get inside them. I hope they get those Nazis, I thought
. . . we've got to. They're the cause of it all."
Windy paused with a wry face. "And that was my
bit of work, salubriously short. I'll do better next
time.

"Of course that was all I saw of it," said
Windy. "There was quite a lot going on that I didn't
see. When you're in a plane, your mind is too concentrated on the job to take in many details."

This was generous understatement on
Windy's part. The French were putting up a ferocious resistance—fighting back blow for blow.
The American ships were pounding the coastal
batteries, the dive bombers were whacking hell
out of the ships. War flamed all over the sector.
Over the airfields the Wildcats were clawing the
P-36s when they could get at close quarters with
them. The French planes were fighting in groups
of three and roaring down to break up the American fighter formations. American control of the

air had to be maintained at all costs. That meant not a French plane must be left in the air, or allowed to take the air. If the fighters could knock out the Vichy air force the landings could be effected in double time. The ships had to be protected too; at any moment, French bombers might take off to attack the American battleships.

Chapter 3

"THAT WAS some air battle over Cazes," recalled Tommy Booth. "Our boys made one big mistake. They did not keep together. The enemy fliers took good advantage of it."

"They certainly did," said Chuck August, who was in the third section assembled for a second strafing attack. Chuck is a warm, rangy kind of fellow with a personality rather like a summer day.

"As we went in behind Spanky," went on Chuck, "I noticed my wingman was missing, which didn't make me any happier. I closed up behind Spanky and we went in at full throttle, diving east to west along the runway. There was an anti-aircraft battery firing rapidly. I made for it, opened up with all guns. Strafing that way gives you a feeling of terrific power. As those guns blaze you feel as if you had suddenly gotten safer strength. You feel incredibly tough and confident as if nothing could stop you. The .50-caliber bullets splashed up divots of grass round the emplacements and struck sparks from the guns and concrete. As I got near the target I saw the gunners begin to run. That put me on the top of the world.

"Everything was working fine till something hit me. My Wildcat jerked and shuddered. I thought she was going out of control, but she was all right. It was only a jar, but the plane didn't feel right now.

"There was a Douglas bomber beetling out over the airfield, so I let go my incendiaries. I don't know whether I hit it because there was no time to see. Another set of guns had opened up. My windshield had fogged over except for a small space which wasn't helpful. As I formed up again on the other side of the run, Spanky told me that my right landing gear was dangling. Some of that flak had hit me hard. When I got back I would have to land in the drink beside the carrier. Not a pleasant thought, but it would have to be done. I wasn't going back yet, not for a long while. Spanky was just telling us we could go in again when Ed Laake whooped warningly, 'Watch it, boys! To your right.'

"Six or eight of the French planes came in flying at about 2,500 feet. I forgot about my landing wheel. When you see an enemy for the first time you don't have much time to think about anything. That comes afterwards. I was tense, as everyone is, but I seemed to know just what to do. We had been training for this kind of thing. I was very conscious that we were fighting against the Axis, but when I saw the markings of the Vichy fliers, showing we were up against the Escadrille Lafayette, I was rather let down. The squadron had a history and a reputation. It would be a crack outfit, I figured.

"'Two each, boys,' said Spanky. 'Keep together this time.' We were soon in the middle of them. I picked out a P-36 but I overshot him at the first attempt. You are liable to do that if you come in too fast. We were all too anxious because we hadn't been in action before. I cussed myself and came round in a tight turn, at which the Wildcat is a honey. My position was just right, and I made a high attack from the beam and gave him a long burst. The .50-caliber bullets hitting at about sixty a second seemed to rip him open like a can opener. He stopped in his line of flight, turned turtle, and went down in flames. 'Tallyho,' said someone in my ear. I saw another pair of enemy planes, a P-36 and a Dewoitine 520. The pilots seemed to be talking to each other.

"I got in close and fired my port guns. The P-36 shuddered. The weight of metal you put into them with these .50-calibers appears to jar them off their line of flight. I got in to fifty yards, feeling strangely elated. I was sure of hitting him now as I gave him a burst with all guns and pulled up over him while he was hanging in the air and rolling about with a convulsive movement rather like an animal in pain. I figured the pilot had either been hurt or killed. Then the red-and-yellow-nosed plane turned over in a slow roll with its engine running and began to fly on its back. It was like watching a beginner crash in a training flight and being able to do nothing about it.

"It went down quite slowly. A plume of dark smoke spurted from the ground where it hit. I looked round for Spanky Carter but couldn't find him. There wasn't a Wildcat in sight. The French had broken us up properly. They themselves were not flying in any kind of formation, but they were milling round in pairs on the principle of one plane coming to the help of another. There were too many of them in the air near us to be healthy.

"Where were those Wildcats? I seemed to be alone with all these enemy planes. Two of them came down to attack me, both fired at me, missed, and passed over. Then two more got behind me. Wisdom told me to get out of the battle, try to re-form with the others and come back. I thought I would be able to shake the two Frenchmen off my tail, but I soon found that was just wishful thinking. In spite of all my defensive skill, they stuck there. I tried to out-climb them. We all of us angled, then I dived. They were there when I pulled out.

"I got frightened. I say now I have never been so frightened in all my life. I tried to climb, intending to come over and make a high side attack, which I had practiced to perfection. They followed and got in the same position behind me. I was consoling myself they were rotten shots when their bullets started hitting me. That was the most awful gosh-darned sensation. I could hear the lead they were throwing at me clattering against the armor plate behind my cockpit. A terrifying noise. I got very scared. How long would

that armor plate hold out? I'd got to get rid of
them. But how? If only there was a Wildcat about.
I scanned the sky. Then I saw one in the distance.
He was busy strafing a truck coming along the
road southwest of the airport. I called him, but he
went on strafing. I was badly jerked when a burst
of bullets made a hell of a crack behind me. This
time they jolted the plane. It couldn't take much
more, I felt sure. If I didn't shake off these Frenchmen, they would shake me down. I was doing well
over three hundred m.p.h. but they were sticking.
I gave the motor the gun and dived till I was ten
feet from the ground.

"They followed, and then I saw Windy
Shields. I could tell it was Windy instantly. I could
have kissed him. Windy got wise to the fix I was
in and promptly got on the tail of one of the
Frenchies, the loveliest sight I ever saw. Windy's
move was the finest piece of flying I ever want to
see. He came in low, guns spitting. The French
pilot saw him and broke away, giving me what I
wanted—a chance to climb. I zoomed up and
round and came down again heading for beam of
the P-36 that had been following me. I gave him
a fairly full deflection shot and got him! The plane
burst into flames, first a deep orange color and
then a flood of dense black smoke. I saw the pilot
jerk back the hood and try to get out. He was black
with smoke and seemed to be smothered with oil.
I saw him jump, but he couldn't get his chute open
and fell to the ground about fifty feet from his
plane.

"Windy cheered in my ear. 'Tallyho, Wildcat! Good shot! Oh boy what a shot!' And off he went like a crazy man after the other P-36 that was going south.

"I kind of stopped for breath, and set off a bit soberly across the airfield. Whew! I had been lucky, but I was still out of formation and stalling round like a lost sheep. The airfield was beginning to show signs of war now. Five aircraft were burning in various parts and I saw a long black scratch near the south boundary where an engine had struck the surface and skidded into a ditch.

"There was smoke belching up all over the place. The guns were keeping up a lot of fire with small stuff. I realized that I would be better off with a wingmate, so I called over the mike. No one answered. Then I saw a Wildcat strafing a gun emplacement. I decided to take a position over him and we'd stick together. I watched him go down to do his job with growing satisfaction. He was flying into what looked like a terrific fire. When you watch a strafe from that angle it seems a hell of a lot more spectacular than when you are in it. This guy was quite fearless. I wanted to cheer him. When he dived into the ground and burst into flames, I felt sick.

"I only had one idea then, to get back to the rendezvous point. There was a lot of talk going on. Everyone was going to 'play ball' but I couldn't locate any of our own Wildcats. I began to wonder if they were all shot down. Could we have taken such a licking? Might be, but I wouldn't think of it. Well, if I was on my own, I still had a job to do.

"I climbed to a better altitude and checked over the objectives on the airfield that I had intended to strafe before I left the target area. I made one run over some parked aircraft. A gun crew fired at me, and a man took a pot shot at me with what looked like a tommy gun. He shook his fist pathetically. I cussed him and knocked off a bomber. It subsided gently on the ground as if a giant had suddenly sat on it and splayed out its undercarriage. Then I heard Windy calling for help. 'O.K.,' I called back. 'Don't worry, I'm on the way.' I saw a bunch of French planes ahead. They were in pairs, as we should have been. I was higher than they were. When I went in to attack, they scattered like a flock of birds fired at with a shotgun. They were doing the right thing I knew. I had the advantage of height over them. I picked out the two of them following the other Wildcat, which I thought was Windy, and got into firing position behind them.

"Then I suddenly found I was losing speed. I pulled the nose of the plane up to fire, but she just took up a stalling position and I lost my speed. I cussed and stuck the nose down, and checked the instruments. I had about sixty gallons of fuel, but oil pressure was zero. The cylinder-head temperature was normal, which was good. I might be able to make for Medouina airfield where some of the boys might be waiting. Underneath was what looked like the world's worst terrain for a forced landing—hills, rocks, and gullies. I was at about 1,100 feet when my motor let out a noise that was like a cracked bell sounding over a radio at full blast. Then came a terrible vibration. The entire machine got the jitters. It was so violent that it almost shook the stick out of my hand. Then it stopped.

"I knew all was up. I tried to turn the machine over and jumped. I flunked it, and my left leg hit the stabilizer, which sent me spinning down like a top. I pulled the rip cord, and spread my arms and legs to check the spin. You do this kind of thing automatically. I was afraid the parachute was going to wrap itself round me and kind of prayed for a split second, but it opened a few seconds before I hit the ground.

Hit is hardly the term—I crashed very heavily and painfully because I was swinging like a pendulum. When I got my breath I found myself lying on my back being dragged along by the parachute. I managed to pull the shrouds and thus collapse the chute. I lay there a while feeling pretty low. I seemed to have done a poor job for Uncle Sam. What a fool I had been. I thought of my kid brother at school who thinks I'm quite a man."

Chuck caught his breath reminiscently. "I figure I was very lucky as it all turned out—very lucky."

"More than lucky, Chuck—that first encounter was some dogfight," recalled Lieutenant Wood ("Woody"), who was in Hank Weiler's section with Abe Conner as his wingman. Woody is one of those quiet men who say very little, and that with a distinctly droll sense of humor. Before he came into the Navy, Woody was a composer and musician of some note. Naturally, he is still crazy about music, and when he isn't flying, he is playing. The squadron boys call him "the pilot with the perfect pitch." Engineering and flying both have musical meanings for Woody. He can tell you the revolutions per minute of the ship's engines by just putting his ear against the side of the ship.

"Things were happening all around us," said Woody. "The air was full of planes. I saw a Dewoitine 520 coming up from below and to my left. He was firing at me but not hitting. As I turned towards him, I saw a blazing plane plummeting down near by, with the pilot bailing out. My man was fast. I made a spin on the inside of his turn to the right and landed below and behind him. I then got inside of his turn and he tried to shake me off by doing Immelmanns, quite old-fashioned tactics. I stayed on his tail and finally gave him a burst at full deflection. He pushed over so suddenly that I lost him, but I saw several chunks of his plane flying. When I picked him up again, I saw a Wildcat diving after him, his guns blazing. The 520 was on fire and crashed in flames. "Nice work, Short Man,' said Tommy Booth quietly. So it was Little Harris who shot him down.

"Then I picked a tartar . . . another Vichy 520 was ahead of me and quickly got on my tail. I remembered that I still had my bombs. I jettisoned them right away, and the plane immediately felt a lot better. I took a chance and let the Vichy pilot get very close.

"Then I closed my throttle quickly—a good dodge if it works. He overshot me, and I picked him up in my sights from a perfect position on his tail. He was quite a flier and gave me a good dogfight, but my Wildcat seemed to be as fast as it ever had been, and although he went up steeply I managed to keep the inside of the turn and got in a two-second burst as we both spun out. I recovered earlier, but he had some trouble and went from a left spin to a right, spun to the ground, and all that was left was a solid sheet of white-hot flame. I heard the Skipper say, 'Come on, Boyd. Let's give him another squirt.' So I joined up with them. I then found I was running short of gas, so I made for home. The ship wasn't where we expected it and couldn't take us aboard. I had about two gallons of gas left, so I gave them the forced-landing signal, and after about five passes they let me land. They told me, when I got down, that Abe Conner had landed in the water, but had been picked up by a destroyer. Eus Brown of Blue squadron had also run out of gas and his plane had sunk immediately. He got away with a bad cut on the forehead.

"I suppose one of the most interesting sights of that trip was passing over an Arab village at about ten feet. The big brown huts looked like chicken croquettes. I could see several Arabs standing round in their burnouses. They smiled big smiles and waved. There were quite a few holes in our planes. We only had time to drink a cup of coffee and expect a sandwich, which incidentally didn't come before it was time to get off again."

"In spite of Woody's rural reminiscences, we seemed to be taking quite a pasting," said Spanky Carter. "The French pilots weren't aggressive, but they were doing a good job and sticking to the rules of the game."

"The unwisest thing they did," put in Tommy Booth, "was to keep on trying to break off combat by diving out of a roll, although their zigzag evasive action wasn't so bad."

"But they taught us something," said Spanky.

"Spanky is ready to take anyone on at rowing rubber boats and digging slit trenches," laughed Tommy.

"I got separated from the gang and three Vichy fighters came from nowhere on my tail," Spanky said. "I did everything I knew to get them off, but they kept on. It was just one of those things. I got a shot at one and turned him off with smoke coming out of his motor. Then the other got me at close range. He hit my plane behind somewhere, and the control became difficult. The best thing to do seemed to be to head for the sea and try to make the carrier. That Vichyman on my tail was smart and exceedingly aggressive. He came in at me again. His second burst shot away my oil-cooler lines. I began to lose height rapidly and was heading straight for the drink. You get really mad in a case like that.

"A bunch of bullets hit the back armor. I couldn't do anything about it, so I stuck her nose down. A plane showed up on my right then. I saw it was the French pilot who had shot me down.

He was grinning like mad and waving his hand. Then he started circling round. He was still overhead when I made a crash landing on the water. Quite a chivalrous guy, he seemed. I was gratified, of course, but too busy to give it much thought. Then I got out of the plane before it sunk, inflated my Mae West, and blew up the rubber boat in which I stowed myself. A couple of Wildcats passed overhead going out to sea, but they didn't linger, so I guessed they were low on gas. The obvious thing to do was to paddle for the shore, but immediately I did that a French machine-gun nest on the beach started to fire at me. You can bet I took evasive action. I began to paddle for the open sea. It wasn't pleasant with the bullets flocking round and a rubber boat does not give much protection. To hell with getting shot at like that. Once or twice I looked back. The docks at Casablanca were smoking, and the shells from the battleship were howling over. I hoped they got those gunners who potted at me. Later I rested a bit and watched a dogfight between six P-36s and a couple of Wildcats. I envied our boys up there and felt a bit depressed at getting shot down."

"When I got back to the ship, as far as I could make out we were six planes missing," said Tommy Booth. "It isn't a happy feeling for a squadron leader. We were short of Carter, August, Shields, Taylor, Seiler, and Mikronis, who the boys call Nick the Greek. We had heard that Abe Conner had fallen in the drink and had been picked

up by a destroyer. Mac Wordell hadn't come in,
Ed Seiler and some of the others could have
landed on another carrier. Mac would come back
all right, I felt, but I could be forgiven for feeling
uneasy. I tried to convince myself that they would
all turn up. There were so many things that could
have happened to them.

"A call came through, 'Help badly needed.'
A battery was shelling our landing. I called my
section together, warned them to keep together
this time, and we hopped off again. We were feeling a bit mad, so we gave that battery hell. We
put it out of action in record time and got back
with one man short. Tag Grell had run into some
machine-gun fire and called that he was in trouble.
Short Man said he had seen Tag force-land on the
sea. Tag would be sure to come back. I couldn't
help wondering about Mac. He had got down we
knew. The plane-to-ship radio had picked up his
last call—a real Red Ripper message. 'I'm all
right, you go and get those bastards.' Yes, Mac
would turn up, I was sure."

"I'm sorry I couldn't make the carrier that
trip, Captain," said Ed Seiler. "Dub and I ran low
on gas and had to get aboard another carrier, where
we had to wait two hours before I could do anything.
They were pretty busy then." Dub Taylor was Ed's
wingman in the last section of Tommy Booth's formation in the first attack on the Cazes airfield.

"Dub and I arrived and went down to attack
in pairs," related Ed. "Like the others we got separated from the rest of the division. I was figuring

whether I would make an attack individually when I found myself four or five French fighters. 'Let's take these characters,' I suggested, and we went in. I overshot just like everyone else, and missed. There was a bank of cotton-wool mist screening the airfield that gave excellent cover. We flew above it for a while to see if could get over the French planes, but they were too smart, although we did mix in one melee with shooting at fifty yards range. We were at a disadvantage because we had not yet let go our bombs. I realized that, when a Vichy yokel got on my port quarter. He was distinctly a spirited character and seemed to want to show off his flying. Instead of opening fire, he kept whirling round like a gnat. I managed to duck every time I thought he was going to fire. I gave him one burst that notched his tail I figured, but he came again stunting like mad, so I opened up, ringing him just behind the pilot's seat. That must have put the fear of God into him, because he made off into the mist. I went down after him, came out underneath the clouds and let go my bombs. I slowed down to see if they would work. They burst in bright yellow flashes. With them off my mind I was ready for anything, and headed for Medouina airfield, our rendezvous, where we were to re-form to concentrate for another attack.

"I found Dub Taylor circling round, and we joined up together. Two more Vichy boys came out of the clouds but they seemed to be going somewhere in a hurry and were higher than we were. Dub, whose radio was off, signaled to me they were two angels up, so we went off. I tried to sneak under them to get into the sun, but one slipped away on the far side. We got a shot at the other, but he wasn't in a fighting mood and beat it. Over Medouina, four Wildcats were circling, so we went over, to find Tag Grell leading. I called Spanky but couldn't get a reply. We called the ship and said we were coming back. Tag pointed to his radio and made the thumbs-down sign, so his was out too. We followed him seawards, and then I saw my gas was running low. Down below one of the other carriers was swinging into wind to land planes. When we landed on the other carrier, after we'd made the intelligence reports, we went to look at our planes. Stew Ball and Dub Taylor had had their planes hit several times. 'You should see mine,' said Stew, "I'll bet it's got more holes than any of yours.' Dub quietly pulled him over to his plane and said, 'Look.' Stew counted sixteen. 'Hell,' he said, 'I'm not going to show you mine after that.'

"We had to get in or flop in the sea. I flew low and let down my tail hook several times, which is a signal that I was nearly dry and had to land. The landing signals officer waved me in. The others followed. Tag circled round and made for our own carrier. This carrier was busy—planes were landing at the rate of one every two seconds, it seemed. We reported to the intelligence officer and gassed up, intending to go back and join our carrier, but there was a hop on, something was going amiss somewhere. They wanted every plane they could have, so we ourselves were quickly organized into a combat patrol. It wasn't long before our own carrier came through calling "Cagey" Hammond, who was leading on the combat patrol. 'Hammond, take your fighters to Fedala to attack enemy fighters attempting to bomb our transports. Expedite!' Eight of us hared off, delighted to be out and doing something instead of circling the ship. We heard the fighter director officer calling us again before we had made it. 'Expedite Hammond.' I'm expediting,' answered Cagey.

"We got to Fedala. There wasn't a bomber in sight. 'Let's take a look at the transports,' said Cagey. He split us into four pairs and we went over. The air was clear. 'Back to Cazes,' said Cagey. Cazes is the Casablanca airfield the squadron had originally attacked. The intelligence report had been dead right for there was a row of Douglas bombers gassing up on the airfield. The French seemed to be doing the craziest things. There were no fighters in the area to protect the bombers and they were going to send them out alone to attack our ships.

"'Here we go, boys,' drawled Cagey. We went down in pairs. I was leading the second section of four planes and came in at about ten degrees. With the excellent arrangement of guns on the Wildcat, it is difficult to miss on a strafing job. I suppose I opened up at six hundred yards although when you're doing four hundred m.p.h. six hundred yards isn't much time in your life. This six hundred yards nearly ended mine. The bomber exploded in my face. I could hear the explosion above the roar of my engine. The debris spattered all over my wings and screen. The old Wildcat leapt in the air rather like a horse taking off for a jump, and that was that. A nasty feeling flying through a burning bomber, but worth while under the circumstances, and certainly quite a tribute to Mr. Grumman and his machine.

"Dub Taylor was doing a good job on a gun emplacement that was throwing some small stuff at us. He came in on an angle and opened fire. The gun never fired again. We climbed and came down for another strafing run on the bombers, giving them another going over. They all looked as if they were out.

"That airfield was a pathetic sight. It looked like a child's toy after the little owner had become displeased with it, and had peevishly stamped on the planes. There were five bombers in a line squashed out in grotesque attitudes, and two burning fiercely with their undercarriages splayed on either side. One was cocked on its nose with its tail burning like a torch. Three fighters were cracked up in equally melancholy positions, and there was a wing of a plane all by itself as if someone had thrown it away like a match stick. The guns were out for the time being. The strangest thing was that we didn't see any soldiers. The gunners had either taken shelter or were knocked out. Just after that plane blew up under my nose,

I got a laugh. There was an Arab with a donkey walking along a road near the airfield when the blast occurred. He just went on walking, without taking the slightest notice of us. He may, of course, have heard the President's speech, had unequaled faith in Allah, or perhaps he was deaf. It came to me then," went on Ed, "that for aviators, war is a rather impersonal affair. It isn't noisy and dirty. It's kind of aerated, as it were. You don't get excited about the horror and the dirt and the noise and the smells. You're just there, doing a job."

The fighter squadron was seeing only a small part of the action.

"We only saw our own little bit of the show also," chipped in Max Eaton of the High Hat squadron. "My memory of the first day isn't so clear. There were hops coming and going and general excitement. I believe Pete Carver, our skipper, made two hops and then in the third his engine conked just after he cleared the deck. He managed to jettison his bombs and landed in the water. He and his radioman whipped out their rubber boat and were in it just as the plane sank. They were picked up later by a destroyer and we never saw him again for the rest of the action. Ralph Embree automatically became skipper. Ralph grabbed the job with a vengeance and went like a house afire from then on. Ralph's boyish exuberance for the job was really something to see. I often caught an impression of him with his face all lit up and his eyes shining with excitement; he reminded me of the leader of a gang of boys going out to terrorize the neighborhood on Hallowe'en.

"Ralph was really a terror. The closer the anti-aircraft fire came to him, the more it seemed to amuse him. We used to hear him chuckling over the radio.

"He worked harder than anyone and he never lost his temper or jumped on us, and he was always taking the big slice of danger. I always remember a glimpse of Ralph, taking off down the deck with a stick in one hand and munching a big ham sandwich in the other, which he waved to the crewmen as he went off. Ralph admitted afterwards that all this was an act. He says that he was just as scared as anyone, but he was trying to whip our spirits into shape and not attract attention to himself. He had the know-how and the courage to do the job anyway, but instead of making it a grim and depressing business, he played it like a thrilling and amusing game.

"That guy's spirit really was contagious and even the fellows in the squadron who were cynical to this kind of enthusiasm caught it without realizing it. They needed it, too, when I tell you that every one of our planes was hit by flak. On the second hop, we lost one of the lads. When I heard the news, it struck me as being a major loss, because he was such a swell guy, as Irish as County Cork, and always able to see the funny side of everything."

From zero-hour early that morning war had been steadily blazing and spurting like a bush fire along that sector of the northwest African coast. The heavy guns of the coastal batteries were crashing out great blobs of smoke, and the air was crackling with radio talk. Dark, noisy shapes that were planes scudded here and there dodging behind clouds, diving precipitously, and bolting seawards. Along the narrow roads sheltered by the tall trees, little plumes of dust rose and clung to the wake of hurrying motor vehicles, and Wildcats could be seen stalking them almost laboriously, dipping below the level of the trees, then yowling to the upper sky in sharp arcs.

Across the rolling country, lined with tall trees and narrow roads, the town of Casablanca, its dark lines of docks looking like a mouthful of black teeth under the white-façaded face of its residential section, was giving up clouds of black smoke.

Offshore were the transports, the great, towering bulks of the battleships, constantly moving, and the destroyers darting here and there, screening their charges. Guns were booming and shells whistling. Occasionally the surface of the sea would be disturbed by rising plumes of water as a depth charge or a shell detonated.

Chapter 4

ALL THROUGH that first day the dive bombers continued the attack over Casablanca Harbor. Below them, huddled in angles of the jetties, were their targets, destroyers and submarines, and the massive buff-colored cigar shape of the beautiful battleship *Jean Bart,* with its anti-aircraft batteries spouting from stem to stern. As the Dauntless dive bombers were in full dive two Curtiss H-75s closed in to attack. A pair of escorting Wildcats pounced on them, and the four planes tore away to the southeast in a mad gyration, guns popping and engines howling. "They looked as if they had been rolling into a ball," said a dive-bomber pilot. "I saw one French fighter fall in flames on a building in the docks. The other limped home with his tail blasted by .50-caliber bullets."

As the pilots leveled out over the roof tops and dropped their bombs, the waterfront became terraced with smoke from the explosions. Some of the lighter debris floated in the wind at one thousand feet. While the first section of dive bombers climbed away and formed themselves into a defensive fighting formation for the return trip to the carrier, another section took their place. The first squadron got back to the maneuvering carrier, three planes short. The pilots sat in their planes on the flight deck as they gave their reports to intelligence officers and drank the coffee the excited mess boys brought out. New bombs were fitted to the bomb racks, guns were reloaded, and the fuel tanks replenished.

"When our pilots got back from the first hop there was bedlam in the ready room." Fred Akers was speaking. "Honestly, you'd think they had been to a ball game instead of a battle. They were all too excited to make their reports. Everybody wanted to talk at once and nobody had anything useful to say. Getting details out of them was like pulling teeth. They gave me a rough ride for a while. When I did manage to get home a question, they all started shouting together. I got mad then. 'Stop talking, fellows, for Mike's sake, and get on with it. There's a war on.' That quieted them. Then the bridge called . . . ten more planes were wanted for a show. That broke up their concentration again. They jumped up; all wanted to go. Hank Weiler was flight officer. He made 'em pipe down and sorted out the ones who had planes and the ones who hadn't. They were detailed and went off to their planes on the double. I got to work on the chaps who were left. They were pretty melancholy about it too, but they began to give. The reports had to be collected and analyzed. We needed that information immediately for the task-force commander!"

The Padre did a swell job. If he didn't pass the ammunition, at least he gave the crewmen an idea of what was going on. Whenever his "Here it is, men," came over the ship's loud-speaker, everybody who could listened. It went like this: "We've just heard our dive bombers have attacked the ships at Casablanca. They have stopped a big one coming out. . . .

"Now the news has come through that we have destroyed three large bombers on the airfield, and listen . . . one of the pilots on the other carrier saw a submarine coming straight for his ship as he was going home. He dove on it and got a couple of pot shots. You know, we've just had a couple of submarines on our beam too. The destroyers dropped depth charges and that was all we heard. Just now three enemy ships tried to get out of Casablanca Harbor. One of our big battlewagons turned them back. . . . Everything is ticking like a clock.

"Our pilots are doing well. There have been casualties, of course, and a few accidents. One young man went over the side taking off this morning, but they fished him out . . . I'll be coming on again very shortly."

"Back in a flash with a flash," mimicked someone. "That isn't the Padre really," remarked Ed Seiler.

"You know we took aboard the original Winchell, wrapped in one of those copies of *Life*."

The Padre soon came on again, very excited. "Here it is . . . A French cruiser is coming out of Casablanca under a heavy smoke screen and . . . uh . . . and there's another one ablaze on our starboard beam.

"The guns of one of our battleships have got it. They say that it can be seen plainly from the bridge. Now news has just come through that our planes are still covering the landing of troops and holding their own against the enemy. This is the third hop for some of them." They cut the Chaplain off, then, and the bridge came on . . . nine planes were wanted for a bombing attack on the three French warships.

"Dive bombers, by gosh, no fighters." The pilots, hunched in their armchairs, were making long faces . . . "And no sandwiches," moaned another. "What kind of a ship is this?" Bridge called again a second later to say enemy bombers were about four miles away . . . "All available pilots to their planes." The boys scuttled up, but came back a few minutes later. It had been a false alarm.

Then we heard that a section of the Dauntless bombers under Lieutenant Embree was called to attack the heavy cruiser *Primuguet*, which was keeping up a regular fire on American transports. The bombers scored three direct hits, and left the big vessel with smoke pouring from gaping holes in her decks. Her guns, however, continued to put up a heavy barrage.

Forming up his squadron to return, Lieutenant Embree called to Ensign Warta. "Get home,

Warta . . . quick." Warta looked behind him, and opened his throttle.

He warned the carrier that he would have to make a priority landing. He had a casualty aboard.

"We were taking in planes as fast as we could, dodging the subs, which were making operations ticklish. The ship kept moving and changing her course, which made it difficult for the pilots," recalled Bill Stewart, a Navy flier who superintended the landing aboard of the planes from dawn to dusk. "You have to work quickly when they come back. Some of them are bound to have priority because they are short of gas. If you don't get them in, they'll drop in the drink. I was trying to get one of the fighters in when I saw a scout circling round and giving me the sign that he had to get down. I ordered him straight in and as he came by me fairly low, to turn into the wind, I saw that his radio gunner was hanging out as if he were sick. I could see him quite plainly, one arm over the side, his face turned down and his mouth open. It didn't need a second look to see why the pilot wanted to get down. I warned the corps men and they were waiting with a stretcher-bearer as the pilot landed."

When they got him out, radio gunner Patterson was dead. He had been hit by the anti-aircraft fire through which the plane had flown in an attack on more of the shore batteries. "Shall I take you back?" Ensign Warta had inquired previously when Patterson told him he was hurt. "No, sir," answered Patterson, "I can fix it. It's nothing nothing much." As they went down, Patterson called, "Take your time. And give me a chance to shoot." Patterson died fighting for his life. Although his leg had been shot off at the knee, he had calmly set to work to make himself a tourniquet out of his silk muffler, but he must have lost consciousness before he had fixed it. Had Embree not signaled to Ensign Warta, flying Patterson's machine, he might never have known the young gunner was dead. Patterson was not the kind to detract his pilot's attention from the task they set out to do.

"That kid was plumb crazy to get into something," said one of the plane captains. "Listen to this. When we knew there was to be action, everyone was trying to get in on it. There wasn't a man aboard who wouldn't have given his month's pay to get out there with the pilots. It kind of broke our hearts to see them go off. Patterson felt the same way. One of the boys offered him $400 for his place as gunner of that plane. The kid just said there wasn't enough money in the whole of America to stop him, and off he went. His pilot thinks the kid got a Vichy plane before he died. We figure that he kept mum about his wound because he was afraid his pilot might break action. He sure was the right stuff."

As radio gunner, Patterson's job was to defend his airplane from attack from the rear and to undertake the greater part of the communication. The pilot of a dive-bomber has plenty to do. He must do the bombing and use his forward machine-guns. He relies a great deal on the man in the back seat.

The death of one man in an action-crowded day is but an incident in the orderly hurry of a carrier in action. Five planes had been hit in that operation. On his way back to the carrier one of the pilots spotted four submarines in a group heading towards the carrier. Four scouts hopped off with special anti-submarine bombs. Another submarine got within range without being detected and attacked. An alert lookout saw the track of the torpedo and gave the alarm. "The carrier turned just as a dive-bomber pilot was preparing to come aboard," recalls Bill Stewart. "As the pilot made his approach he was waved off. Later a crewman told me that the tin fish missed us by five yards. It was a fine bit of evasion.

During the day, the water in the area was becoming infested with submarines. The carrier kept moving in irregular patterns, coming into the wind only to land her planes. At intervals new sub contacts would be reported, and our escort destroyers were constantly maneuvering and dropping depth charges which would throw up deadly plumes of spray.

"Once when the ship was reported under attack by torpedoes," laughed Ed Kelly, "they were telling Tommy that if he had to land ashore he could make for Port Lyautey, which was in our hands. Tommy didn't like that. I heard him answer, 'What the hell are you telling me all that for? We want to come back to the ship.' I guess we all felt that way, and it wasn't cheery to be told that, even if it was only a precaution." Shortly thereafter

Lieutenant Winters of the Blue squadron received a call that anti-aircraft guns were operating at the northeast edge of El Hank racecourse. He led his section of eight planes into the attack and went into a dive from sixteen thousand feet, making an erratic weaving approach. Each plane dropped two small bombs. Immediately after they had dropped their bombs each machine turned around at low altitude and made a fast flat strafing attack on the target with 50-caliber guns. The battery was silenced. On their return, the pilots reported that the guns were covered with debris, and that there was no sign of life.

The French cruiser *Primuguet* was still firing after the first bombing attack so Lieutenant Embree took six more of his dive bombers against the cruiser. The Vichy gunners were ready and put up a heavy curtain of anti-aircraft fire supported by shore-based guns as the Dauntless bombers swooped down. Four pairs of French fighters attempted to attack between the dive bombers and their fighter escorts, but their interception was bad, and the American pilots swooping down in line ahead were able to drop their bombs without opposition from anything but the gunfire. The leading dive bomber scored a direct hit fairly amidships. Jack Raby, leading the Fighting Blue group which was screening the attack, yelled "Bravo" over his radio. "It was the most beautiful thing I have ever seen," he said later. "Superb aiming. The debris went up to about a thousand feet. It cheered us no end, especially as that cruiser was working for Hitler. It wouldn't be much use to him after that."

Three machines of that flight were badly hit, two landing in the sea. Fighting Blue squadron is a comparatively young organization commissioned just recently.

Chapter 5

"I SEEM to have missed a hell of a lot that first day," lamented Mac Wordell. "I get madder every time I think of it. The idea of my getting shot down on the very first hop of the very first day isn't exactly cheering I must say. I'm sorry that you were all worrying about me so much. The truth is that I was worrying much more about the rest of the fellows. I hated having to leave Tommy Booth with all the work to do. No, I won't admit that it was bad luck."

When Mac gets talking like that, there's a flash in his eye, and his jaw gets a more determined set. It is a habit he has, although you have to know him well to notice it. There's a goodly portion of Scots-Irish wrapped up in this New Englander.

"We finished up that first hop with six of the boys missing," went on Mac. "I would have to be one of them. It happened over Fedala. When I got my section over the beach I could see the transports landing troops on the beaches east of Fedala. There was a sizable fire burning in the oil-storage area near the bend in the Mellah River. The heavy black smoke was blowing slowly across the area completely blanking it out from our view. The boys arrived and took up their positions in a huge defensive circle over the transports and landing area. I had Andy Andrews, Bus Craig, and Hubie Houston with me; Cagey Hammond had Pete Bolt, Art Cassidy, and Stew Ball with him. Jake Onstott had a group, and Danny O'Neill had another. We were loaded and ready, but there was absolutely nothing doing. This went on for half an hour, I suppose. Hell, I thought, if there's a scrap, we've got to get into it. I was a bit anxious as was everyone else. I decided to go down to look for trouble.

"All I could see was a couple of our own planes spotting. I was disappointed, I admit. This patrol seemed to be empty and uneventful. It seemed hard to see the battle going on below and not be taking part in it. I think every man in the squadron was looking for a fight, and all that was happening was that we were making a very routine combat patrol. We swept round over the airfield at Boulhaut in a wide circle. No planes, no troops. I began to get disgusted. It looked as if we were going to miss the show. I called the ship for instructions. There were no instructions."

"There was quite a lot of talking at the time," remarked Bus Craig. The ship's recorder picks up every word spoken by the pilots in action. It preserved the record of the bored patrol:

Andy from Mac: *Let's investigate this down below.*

O.K., Mac.

Later, Mac spoke to Andy: *Nothing but our planes around here. Let's try to knock out some of those A.A. guns firing at us.*

Five minutes later, with a touch of Irish in his voice: *This is Mac. I can't locate a darned thing. Anybody see them?*

No reply.

A little bored: *This is Mac. O.K., upstairs again.*

Two minutes later: *This is Mac. Those boats are doing a swell job down there. See, they're putting them ashore now.*

Mac to the ship: *Everything's quiet. Have you another mission for us?*

No reply.

Mac called Jake: *I am heading south to investigate things round Casablanca. You stay here.*

Four minutes later, Mac called again: *Cagey, there are four destroyers and two cruisers steaming north at high speed out of Casablanca. They're heading for our transports. The destroyers are laying smoke. I am going to attack them with four planes.*

"It was the wickedest sight you could imagine," said Mac. "The four destroyers were speeding northwest towards our lines of transports. I knew by their four stacks that they were Vichy boats. They could do a hell of a lot of damage before they might be spotted by our naval craft. We would have to stop them. I announced my intention to the ship and got no answer. Then I noticed that the destroyers were laying a smoke screen for two light cruisers. This group was trying to dash out to blast our transports. I decided to take a chance at those babies with what I had. Fifty calibers would have to do the job—there wasn't anything else available and time was short. I figured that we would hit the destroyers first and the cruisers would come next.

"The thought of the French fighting against us didn't seem possible to me even then, but they were going to knock hell out of our transports, and that mattered. But could they? Not if we could stop them. We had a common task ahead, to lick the Nazis—nothing else mattered. The men on the ships down there had their orders. They were going to carry them out. We had our orders. If we didn't stop them, there was going to be one hell of a slaughter on that line of transports.

"I called the boys in my section. 'O.K., gang, this is it.'

"'Right,' they answered.

"I gave the signal to attack and nosed her over grimly. This time it was for keeps!

"The approach was just what you dream of when you are figuring them out. We were turning in down wind, down sun, pointing for the stern of the last ship. We picked up speed to three hundred knots. Looking into the sight, I could see the Tricolor on the stern of the last ship growing larger. A grand and glorious feeling! It was in the bag! I started firing at about four thousand feet as my sights began to travel down the center line of the last ship in column. I could see the tracers were squirting on the decks and bouncing off. I almost felt that I was running into my own ricochets. Actually, I was seeing the red pencils of their tracer fire coming up at me.

"It wasn't until after I was nearly over the leading ship that I almost subconsciously heard a noise—the same kind of noise you hear when you jam a screwdriver into the top of a can of milk—and there was some dull thudding, like hitting a metal blade with a hammer wrapped in a cloth.

"It was only when my first attack was over that I realized my plane had been seriously hit. The oil was streaming out of the oil cooler, and the cockpit was filling with smoke. I knew I would have to land or get altitude to bail out."

Heard over the radio it sounded this way:

Andy: *Mac, you're on fire.*

Mac: *I know. It's a left ammunition can. My oil cooler is shot up. I am going to land as near Fedala as I can get. Will you go ahead and find that little field southeast of Fedala.*

O.K., Mac.

Andy, there's no oil pressure now. I am going to unload my guns in the water. Keep clear . . .

Soon Andy called: *Mac, there's a good-looking field over here.*

Where, which side of the railroad is it? I can't see it from here.

West side, Mac!

Can't see it. Hubie, you drag the field for me.

Hubie went down to investigate: *Hell, Mac,*

you can't land here. This place is full of cows.

The hell I can't. I've got to. The engine has conked out.

"Mac, you may not believe it, but I said a prayer for you when I heard you tell Andy to go ahead and find a spot for you to land," remarked the Padre. "I recognized your voice."

"Padre, I needed your help then," said Mac. "Suddenly Andy called that he had found a landing field. I got over and found that it was a pasture full of cattle and black rocks. If I was going to land, I'd better play safe, which was why I dipped my nose and emptied the guns into the water. The motor was now doing about two thousand r.p.m. I said a prayer—not quite the Padre's kind, but it worked. The plane slowed down, dangerously. I thought she was going to stall on me as the wing went down to the left, so I stuck on a lot of right rudder and managed to steady her. My wheels touched but my flaps wouldn't work, so I went on very fast till the left wheel hit a rock and came off. I heard Hubie calling me, 'Hell, Mac, you can't land here—it's full of cows.' 'Damn the cows,' I said, 'I'm down.' I was, too. The plane was rolling along on the right wheel and left wing tip until it hit a shell hole, where it stood up on its nose. My shoulder straps kept me from bumping *my* nose. The plane gradually settled down in a normal attitude. Hubie was circling round and called, 'Are you O.K., Mac?'

"'I'm O.K.,' I yelled. 'You go back and get those damned destroyers. Get all the boys to get them. Blast 'em!'

*"'We sure will, Mac. We'll fix them. We sure
will.'*

O.K., gang, I'm signing off.

"I heard Tommy talking to Boyd just before I
shut off my radio. It made me feel good to hear
him, but I had other problems, the first to beat
out the fire. I did this with my gloves.

"I looked up to see Andy, Bus, and Hubie flying off. I've always thought that my section was
the best fighting four in the whole Navy. I was
positive of it then, and proud of them, even if I
was grounded for the duration. I sat there a bit
listening to the radio. I heard Tommy telling Boyd
to close up for an attack. I called him, but he didn't
answer. Then a shell came over and burst so near
that it rocked the plane. It seemed the time to get
out and make myself scarce."

After Mac had made his first run, Andy, Bus,
and Hubie joined up on Cagey and made another
run on the destroyers. Mac's attack had caused
the destroyers to turn to port for a while, but they
came back again and headed out towards our
transports in a separate column. The second attack, led by Cagey, made them break formation
again. They then turned away from the transports
and began to mill around before turning back towards Casablanca. The two destroyers that Mac
had attacked were already beached, and one of
the light cruisers looked as if it was in trouble.
Cagey led his section in a fore-and-after run, each
machine peppering the vessels with long bursts that
raked them from stem to stern. There was so much

smoke pouring from one of the light cruisers that the pilots had to fly on instruments for some seconds. The destroyers were also putting out a lot of smoke. With each successive attack, the anti-aircraft fire from the vessels diminished, and finally the pilots were merely making unopposed runs. The ships had broken from their formation in confusion. It became impossible to attack more than two ships at once, because of this dispersement.

As the attacks did not take place until the planes had been circling Fedala for two hours, the Wildcats did not have much gasoline left and, as each strafing run was made at full throttle, this was rapidly diminishing. After his second runover, Andy suddenly realized that he only had twenty-five gallons of gasoline. He called Cagey.

"One more attack, Andy," replied Cagey. They went roaring down again. When that was over, Andy was looking anxiously at his gas gauge and wondering whether he would be able to get back to the ship without having to swim.

Cagey called again. "One more attack, Andy." Andy was then resigned to having to make a forced landing. "O.K., Cagey, let's go," he answered. Down they went and gave two of the destroyers another stream of lead.

"I figured that I could just about coast in to Fedala and land next to Mac's plane, when we made that last attack," said Andy, "but the gas held out. When I got back to the ship, I had about a thimbleful in the tank. I guess the Gremlins helped me. If Bill Stewart had waved me off, I couldn't have taken it. That's just how it was with me."

Planes of Fighting Blue also attacked the cruisers and destroyers, and the transports were saved by the determined attack of the Wildcats.

"We got a report that some French warships were coming out of Casablanca Harbor to attack our transports off Fedala," reminisced Max Eaton. "They would have done terrible damage if they had gotten there, and we were all ready to go after them when we heard that the fighter patrol acting as an umbrella for the landing operations had spotted them and attacked. Listening to that on the radio was surely dramatic. I don't know whether those two cruisers and destroyers would have had a hope, but as we took off, we could see our heavy cruisers closing in. President Roosevelt in particular should have seen one of his super-battlewagons romping in like an angry bulldog whose pups have been harmed.

"This was where we came in. We climbed and circled into position over one of the Vichy cruisers and plastered it with bombs. I think some of the destroyers were hit, too. I remember that the cruisers sent up a lot of black smoke. The pilot diving behind me said that my bomb landed amidships. As I came out of my dive, one of the destroyers close by started shooting at me. Shackleford raked it with his guns, and I noticed some flames spurting up. Jack hit it squarely, and so did some of the others. The ships then withdrew to Casablanca. Two of the destroyers were beached. The strafing had been so effectual that not one of them lifted another gun at us. We made two attacks on those ships, looking back, I would say that their not getting out to attack our transports was the turning point of the naval battle. That afternoon we attacked the coastal batteries of El Hank. There were seven or eight turreted naval guns there in cement pits, hard to see and well dispersed. Only a direct hit would be decisive. We knew that, but while diving on them it wasn't very easy to pick them out. They looked rather like little vague doughnuts."

The Padre smiled at Mac. "I put you into my report, Mac," he said. "After all, you are quite an important man on the ship. I couldn't help wondering how the boys would get on if they hadn't got you to teach them their songs."

"I'm sorry I missed your blow-by-blow accounts, Padre. I'm told they were pretty snappy," retorted Mac. "How did you manage? Suppose it's the Irish in you."

"No, just training, Mac. When the Captain suggested that I should do it, I jumped at the opportunity, but of course I had to make the proviso that it wouldn't be allowed to interfere with my work as a priest, should there be any need for me to administer Sacraments to the dying. That is my job in battle, after all. Fortunately, there wasn't much call for it. As for my being able to do the broadcasting—well, I suppose years of teaching help us to develop a gift of the gab. In this case it wasn't difficult for me to extemporize. The difficulty was to keep to the facts because I was excited. Just like everyone else on board. There was no need to dramatize anything, of course. We were living drama. Anyone who heard those plane-to-ship and ship-to-plane conversations realized that. They were pretty steep some of them. Once I heard some bad language, but it wasn't really bad. Speaks well for the Navy pilots, don't you think?"

"Our squadron especially, but we knew you'd be listening," kidded Mac. "We've a great respect for you here, Padre. Besides we're exceedingly salubrious. All our boys read nursery rhymes in their spare time, and the married ones write to their wives all day. But honestly, you did a good job, Padre."

"I'm truly glad." The Padre was very happy about it all. "The Captain's idea was for me to give those broadcasts over the public-address system so that the hundreds of men whose battle stations kept them below deck—I wonder if you pilots ever think of them?—could get an idea of what was going on. Put yourself in their position for a while—cooped up in a compartment often below the waterline, with nothing to do by the hour but to wonder and wait. Of course, they have the tension of being ready all the time to rush out for fire fighting or damage control, should the ship be hit in adjacent compartments. If they get hit in their own compartment, they won't have a chance to do that. We felt that to fight the ship at its best they ought to know what you experienced—it would help to relieve the monotony of their job. It was a good idea of the Captain's to remember them down there and, I should imagine, a great comfort to them. The Captain figured in advance that every one of them would appreciate knowing what was going on outside and what our planes were doing. There was another thing too—we needed to set their minds at ease. Whenever there was a concussion thud, which they knew instinctively is a depth charge, it would help if they knew just what was happening. I mean, if we caught the sub or not. I couldn't tell them that, but I did my best. They told me afterwards that what they liked most was knowing which squadrons were going off and what objectives they were after!"

Chapter 6

THE NAVY planes were back at their job early in the morning of the ninth, the second day of the action. French shore batteries were offering sharp resistance. It seemed that the near misses and strafing that had been so adequately undertaken by the dive bombers and fighters respectively could only silence them temporarily. Only direct hits from heavy bombs would put these guns definitely out of action.

It was a brilliant dawn, with a freshening wind freckling the sea with whitecaps, and visibility almost as good as one could wish. As one of the husky plane captains put it, "Just a grand day for a scrap."

Dog-day had been a great experience for the squadron, a fast and furious fighting day, an exacting test for the utility of naval aviation supporting troop landings. Control of the air was essential, and could only be achieved by elimination of the Vichy air force. Army planes on carriers were waiting to use fields the enemy was now controlling.

Until we had obtained control of the air to enable the troops to capture the airfields, those planes could not take off.

The losses of the day before meant some changes in the squadron's flying arrangements. Cagey Hammond took over Mac Wordell's section. Hank Weiler, the flight officer, whose duty is to arrange who flies with whom, when, and how, and to keep a record of the trips, did his best to make the changes so that the same bunch of fellows who knew each other were together; when this was not possible he paired off a new wingman with a senior and experienced pilot.

The night before, Commander Hoskins, the executive officer, had read a message from the Captain that had touched the spot. It came up with the plan of the day in the wardroom that morning, with the preface by the "exec." We're so proud of it that we can't resist publishing it again.

The outstanding performance of the ship and its air group on Sunday, 8 November 1942, surpasses any known achievement by a carrier and its air group. The cheerful and willing manner in which pilots took off on a total of two hundred and three flights to engage the enemy on land, on sea, and in the air in a single day constitutes a bright page in the history of the ship. The efficient handling of planes and ship by the officers and crew of the ship made this remarkable performance possible. Several men have made the supreme sacrifice in fighting our country's cause but our aircraft have made a major contribution to the successful landings by Army troops at Fedala and Port Lyautey. I take pleasure in saying "well done."

It was signed "Commander Task Force."

The pilots and ship's officers clustered round reading it. It was good to hear that the task force commander felt we had done a good job, but every pilot was probably feeling he could have done a better one. Our mood had changed from that of yesterday morning. The whole ship's personality had settled to an attitude of grim confident efficiency. We were fighting—and fighting well. We weren't excited about going into battle any more. We knew what it was like. All that remained now was to go in again and fight harder. Today was to be a crucial day, with our task that of following up heavy punches with knockout blows. Someone had said that we must crush the resistance today or the landing would be thwarted and the show might go on for weeks. If Sunday had been busy, this was to be a rush job. We had been up since 0400, half an hour before general quarters, and were waiting in the ready room. Tommy had warned us we might be in the air most of the day. He explained that our task would be the same as the day before—to patrol the area, destroy any hostile planes in the air and on the ground, and support the landing force in every way possible.

The Captain, in his report to the ship of the first day's action, gave a good hand to the Chaplain's blow-by-blow account. He also told us that some of our ships had been hit but none were put out of action. He struck one ominous note when he added "yet" to that, saying, "The enemy is concentrating its submarines in this area. It will be a miracle if all our ships escape. Keep a sharp lookout, all of you. So far our squadrons and the ship's crew have done a marvelous job. I must say I have never read a message giving higher praise than the commander of the task force gave us yesterday. But we must keep on hitting the ball and hitting hard if we are to complete our mission successfully and arrive safely back home."

Home, which seemed quite a space of time away at that moment, was from where we had sailed on that morning in October. To be on a U.S. Navy ship leaving its base provides a panorama of views and emotions for the crew and flying officers. It is a kind of mechanism departure and fundamentally democratic. Officers driving through the air base give lifts to the crewmen. The share-a-car principle is highly developed in this man's Navy. On an embarkation trip, an automobile is not much use unless you have a wife or somebody to drive it home when you've gone aboard. You can't just park it until you come back. Every ship berth has a parking lot. Most of them are taken up by the sacred spots where only the automobile of the captain and the senior officers can stand. That morning, there were cars flowing in steady streams to the ship, in infinite variety, some slick and glittering toys and some of them decidedly on the aged list.

Ed Seiler has quite an "expensive" proposition, a kind of squadron sweetheart that was high-pressured onto him by Hubie, Pete, and the Short Man for the magnificent sum of $125. It makes strange noises and it wheezes, but it goes, and when the local rationing board decided that Ed was a Navy hero and allowed him to fit four re-capped tires, its value and utility curve ascended sharply. As Ed had no wife to act as return driver, we were spared the pleasure of bidding good-bye to that familiar jalopy.

Wherein is a tip to prospective wives of Navy fliers: learn to drive the automobile. Then you will be able to do the embarkation stunt in approved style and get a first view of the carrier when it returns and embarks.

News coming over the radio was encouraging. The Vichy radio had announced yesterday that American troops had infiltrated at some points in Algiers and followed it with a communique saying that fortifications in Algiers were burning after being shelled by British destroyers. The British radio stated that American forces of all types, supported by the British under the supreme command of General Eisenhower, had successfully landed in North Africa.

Those communiques were of the greatest interest to us, even if we were very close to this second front. By studying them, we kept track of what was going on. They were read and reread a hundred times more attentively than one scans a daily newspaper at home, and they were discussed endlessly. Arguments mushroomed as they will among men; everyone wanted to know how long the French would fight. We heard, too, that the American Navy fliers had destroyed fifty-two French planes yesterday. We'd make it a hundred today, if we got the chance.

This morning was not like yesterday, starting off with its tense excitement, the prayers, the pep talk. We had undergone our baptism of fire and survived, even if we had lost some men and planes. There were short silences when the conversation sagged. Pilots, fidgeting with their straps and pistols, would hunch together talking in low voices, but each man had his ear focused on the loud-speaker system. They were keener than ever to get a hop then. While waiting, some of us were holding our own committee of inquiry on Mac and Tag Grell. Tag was worse off than Mac because he had fallen in the drink. The Short Man had flown round some fishing vessels he had seen near by and signaled to them to pick up Tag. There had been some strange ships hovering about. With so many submarines in the area, and known to be coming up on our heels, one of them might have surfaced and taken him aboard. Tag was one of the married men, too.

We had to wait some time for anything to happen. We began listening to the jukebox and collecting and airing the new gags that spring up among members of a squadron overnight. Rumors began to circulate that General Doolittle had been called to finish the job we had started. Doolittle was due to arrive at any moment with his Army planes. The Doolittle gag was running high all through the battle. A ginger-haired pilot from the dive-bombing squadron stuck his cheery mug in the door. "Hey, fellows! Where's Doolittle? Gotta message for him."

"Can't tell you—we know, of course, but under the terms of the Geneva Convention we're not permitted to say. He's a military secret! Didn't you know that?"

"You're off the beam! Everybody knows—he's waiting till we drop some cement bombs to fill those holes on Cazes airfield. Then he'll land those Army planes. Army planes can't land in holes like Wildcats."

Gaff was being tossed here and there most of the time, over a musical background provided by the jukebox. There would be a lull sometimes, then you would hear a pilot kidding along in a loud voice . . . "And all of a sudden there were enemy planes all around me".

"Magnificent—just magazine stuff!"

"But seriously—I'm not through yet. I shot one down and then the other, and another came. The pilot got out and began to crawl up my wing tip with a shark knife in his mouth."

"Gosh, what did you do?"

"Well, kid, I shot him down three times, but he came back, and began yelling at me over the radio."

"What did he say?"

Everybody roared the answer, a hilarious chorus—"Where's Doolittle?"

Tommy Booth came in to break it up. "Boys, there's a lot to do today and we've got to do a hell of a lot better this time. We lost six good men yesterday, principally because we didn't keep together. I'm relying on you to do better today."

A mess boy followed, smiling broadly. "We'll have sandwiches on the flight deck for you today, gentlemen," he said. "The chief steward is sorry about yesterday, but they were sent down to the men's mess in error." We cheered.

The Padre came on the loud-speaker system. "Here it is—We have just heard that enemy bombers are attacking our forces at Safi."

Safi was not in our area, but there was a chance we might be sent to help. We waited impatiently. And presently the bridge called for planes. Not our squadron though, but the Blue squadron. The next call brought us to the flight deck to take off on a combat patrol over our area at Fedala. Tommy Booth had just got off when the ship made a hard turn to the right. We heard afterwards that the torpedo had been seen just in time. Those crewmen on the lookout were doing a good job. When a submarine is near, there is a sudden blast of noise, then splurges of activity. Destroyers were dealing with this one. We could see the depth charges throwing up feathery mountains of spray. We counted eight of these explosions as the ship swung back into wind.

Tommy brought us over Fedala, which we knew like the main street of our home town by this time, and set us to flying round in a wide defensive

circle. We had a good view of the war beneath.
Our troops were still landing. Some French ships
were burning, and the big French guns were firing steadily. The concussion of the harbor buildings must have been terrific. Sometimes pieces
of debris flew up as the great stabs of fire welted
out. To the southwest, a big fire was spreading a
dirty black smoke screen across the countryside.
The shells from our battleships were bracketing
the shore with high explosives. Occasionally the
fifteen-inch guns of the *Jean Bart* would belch a
salvo through the haze.

We circled for a time, keeping a good lookout for enemy fighters. The sky was empty, except for a few clouds and black patches of anti-
aircraft fire in the distance. Away from the town,
the countryside was sleeping peacefully: serene
and rolling away to the south, without a sign of
life, as if it were ignoring the bombardment.

Tommy Booth announced he was going down
below to see what was doing. This is just like
Tommy, doing things himself first before asking
anyone else. A mission like that is dangerous. The
French might have brought up more fighters and
anti-aircraft guns. We waited, circling in formation at twelve thousand feet, watching him and
Boyd darting here and there, the dark wings of
their Wildcats showing sharply against the green-
brown countryside. Twice they flew across the
green carpet of the airfield. The blast of anti-aircraft we expected to see did not show. We heard
via radio a ground officer call from the beach,

"There's a French plane strafing our troops—you've got to get him."

"We're coming," answered Tommy.

"Leave it," countermanded the ship. "Take a look at the enemy transport, Fedala–Casablanca road."

Tommy hurried off, leaving us with Cagey Hammond, the next senior pilot. Just after Tommy had gone, Hammond called Dub Taylor. "Dub, there's a plane down there. Look—nine o'clock." A plane was coming in under us. The chances were ten to one that it was the French plane that had been sneaking across the beaches. He would be worth getting. Cagey took his section, four planes including his own. They were going down like dark plummets, their silhouettes sharply etched against the sky. We waited, circling, keeping our eyes skinned. That peaceful, placid-looking sky might produce fireworks any second. We wouldn't be caught this time, as yesterday. I guess we all felt the same about that. Cagey and Dub broke off their dive suddenly, Cagey reporting, "Careful, you fellahs. Looks to me like Sweeney."

"It is me!" Sweeney's familiar voice came out. Sweeney was making a photographic reconnaissance in a specially equipped plane. We could see the belly tanks that had been attached underneath the wings to increase the flying range of his fighter. Our four Wildcats climbed back and the division formed up again. It was dull sitting up there like vultures waiting for something to happen! The French were either holding back their aircraft or the work we had put in on them the day before had been too hot for them.

Then Tommy Booth called for us to meet him at the southeast end of the Fedala–Casablanca road. "We're going to attack some trucks, bringing up supplies." Tommy's tip-off had been 100 percent correct. Along the narrow road leading to Casablanca was a long convoy of motor trucks. Hustling along, each throwing up a telltale plume of dust, they looked like tea-stained lumps of sugar sliding along a chute. "Make sure of them this time," urged Tommy, and we went down at about 240 knots in pairs. Tommy's .50-caliber guns began to speak, and the first truck swerved off the road into the ditch. Another hit a tree. Machine-guns began to squirt at the Wildcats as they went over, a roaring deadly aerial chain of destruction, slashing forward progress of the motor convoy. We zoomed up at the end of the run that must have covered the whole fifty of them.

"Once more," ordered Tommy. We went in again from another direction, guns blazing. The trucks were already smoking and turning. That road was a pathetic sight, striking evidence of the relentless destruction of war. The vehicles had stopped in tragic disorder, some capsized in the ditch. As far as we could judge, not one was moving. The drivers were probably dead or had taken cover. We heard afterwards that six out of the fifty had been burned, eight were ditched, and nearly all damaged. The terrific destruction handed out to the first units completely blocked the progress of the convoy. They were packed with troops. "Well done, gang," said Tommy. "Join up and we'll head home."

We went hurriedly to the ready room when we got back from that trip. We munched sandwiches and drank coffee in between giving our reports to the intelligence officers, while the men were gassing up and recharging the guns. The bridge had word of tanks heading toward our bridgeheads and sent us off again. In a very short time we were back over the target, with the port of Casablanca showing a chain of bonfires. We inspected the roads carefully. There were no tanks visible, just the abandoned trucks we had strafed. Tommy announced that he thought he saw the tanks and left us to go below and investigate, only to find they were haystacks.

The ground liaison officer called again, saying, "That French plane is strafing our troops again. He comes in from the east, strafes us and then disappears. Can't you get him?" There was nothing we would like better.

Four of us went over the beach and hung around. We could see nothing but our troops. Tommy left the rear section to patrol for a while. The rest of us were to return to the ship. We were on the way home when the ship warned us that Vichy tanks were heading towards Casablanca. We found them. They must have been tipped off that we were coming to attack. By the time we got there they had taken shelter off the road under some tall palm trees. Anti-aircraft guns began to spit at us but with wild aim. We came down below the level of the tree tops and methodically filled them with slugs. Tommy told us to "get them from the side." We gave them plenty, leaving them burning under the trees. Having completed our mission, we headed back. On our way we saw some of the results of the work of the High Hat squadron, now being led by Embree, and the fire of the U.S. naval guns. A fair-sized Vichy cruiser was beached with black smoke rising from its stern and a destroyer lay miserably on its side, its red-banded funnels barely showing above the water.

We had had no casualties that day, we learned after arriving at the ship. Embree had arrived back on the flight deck with his plane looking as if it had been passed through a mincing machine. His section had been strafing a line of enemy tanks and transports trying to sneak in towards the city of Casablanca and immediately attacked them. It was a battle of angry Dauntless dive bombers, veritable tanks of the air, against the crawling armor of the land troops. The conflict was short and sharp. One tank got a direct hit, another burst into flames, two were overturned by near misses. The French soldiers were fighting hard during this attack. One section set up a .50-caliber machine-gun on the road and fought the American planes shot by shot. One of Embree's pilots remarked, "It was just cold hard fighting courage. They had probably done the same thing when they faced the Germans in France. We went at them again, and again, and finally the gun was silenced."

"We had quite a busy day and plenty of opportunity to study the countryside," said Max Eaton. "I remember seeing some cows grazing in a field, which reminded me I hadn't had a glass of milk for a long time, and there were plenty of goats and pigs. Scouting for targets, we could hear the ship talking to its squadrons in the air. Once I heard Jocko talking to his planes. One fellow asked, 'Is that a tank down there?' and Jocko drawled, 'It looks to me like a tired camel. Leave it.'"

Embree and his radioman, Eardeley, surely used up a good many of their proverbial lives on this attack. One truck they were strafing was snaking along the road. Suddenly it headed for the field and Embree, so intent on concentrating on his target, flew his plane head on through a roadside eucalyptus tree.

Embree is a stocky, rather pink-faced fellow, who looks much younger than he is, and he achieved the distinction in this action of putting in more hours in the air than any other pilot.

We also found that Jack Raby's Blue squadron had been in the luck. It was definitely Jack's day.

"May I say that Jack's quite a character—as tough as they come," put in the Padre. "I have a confession to make. I felt, in a moderately pious way, quite a hero, getting up at two every morning after about five hours' sleep to say Mass before going to battle stations. It was difficult to get to bed early, too, after action. So much to do, so much to talk about. There was a great temptation

to stay another hour in bed, but I knew that some
of the officers and men wanted to attend Mass and
take Holy Communion. The third day was the
worst. There was Jack on his knees and swaying
to and fro. I had warned him the night before to
stay in bed, but Jack turned up, dozing like a tired
bulldog. Poor old chap, he was half asleep, but
there he was with the others wanting to make a
good start for the day."

The Padre smiled. "Jack had quite a day. We
could hear him over the radio, snapping out his
orders and going in. When he called out, 'Got
him—got him!' and then, 'Got another—right on
the nose!' everyone strained to listen and thrill at
that fighting flier doing his job."

Blue squadron had taken off before the Red
Rippers just after seven on a similar mission to
the one we had the day before to go out and destroy any enemy planes they encountered over
their area. They ran into two groups of Vichy
fighters, taking off either to attack or to fly inland. Jack got his boys into a cloud formation
before the Vichy pilots had seen him and then attacked the leader of the French squadron at close
range.

He caught his victim unawares with a sizable
burst of fire. His bullets tore big holes in the
enemy's fuselage, and the plane rolled over and
went down. This Vichy squadron was game. They
turned to attack the Wildcats. The enemy leader's
wingmate got on Jack's tail with another H-75
supporting him. Jack, headed for the cloud and

the H-75, followed to snoop for him. "It was the damnedest thing you ever saw," said Jake Onstott, flying with Jack. "The skipper went in that cloud with the Frenchman on his tail, squirting all the time. Then Jack came out heading south. One of the Frenchmen was to starboard, the other must have lost himself in the cloud. Both planes were fully extended. Anything might have happened with the odds against the Wildcat because of the Vichy plane's nimbleness. The Vichyman seemed to be an experienced flier. He turned in sharply in wonderful style and tried to get Jack on the starboard side. Jack saw his ruse and flipped his Wildcat over. The sinister looking red-and-yellow-striped nose of the French plane seemed to be only a few yards from Raby's quarter. The boys of Jack's section thought they were going to collide, but Jack was quicker with his guns—a second perhaps, or half a second. Just enough. His bullets got there first. The Vichy plane blew to pieces in the air, its lightly colored nose falling like a bomb".

"It was the finest bit of flying I've ever seen," said one of Jack's pilots. "Better than any movie."

Blue squadron was outnumbered in that encounter by two to one. The French pilots were fighting mad. They had probably been told they could outmaneuver the Wildcats. They broke formations and fastened onto the Wildcats in pairs, attacking persistently. It soon was a good old-fashioned dogfight, but the Vichy pilots were at a disadvantage because their .30-caliber guns were of little use against the armor fitted to the American machines. Unless they got a direct hit on the Wildcats in a vital and vulnerable part or killed the pilot, the machine kept on flying. One Navy pilot who had lost his wingmate preferred to take on six of the H-75 pilots instead of evading action. They all jumped on him at once—two on his tail, two on his flank, and two from ahead. It looked as if they were filling him with lead, but he finally fought them back and kept coming for more. He eluded them by diving through the clouds. When he pulled out of the dive, one of the H-75s was still hanging on—and giving him frequent bursts. He stopped firing suddenly, and the American pilot guessed that his ammunition had run out. He climbed sharply and came round in a tight circle, his guns aimed at the enemy's motor. Three short bursts of his .50-caliber guns—they were his last shells—brought the usual result. The H-75 went down burning with the pilot standing up gesticulating wildly. The five remaining Vichy pilots attacked Lt. Casey Childers. To elude them, he too spun down till he was almost on the ground. Again, one of the excited Vichy pilots followed him down only to be raked by that terrifying .50-caliber fire. It was a battle of modern American planes against outdated ones and American resource and determination against the Gallic courage and temperament.

The French appeared to be bringing their planes from the Port Lyautey airfield to our section of "country," but Raby's boys had intercepted and beaten them off. Jack got his squadron off again to attack Port Lyautey airfield where it was presumed the French were preparing to launch a bomber attack against our battleships and transports. Finding no planes in the air but many on the ground, he decided to strafe them and knock out the airfield defenses, which seemed to have been augmented. The squadron got a bit reckless as the French gunners were getting their eye in. "Go for 'em," said Jack over the radio. "Knock 'em cold."

A minute later the ship's radio picked up a message from Ensign Wilhoite: "They got me." It was followed by a gasp and a silence.

"We'll get 'em for that," snapped Raby's voice. He told the ship he was going in again.

One of the pilots reported having seen what appeared to be Wilhoite's plane spread all over the ground, where it had crashed after he had attacked a gun that had been spraying .50-caliber shells at him. Wilhoite had done plenty of damage before he was hit; the squadron reports credited him with having destroyed two French bombers on the ground and silenced a gun emplacement. The other pilots dealt with the set of guns that had got him. Raby brought his squadron back with several planes hit badly. Ensign Gerhardt made a forced landing in the sea and was picked up by a destroyer. Two other pilots landed on another carrier.

Lieutenant Winters had picked up some nasty shrapnel wounds in the leg and hand, but he managed to fly home although in great pain, and he did not bother to ask the ship for a priority. As he was carried below, he beckoned to a mess boy and grabbed a sandwich. "This kind of work makes you hungry."

The dive bombers had been out all day bombing shore batteries and ships. One got back minus flaps and landing gear, and crash-landed on deck. Others came in severely holed.

About midday, the Padre came on the announcing system again. "Here it is. Everything is going well. Our troops are landing in great numbers at Fedala, and it looks as if we have gained control of the air over that area. Red squadron has been over and met no enemy aircraft."

Later he made a utility appeal. The metal smiths had run out of adhesive and medical tape, with which they were repairing the bullet holes and shrapnel gashes in the wings of the planes. "Anyone of you who happens to have any Scotch tape, will you please turn it in?" he asked. There was a rush to turn in anything available, and scuttlebutt reported that someone had secretively contributed a card of bobby pins.

The Red Rippers were chafing a bit because Jack Raby's squadron seemed to have been getting all the fighting. Later came the news that Army planes were due to land on a captured airfield. Naval aviation had won the first round. The operations were working clearly to plan and demonstrating one outstanding thing: if you can knock out the enemy's air force, troops can land with comparative safety with air support.

At midday, a section of Blue squadron was off again on a mission to Medouina. The Vichy air force were again assembling bombs to attack our ships. How swiftly the Navy planes struck is shown by the report that not one of these bombers left the ground. When our planes went over the airfield, a report was received that enemy troops were proceeding along the road to Casablanca. The Wildcats turned them back in the face of a heavy crossfire that did some damage.

One pilot on that hop, Lt. Edward Micka, was killed. He was flying in fast and low, shooting up a bomber on the ground, when his plane received the full force of that bomber exploding. "We saw his plane literally disintegrate," said another pilot's report. "There was no chance for him to survive."

When that particular flight returned, there was plenty of work for the plane crews. One pilot whose plane had been hit twenty times was carried to sick bay with severe wounds, a tribute to the increasing accuracy of the French fire, and his own courage in making repeated attacks. At sunset, as the planes were coming in, the Padre was burying young Patterson, the radio gunner who had been killed the day before.

"It was quite a simple affair," he said. "just the last rites for a brave kid who gave his life for Uncle Sam—and for our way of life. It took place on the hangar deck to the accompaniment of the rumble of the guns of our ships attacking the port of Casablanca. As many officers and men as could be spared from their battle stations attended. I spoke very briefly: 'This man has been killed by enemy fire in action. Before this battle is over, we may also meet death. We must not be morbid about such a thought, but we must face the fact. If death comes, may it find us in the grace of God. Let us say the Lord's Prayer for the repose of the soul of our shipmate, and hope that God will ease the natural pain of sorrow that will come to his mother when she hears that her son is dead!'

"As I finished the prayer, the ship went into a wide turn to starboard, and in the middle of that turn, the boy's body was committed to the sea. The marine guard of honor fired a salute, and the bugler played taps.

"By a coincidence, the dive-bomber squadron to which Patterson had been attached was returning from its latest mission and was circling overhead as if in tribute to his memory.

"It was a brief but slow and solemn ceremony. When it was over, the men returned to man the battle stations' whole complement, and the ship that itself seemed to have paused to honor the brave youngster to whom a chance to get a crack at the enemy was worth more than money, turned into the wind and continued with the urgent business of landing the planes that came out of the darkened sky at regular intervals."

In the wardroom that evening, we had time to take a longer view of the operations in which we had been engaged. We had met the Vichy air force, which was Hitler's first line of defense in North Africa, and if the Red Rippers had not entirely covered themselves with glory, they had done a good job.

We had expected air fighting to be fast, deadly work. Our first clash with the enemy had shown that it was just that, and a lot more. The speed of the operation gives no time for correction of errors, and if one man fails to keep formation, the others are at a disadvantage. We talked the whole thing over rather seriously that night and although no one mentioned it, we really missed Mac, Spanky, and the rest.

The program of the invasion showed up clearly in the resume of the news of the day. An American supply ship had docked alongside the quay in Fedala Harbor and troops were landing without resistance. Vichy had announced that an armistice had been signed by the government in Algeria, and the Army planes had arrived. A number of carrier-based planes had landed at Safi, the first airfield to be taken by our troops.

There was plenty of work ahead of us, we knew. The French shore guns and the big *Jean Bart* were still resisting in Casablanca, and planes were expected to be brought from airfields farther inland. The whereabouts of the French bombing squadrons known to be in the neighborhood, but which had not put in an appearance, was a mystery. Some of the pilots had personal scores to even up. Bus and Rubie were collectively mad at an anti-aircraft battery that had put some stuff dangerously near them. They were planning to go and strafe it if Tommy would give his O.K.

"I want to get that fellow who has been strafing the troops on the beach," said Hubie. "I'd like to get that son-of-a-seacook."

"You're a bit too late, Hubie, I think." It was Woody speaking. "Yes," said Woody, "it happened like this—for which I am extremely grateful. Hank and I suddenly sighted the Phantom Raider. It was quite different from any other plane we had seen—as far as we could make out, it was an ME-109. It was painted dull black all over and seemed very fast. It was the meanest, dirtiest job I've ever seen. Hank made a pass at him, but missed. The other plane went on. I crammed on full power and made a shallow high-side run.

"I opened fire from 150 yards and gave him all guns. It was a long burst. I felt this was a job that had to be done extra well. I kept firing until he disintegrated in my face. As a matter of fact, I was forced to pull up very violently to avoid the pieces of the plane and the flames. There was so much oil—I suppose it was German oil—on my windshield that I could hardly see out. The wing was also covered and had been hit by something from the ME-109. Fortunately, I was undamaged. Hank and I then returned to the ship, and I was feeling exceedingly happy. We wouldn't have that ground officer moaning about the Phantom Raider any longer.

"Incidentally, just as we were getting to the ship, there was a bit of excitement. A submarine had been sighted taking cover between two fishing boats. The ship's heavier anti-aircraft opened fire on it. They may have sunk the submarine. These sub commanders are certainly clever at taking all the cover they can, and of course, one is never sure about the loyalty of those fishing boats. They were probably in cahoots with the subs. All I hoped was that Tag wasn't aboard that sub. It would have been a bit ironic to be sunk by our own shellfire."

The air opposition had been stiff and more effective, but the Navy planes had done considerable damage, pounding shore batteries and harbor defenses, and destroying planes on the ground at Rabat, Cazes, and Marrakech. In the south, the weather had been too calm and foggy for air operations, and several planes short of gas had landed on the airfield at Saki, the first to be captured by our ground forces.

The most outstanding feature of the day had been the converging of opposition troops at both Lyautey and Rabat. The Navy fighters, however, had been warned in time and succeeded in forcing the troops to retreat from the area under attack and putting out of action most of the vehicles. It had been a good day.

Chapter 7

THE FIRST planes of the Navy air group took the air early on the morning of the tenth, the third day of the action. The Vichy shore batteries were still firing pugnaciously at our ships. The hope that the bombings of the day before had silenced them was vain. Word came that they needed more and persistent attention, to separate the gunners from their determination to fight the Battle of Africa for the Axis.

Everywhere about the carrier was the steady, braced atmosphere of game fighting efficiency. The ship had lived through forty-eight hours of tense action. Her planes had been constantly in the air, landing hard blows on the Axis' African bastion. They had left and returned without letup. In a sense she was making carrier history by supporting this landing operation with her deadly bombs, reaching out hundreds of miles to deliver devastating long-range punches on the ships, anti-aircraft guns, and troops.

Many of the planes on the hangar deck were showing their scars, those patches of adhesive tape. Again, the crewmen had worked through the night getting them in flying condition. Every plane that could be safely gotten into the air was ready for action. The plane captains stood by their charges on the deck, eyeing them like proud and anxious fathers.

The first combat patrol left the carrier shortly after 0615. Jack Raby led two sections of his fighter squadron over Fedala.

"We heard him say he was going down to strafe some guns and cavalry," said the Padre, "and we knew the battle was on again. I was always excited when I heard Jack saying, 'Come on boys. Ready. Here we go.'"

Shortly before 0700, Lt. Ralph Embree took off with a section of the thick, heavy-bellied scout bombers to attack the coast defense batteries at Point El Hank.

It was a bad day for air operations, but fortunately not bad enough to give the Vichymen a lull in which to bring up their forces.

Embree arrived over the target to find it was raining. The visibility varied from one to five miles. The scout bombers came gliding through the clouds, to be met by concentrated A.A. fire, which showed that the French had been busy at night replacing their battered guns. One gun received a direct hit, and two others were rocked by near misses.

On the way back, Embree noticed something that seemed unusual. He led his flight across the bay to snoop. The coast defense guns on the northern tip of the harbor had been trained on the harbor itself. He informed the ship, suggesting that these guns should be silenced, whatever their intention might be.

As the bomb-lightened planes flew home, two small fishing boats were observed five miles north of the carrier. Such small craft had been present all through the action, and might presumably have been giving cover and assistance to submarines. The planes flew down and circled them, but the pilots could see nothing of a suspicious nature. A second later, a submarine surfaced some distance away and fired. Two torpedo wakes streaked towards the ship, but the alert watchers on the deck had seen them, and the carrier moved aside. "It was like a boxer weaving to avoid a punch," said one of the pilots. "I'll admit I held my breath. A few seconds later, another submarine surfaced and fired a torpedo at another carrier. This one missed also."

"Jocko and I were going to Fedala to fly an anti-sub patrol round our transports lying offshore that morning," recalled Max Eaton. "We had left the ship just before daybreak when I sighted a sub on the surface a half mile ahead. There was no mistaking it. It was cruising along unconcernedly. It looked easy meat. I gave my engine the gun, armed my bomb, and got ready to attack. I wanted to get that sub. Then as I got into position for a dive, the sub disappeared, and all I could see was one of those eternal fishing boats. I was mad. I felt like dropping the bomb any how and paying it back for not being a sub. I suppose I was fooled because a minute later I heard the ship say, 'Sub sighted inside fishing boats.' Shortly afterwards I heard, 'Congratulations, No.7, you made a direct hit.' It wasn't me, but I'm glad they got the sub."

The Red Rippers' first job was to take reconnaissance photographs over the area of Petit Jean near Port Lyautey. Bus and Hubie escorted Wally Madden, who was to do the photographing. On arriving over the target area, Bus and Hubie separated from Wally and flew over Medouina airport, where two fighters were seen to be on the airfield. "Do you think those babies could fly?" asked Hubie.

"They don't look like it," answered Bus.

"We'll make sure."

"O.K., Hubie . . . let's go."

The Wildcats swept down over the airport. If the Vichy airmen had been entertaining any hopes of getting those planes off the ground that day, they were blasted. After two runs, the planes were reduced to a mass of charred fragments.

When the two pilots came back to the ship, they reported they could see American landing barges debarking troops inside the breakwater at Fort Kasba. Port Lyautey airfield had been quiet, with nothing to be seen but the remains of some French Douglas bombers and many bomb craters in the runways. There were no seaplanes in the harbor and a French destroyer that had anchored in the bed of the river overnight had not attempted to fire.

"We saw some trucks parked under some trees heading east at Sidi Slimana," one of the pilots wrote in his report, "but as they were surrounded by civilians we did not strafe them."

The pilots had given a lot of thought to the possibility of strafing the civilians. Strict orders had been given to avoid it, but accidents might happen, and that had worried them.

Hank took a section of four Wildcats over the ship. Two fishing vessels that had been constantly in view during the action were again observed. As the pilots went down to investigate them, a large disturbance that might have been caused by a submarine surfacing appeared about 150 yards from the port beam of the ship.

At 0830, Tommy Booth took four planes over Fedala to attack the Vichy ground forces that were moving in to contact American troops. "As we flew over the Cherrat River," said Tommy, "we could see U.S. trucks and troops proceeding along the road to Rabat, preceded by scout cars, tanks, and motorcycles. On receiving a warning from ground intelligence that Vichy troops were moving along the road from Bouznika and the Nefifilch River, I led my flight down, and we strafed fifteen to twenty vehicles. By the time we left all the tanks had been stopped. Some were burning, some had overturned. I reported to ship what damage we had done, and we were called home."

Several of the pilots reported to the intelligence officer that the attack on the tanks had been extraordinarily effective, despite the fact that many of them had taken shelter behind the road-side trees. Tommy Booth told his pilots to attack the tanks from the side when their tops were not exposed sufficiently to make them adequate targets.

Hank Weiler took his section off on a combat patrol over the transports and landing forces in the Fedala area.

"I think the most striking sight I've ever seen in connection with naval aviation occurred on the morning of the tenth of November when Tommy led twelve of us fighters to attack Casablanca," said Ed. "As we left the carrier and rendezvoused, dawn was just breaking. But it wasn't the typical dawn that we've seen before because there wasn't as much light and as much red color. There were quite a few clouds at low altitude, not cumulus and thick, but rather bunched, thin and wispy. When you flew through them you could see approximately fifty feet in any direction, a thin, ghostly veil—thinner than the clouds. In other words, when the three sections of four planes each were climbing to altitude through this stuff you could see all twelve planes but the outer ones were barely visible, as if seen through a camera lens slightly out of focus from where you were flying.

"I got a most intense impression of speed and fury. These Wildcats looked actually furious, fast, formidable. Nothing could stop them, I thought. The sight of these twelve Wildcats tearing through this thin veil was tremendous: we were going up and up and up in this slight climb of one thousand feet per minute. The impression of speed was very strong because the clouds were quite close so that you could judge their speed.

"We usually never get a true impression of speed. We just feel we are floating in space, casually floating in a vacuum where there is little sound and fury. Even a dive is like that. The cockpits are so sound- and cold-proof that the pilot lives in a comfortable world all his own, untouched by the outer world. But here in this vivid moment, the twelve planes were climbing fast, furiously—a dynamic pattern. All the colors were pastel: pale, cold blues, and grays with these wispy, ghostlike clouds whipping by. It wasn't cold and lonely flying there; rather it was an atmosphere of men on a deadly serious mission. We were together, cooking with gas, confident in our machines, in their capabilities. No worry about anything going wrong—nothing had ever gone wrong with these marvelously rugged, dependable, furious Wildcats. We were very hopeful with many fellow pilots *together,* flying in easy, efficient formation, up and up and up through this blue, pale misty morning!"

After patrolling for an hour, Hank called the air liaison officer. "This is Red section supporting you. Have you a mission for us?" The ground officer answered, "Wait." Presently he came on again. "Go and look at the main road between Casablanca and Rabat-Salé."

"O.K.," answered Hank, "Anything you say. We are proceeding to the Casablanca–Rabat-Salé road."

The Wildcats flew north. "Look, boys," called Hank. "Tanks under those trees!"

Twenty-five miles north of the river bridge was a narrow string of tanks and supply cars.

"Take 'em low," said Hank. "We'll go in string." The Wildcats went down in single-column formation, opening fire at one hundred feet and finishing up at fifty feet. At one roadblock, the Vichy machine gunners threw up a heavy anti-air-craft fire. Two medium tanks turned to the fields for safety, followed by the pilots, who went weaving and darting across the fields.

Bus ironed out an old grievance here. On the north bank of the river, he found an anti-aircraft battery that had previously been firing at our planes, particularly at his and Hubie's. As he went over he gave it a burst, before rejoining his section.

The Wildcats' fire seemed to have been very effective. On his return, Hank reported that not only had the anti-aircraft battery been severely damaged, but along the road the burning remains of four supply trucks, two armored cars, and two medium tanks had been observed. All were out of action, and various other vehicles were halted in a state of disorder. The strafing had created a traffic block that effectively prevented the French from bringing up further supplies.

"It was good work, that hop," said the Short Man, who doesn't often say much. "We spotted some light tanks heading north escorted by some motorcyclists, and went after them. I got so concentrated on the job that the boys told me I was chasing a motorcyclist. He was game, too, riding like mad with my bullets splashing all round him. And he got away!"

"The most exciting thing about this trip was that Furney told us to go and look for the enemy vehicles on the other side of the road," said Ed. "So we flew along sometimes with the tree tops higher than our planes, and we could see the tanks and other vehicles hiding under the trees. Then we came back and strafed them through the tree tops."

In this kind of warfare, when bombers have been sent out to attack guns, ships, and airfields, accurate and frequent reconnaissance is essential. Sweeney, who was one of our men on this job, had been out on one of his photographic hops earlier in the day. He went in over Casablanca at ten thousand feet and although the French machine-guns were firing at him, he got down to two thousand feet to take pictures of the *Jean Bart* with her guns firing regularly, but slowly. There was smoke coming from her deck. Over Port Lyautey, he could see American tanks heading towards Casablanca but observed no activity on the roads north of the city. At Port Lyautey airfield, American Army planes had landed and workmen were busy filling the bomb holes with gravel.

Shortly after noon, a report was received that the *Jean Bart* was again indulging in a heavy gun duel with an American flagship. At all costs she must be silenced. As yet she had only been attacked by the scout bombers. Although her deck installations showed damage, and the harbor installations in the neighborhood had suffered, she was still a fighting unit. Orders were given for the dive bombers to be fitted with demolition bombs with delayed fuses so that the attacking planes could make good their escape before the bombs exploded deep in vital parts of the battleship.

Planes of Fighting Blue would patrol the dock area to eliminate any enemy aircraft that might take the air, and to strafe machine-gun and A.A. emplacements.

The American Navy air group had to keep punching. The light punches of the attacking fighters were to be followed by the heavier knockout blows of the dive-bombers.

Embree brought his Dauntless dive-bombers over the target early in the afternoon. The *Jean Bart* appeared a giant steel fortress standing out sharply in contrast to the burnt and destroyed buildings of the shore installations. Her guns were firing in answer to the salvos aimed at her by the flagship.

"Although our fighter escort had thoroughly strafed those gun emplacements," said Embree, "we encountered plenty of fire. It was extraordinarily heavy—that meant only one thing. The French had been busy getting their damaged guns in order and installing new ones during the night. Conditions were fairly good for our task, with cumulus cloud giving us excellent cover for the attack. We pushed over from eight thousand feet."

"A most exciting moment for us in the ship,"

interpolated the Padre. "We heard Embree giving his pilots instructions, and reminding them about opening their flaps. He added, 'Don't bother about that anti-aircraft fire. They haven't hit us yet. . . . Everyone ready? I'm going in.' Again that silence, during which I prayed for those brave youngsters flying into the face of death."

Embree's bomb was a near miss. The next pilot dropped his a few seconds later and made a direct hit on a big warehouse, that vanished completely after the hit. The third pilot was more successful. His bomb hit the after deck to starboard, and a large tongue of flame spurted out. The next plane came in low, and his bomb struck the left side of the after gun turret. The last pilot got another direct hit, planking a large bomb full on the stern of the great battleship. There was a mighty explosion that threw debris a thousand feet. The *Jean Bart's* guns stopped firing and were not heard again during the day.

"It was some sight to see those hits on the *Jean Bart*—she's a big baby," contributed Max Eaton. "We couldn't say exactly, but the fighter boys thought that four of the first bombs hit the ship. I saw towers of flames burst upward, which might have meant that we had hit a magazine."

Embree's planes were out again shortly before sunset. Later the dive bombers were off on three missions, to silence anti-aircraft batteries at the Jetée Transversaille, the shore batteries at Point El Hank, and the anti-aircraft batteries south of a cemetery at Point El Hank. They carried demolition bombs and were escorted by Wildcats of Fighting Blue.

Embree went down first to attack heavy anti-aircraft batteries on the jetty. Because none of the guns were firing, he transferred his target to a destroyer moored near the point. His bomb hit the water a few feet from the slender vessel.

The planes were being troubled by anti-aircraft emplacements on the Jetée Delure at the east end of the Mole du Commerce. Eaton asked permission to go in and silence the battery. He went into his dive from nine thousand feet in the face of heavy anti-aircraft and dropped his bomb at an angle of over fifty degrees, scoring a direct hit.

"Ralph called for a volunteer for what he described as a precise drop on a particular target. I asked for it," said Max. "It happened to be an anti-aircraft battery on the Jetée Delure. Ralph gave me a map with the target circled in pencil. As we approached the city, he directed us to split up and he went across the harbor to attack a destroyer. I went to my objective while the rest of the boys strung out to attack El Hank. The French guns were pumping flak at us as usual. But as we were diving simultaneously on different objectives, their fire couldn't be concentrated. I noticed some tracer going off to the right towards Ralph and I felt as if I was getting in unnoticed, so I got into a long and steady dive and released at about two thousand feet.

"I pulled out and headed straight for the sea. I wanted to wait and see what kind of stuff the bomb threw up but I didn't slow down any. This time as usual it took much too long to get out of the range of the machine guns that were spotted along the jetty. On my left I could see clouds of dust where the lads were dropping their eggs on El Hank. As we went home, we saw quite a lot of submarines, some of them below the surface.

"When I got back to the ready room, Ralph was in high spirits. He said my bombs had gone plunk on the A.A. battery. That made me feel good, but I thought I had better wait to see the photographs before getting really warmed up about it."

Embree then renewed his attack on a French destroyer with his .50-caliber guns. As he went down, the shore batteries on the Point El Hank turned on him. He told the other planes to settle them, while he drew their fire. The ruse was effective, and one of the other pilots scored a direct hit on the battery, smashing it beyond repair.

"The submarines were getting busy that day," continued Max. "I remember a periscope suddenly appeared less than two hundred feet off the port quarter. One of the pilots was just making a landing. The carrier, which had been keeping into the wind for the landings, changed course just after he hit the deck and immediately one of his wheels gave way and the plane stayed where it was. This change of course probably saved the ship because immediately a torpedo hissed by the stern. A sub on one quarter had surfaced and fired torpedoes at us point-blank. It certainly was touch and go all the time."

The last flight was made after sunset, and for the first day since action started, the ship gathered all her planes without loss or mishap.

The ship's crew had been fighting all day with that swift efficiency that only comes from practice and enthusiasm. "We knew our planes were doing well," said one of the plane captains, "but heck, that wasn't enough. We had to keep 'em doing better." "And we," said one of the ship's officers with considerable emphasis, "we had to keep that ship floating and fighting. The enemy had concentrated all his submarines in the area, and they weren't Vichy subs you understand. The presence of carriers was a signal for all the subs to get together. We shall never know how many there were, but with each hour of action we knew we had to redouble our vigilance, and keep the men at top efficiency. All through the day we kept getting reports of submarines. Sometimes the reports came from pilots of planes who strafed them as they were coming home from their missions, sometimes from destroyers. . . . One U-boat surfaced quite a distance from the ship, and immediately everything we had was thrown at it. There were times when it was difficult to imagine we could come through and carry on our routine of getting the planes aboard."

"We were lucky to get a bit of sleep in the afternoon," said Woody, "and we needed it. I was dog tired, but I had hardly lain down when the ship made one of these fantastic lurches, which meant only one thing, that some alert lookout had given a warning in time, and we had avoided a torpedo. I think the most staggering thing I saw that happy day was when I was coming back from the first hop. I was about twenty-five miles off Casablanca when the unbelievable happened. To me, it was like the appearance of the Great White whale in *Moby Dick.* I saw a submarine periscope, plainly visible. As I reported it, the sub surfaced about one hundred yards off the port quarter. I was very excited, and as I reported again to call someone who had something that might be effective I saw the torpedo heading through the wake of the carrier dead astern. The sub captain must have been desperate to get up to he came in quite close, and fired. Quite honestly I was hypnotized seeing that torpedo following the ship, which did not seem to have a chance. I just sat there perspiring. Then the miraculous happened. The ship made a routine turn to receive aircraft, and the torpedo went by, almost grazing the side. The strangest thing about it was that not a shot was fired by anyone. It was a silent drama like a movie with the sound cut off. The sub crash-dived and disappeared. She had been too near for anyone to see her or fire at her. It was a daring bit of work, that didn't come off."

"It certainly was," joined in the landing signal officer. "I saw that one too, Woody—I had just signaled a plane to come in to land, and the ship was moving her stern in to wind, when they saw the torpedo wake heading our way. It missed us not by yards it seemed—just inches. When it went by I heard one of the landing crew say to his pal, 'Tom, I figure we really ought to read that book on *Abandon, Ship* in the library.' 'O.K., Mr. Baker,' said the other. 'Well, I got my knife with me; and we aren't excited are we?' 'Me?' answered the other. 'No, I'm just plumb wild—that's all.'"

All through the trip there, a notice had been displayed urging the men to be prepared to abandon ship, and quoting from the book:

The following true account is quoted to impress upon all hands the fact that even in the case of a rapidly sinking vessel, there is time for cool, deliberate action [wrote the executive officer]: "The experience of B. A. Baker, the *Prusa's* third mate, will give you a gauge by which you can judge your own time in an emergency. After she was torpedoed, the *Prusa* sank in exactly nine minutes.

"Baker was asleep when the torpedo hit. He went to the bridge and got his sextant, chronometer, and navigation books. He stowed them in the boat and helped lower the boat. Then he went back and tried to get the radio operator to leave. Returning to his room, he obtained a sweater, and then jumped overboard. He swam about two hundred feet to the lifeboat. The *Prusa* sank as he was being pulled into the boat."

All that in nine minutes! Lessons we can learn from Baker's experience:

Lt. Comdr. Malcolm T. Wordell in a Wildcat at NAS Norfolk, shortly after Operation Torch. (U.S. Navy)

A candid shot of the VF-41 ready room the day before the first combat. Lieutenant Wordell (in goggles at right) and Lt. Jake Onstott (left) lead their comrades in a few songs. (U.S. Navy)

Looking aft in the Ripper ready room, Lieutenant Wordell (standing, second from left), with Lieutenant Onstott (standing, fourth from left) enjoy a few moments of pre-launch amusement. Bus Craig is to Onstott's left, with Fred Akers behind Chuck August, second from right. Middle row, far left, Pete Bolt, front row, left to right, Art Cassidy, Cagey Hammond, unknown, and Andy Andrews. Note the ammunition cartridges on their belts. (U.S. Navy)

Photographs of VF-41 Wildcats during Torch are extremely rare. This view shows deck action aboard *Ranger* as an F4F pilot prepares to launch. Note the two Piper L-4s far off to starboard, probably having launched and begun their short flight to the beach. (U.S. Navy)

A Piper L-4 begins its run down *Ranger*'s flight deck on 9 November. These military Piper Cubs served as hacks and occasional spotters during the North Africa campaign. The pilot of this L-4 was Army Capt. Ford E. Allcorn. After leaving the carrier, Allcorn ran into French AAA. His Piper was hit and began to burn. Allcorn was wounded. He sideslipped to keep the fire away from the cockpit and set the little plane down. He dragged himself away from it just before the L-4 exploded. (U.S. Navy)

Rear Adm. J. L. Hall (left) and Rear Adm. H. K. Hewitt (third from right) and their staff read a last-minute communique as Maj. Gen. George Patton (second from right) prepares to leave the cruise USS *Augusta* (CA-31) during Torch. The group stands before an SOC. (U.S. Navy)

Wildcats test their guns on the *Ranger*'s flight deck. Today's safety precautions would never permit such a crowd of "observers" during such a potentially dangerous activity. (U.S. Navy)

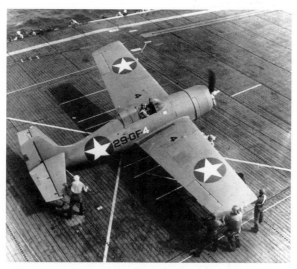

Aboard USS *Santee* (ACV-29), flight-deck crewmen maneuver a VGF-29 Wildcat before a launch. The F4F's small proportions show up well. (U.S. Navy)

A VGF-29 pilot mans his F4F while an armed sentry stands guard, an odd placement as the carrier is no doubt out to sea. (U.S. Navy)

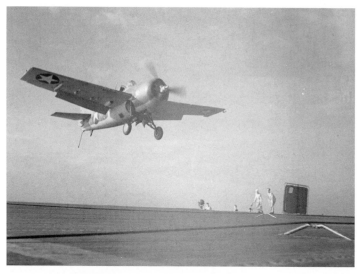

A Wildcat moments before a trap. (U.S. Navy)

Ordnancemen aboard *Santee* prepare to install belts of .50-caliber ammunition in a Wildcat's wing guns. (U.S. Navy)

A VF-9 Wildcat makes an in-flight arrestment, with all three wheels still in the air. Even today, such a trap is potentially hazardous and places undue strain on the tail hook and airframe. Note the open cockpit canopy and full deflection of the elevators. (U.S. Navy)

Ens. Joe Gallano of VGF-29 lost his fighter's tail while recovering aboard the *Santee*. Although the pilot was slightly injured, the Wildcat was jettisoned. Note the raised arresting wires immediately ahead of the F4F. (U.S. Navy)

A flight-deck chief helps the Ensign Gallano from his cockpit. The control cables protrude from the fuselage. (U.S. Navy)

Waiting for his plane's pilot, a young crewman again demonstrates his breed's ability to sleep anywhere and in any position. (U.S. Navy)

The observer of a Curtiss SOC observation floatplane drops a message during Torch. The yellow ring around the American star shows up well. Although considered obsolete, the SOC served throughout the war, even beyond its replacements. (U.S. Navy)

An SBD Dauntless comes aboard USS *Santee*. The LSO, or Paddles (note the frames with cloth strips) follows the recovering aircraft through to touchdown. Note the "cheesegrater" dive brakes now deployed as flaps. (U.S. Navy)

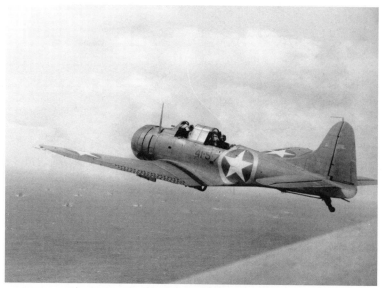

A Dauntless from VS-41 flies over the Allied task force during Operation Torch. Another aircraft that was considered obsolete at the beginning of the war, the SBD saw considerable action in the Pacific. Torch was its most intense engagement in the European theater. (U.S. Navy)

SBD-3s fly over the Allied task force prior to recovering aboard their carrier. Note the lowered tail hook on the Dauntless in the foreground. (U.S. Navy)

The *Jean Bart* lays at her berth following Allied attacks that quickly put the French battleship out of action. (U.S. Navy)

A water-line view of the *Jean Bart*, obviously the victim of much damage from Allied air attacks. (U.S. Navy)

Three SBDs and one F4F from *Santee* landed at Safi airport in Morocco. Intended to function as a support field for refueling, the restricted field did not have a very firm surface, and a few American aircraft were damaged on landing. (U.S. Navy)

Another view of the same scene reveals a French biplane adjacent to the road beyond the Wildcat, Note the wheel tracks in the field's soft surface. (U.S. Navy)

Comdt. (Major) George Tricault, commanding GC II/5. He was killed in action on 8 November 1942 in the first engagements with Navy fighters, but not before he had claimed a shared victory over a Wildcat and another damaged over another F4F. [Service Historique de l'Armee de l'Air (SHAA)]

Sgt. Chef Jeremie Bressieux of GC I/5 in front of a Hawk in France in 1940. On 9 November, he shot down a Wildcat flown by Ens. C. W. Gerhardt of VF-9, who was rescued after ditching. It was Bressieux's ninth and last kill. A year later, he was flying Bell P-39s with the Free French. Remaining in the Armee de l'Air, he retired in 1961 as a lieutenant colonel. (SHAA)

Shown at Casablanca in July 1942, Lt. Pierre Villaceque (left) and Lieutenant LeGrand of GC II/5 flew Hawks against VF-41 and each claimed a kill on 8 November. Villaceque was wounded and had to abandon his H-75 after scoring his sixth and final kill of the war. He remained in the service after the war, rising to the rank of general before retiring in 1977. (SHAA)

Curtiss Hawk 75A-3s of GC I/5 over Rabat, Morocco in October 1942. The export model of the P-36 USAAC fighter, the H-75 had fought well during the brief campaign in June 1940. The surviving Hawks were sent to Africa to bolster the rag-tag complements of Vichy squadrons. Colorfully marked in yellow-and-red stripes on the cowlings and empennage, the Hawks acquitted themselves well, especially since their pilots were experienced combat aviators flying against the game, but untried crews of the Allied task force. (SHAA)

A Dewoitine D.520 of GC III/5 based at Oran, arguably the best French fighter of the war. This squadron intercepted the first Royal Navy strikes of 8 November, claiming four Albacore torpedo bombers. Sea Hurricanes shot down four of the D.520s. There were never enough D.520s to make a difference, whether in France or in Africa. (SHAA)

One of the more modern designs in the French bomber fleet was the Sud-Est LeO 451. Several units were in North Africa, but many of their aircraft were destroyed during Allied strafing attacks. This photo of a Vichy LeO was probably taken before the start of Operation Torch. (SHAA)

The Potez 63.11 was a reconnaissance design with a three-man crew. It saw considerable service in the 1940 campaign, and afterward, in North Africa, and later with the Free French forces. These aircraft are from GR I/23, and are shown over Morocco in 1941. (SHAA)

The similarly appearing Bloch 174 was another reconnaissance type that saw service in Vichy colors, although only one unit, GR II/33 flew them. This aircraft is from that unit, based at Tunis. (SHAA)

1. BE PREPARED. Carry your pocket knife.
Have your life jacket with you at all times. Know
how to use it. Know where your abandon ship
station is. School your own mind *now* as to how
you will act in an emergency. Make up your mind
that you will not get excited and stick to it.

2. DON'T BE IN A HURRY TO ABANDON
SHIP. Experience has shown that men usually
have much more time to abandon ship than they
allow themselves. Sudden sinkings have been
rare. Do not rush.

3. REMEMBER, *USE* YOUR HEAD . . . DON'T
LOSE IT. You've been instructed as to how to
abandon ship. You know what you should do if
that emergency should arise. Don't let the excitement make you forget what you know. Don't
let it *get* you. Keep cool and think clearly. This
business of saving your life does not call for
panic, go about it in a businesslike manner.

"The men on the flight deck were doing a
wonderful job," went on the landing signal officer.
"This action showed us that our training was
standing up to the test. I soon found that we were
working better than we expected. At first they
were slow, but after a few hours they worked faster
than ever we had done in practice operations.
Every second you save in action is valuable. I
suppose we were getting planes in every thirty
seconds, and with a 150 men available to do the
work you expect some things to go wrong, but we
had nothing to speak of. Once a plane came in

with its flaps jammed, and was taken aboard just as if nothing was wrong. We had decided early that we would try to take any plane aboard if it was at all possible. There was one pilot whom I thought we could never get in, but we decided to make an effort. We got him—but only just. He had about two gallons of gas, was leaking oil, and his landing gear was damaged. The pilot landed superbly. The plane crew had him out of the way in no time. About twenty of them practically carried the plane forward. Afterwards the plane captain came up and thanked me for getting his plane aboard. Things like that stay in your mind awhile, even if they happen when you are too busy to think of everything."

"I suppose we shouldn't pat ourselves on the back," joined in Woody, "but that evening when I did have a chance to think, it came to me that our ship was doing a good job. I began to understand why she was one of the oldest active carriers in service. There's quite a difference between a carrier getting lost and covering herself with glory in the process and another doing an efficient job and coming through. I began to get a feeling of supreme confidence in this carrier and her crew. The speed with which the planes were landed and refueled on Dog-day, and stowed away for overhaul, is an eternal testimonial to general efficiency. You have to live aboard a carrier to understand the problems involved in getting such a large number of planes to function and keep out of one another's way in a confined area. When he is short of gas, or when his plane had been damaged, a pilot's one idea is to get down. We're inclined to forget that other people are often in the same jam, and that the ship always has the problem of her own safety. This action taught me a great deal, and, to be blunt, we owe more than we can ever say to the handling of the ship. The astonishing thing was that once you were out of your plane and back in the wardroom or your quarters everything was carrying on as if we were back at base.

"Torpedoes came and torpedoes went, but the routine of the ship proceeded. There was a mess boy who looked after the laundry. He was waiting at my bunk for me when I got in. 'Yes, sir,' he said as he always did, 'I have your laundry for you.' And there it was. Someone had lost a shirt, and the usual search was on. I heard the mess boy saying, as he always said, 'Yes, sir, your laundry's being checked all the way to Africa and back. You don't have to worry. This ship's all right.' It was encouraging to find this atmosphere. When I began the melancholy job of packing up and making an inventory of Windy's personal effects that same mess boy was there to help. 'I'm going to have Mr. Shields's laundry all ready for him when he gets back,' he said. 'He'll sure get back, Mr. Shields will.' Little things, that mean a lot in the morale of a unit.

"Before turning in I began to think of the outcome of it all. We knew now that the French resistance was weakening, but how long they could fight was difficult to estimate. There had already been talk of an armistice. Tomorrow was November 11, I remembered, which would be about as good a day for an armistice as any. With such a comforting thought, I went to sleep."

"I sat up awhile and listened to the yarns of the boys from the other squadrons," said Ed. "We had all got set, and although there was the usual tension, as there always will be when there is a show on, the fellows were feeling much more confident. Someone told me what a swell job one of the pilots had done the day before with his TBF.[1] He went over in the afternoon escorted by three scout bombers. His mission was to silence a coast defense battery at El Hank. He was just getting onto the target when eight French fighters went after him. Now that put the pilot in a tight spot, because a plane loaded with its bombs cannot be thrown about like a fighter. He went straight at the nearest Frenchman and got in a hit before his guns jammed. Then he got out as fast as he could, completely fooling the Vichy pilots, or else they left him to the gunners. He saw some Vichy bombers coming out to attack our landing boats and gave them all he had, previously having tipped off the fighters to come and deal with them. When he finished, he hung on, reporting the position of the bombers, all of which had overshot their targets and missing the American transports. All the

---

[1.] TBF means in Navy terminology Grumman torpedo bomber.

time, the pilot was being heavily shelled, so heavily that he had to make a forced landing in the sea. We all agreed that it was a wonderful job."

The ship's radio report carried a broadcast by General Giraud, the French general who "escaped" from a German prison last spring, appealing to Vichy forces of North Africa. He said, "For two years we have scrupulously observed the terms of the armistice in spite of the violations by our enemies. Germany and Italy want to occupy North Africa, and America forestalls them, asking us for our loyal support. This is our chance for revival. We cannot neglect this unexpected opportunity."

A radio bulletin displayed on the notice board said that Pétain had replied to President Roosevelt's speech to the French people. He accused America of a deliberate and bitter attack against the French in North Africa, saying, "There are no memories or ties between the American Government and the Vichy Government. We are being attacked. We shall defend ourselves to the end." An official statement by Admiral Darlan was broadcast to the French people: "France will remember this tribulation inflicted on her by a country for which French blood once was shed. Our honor demands it."

"I couldn't help appreciating the official Navy communique of that day's operation," went on Ed. "It didn't say very much but it meant a whole lot. The writer put it this way: 'The third day was very much like the second for the Navy fliers, they were getting into a groove. The heavy guns of our battleships were turned on the Casablanca batteries. The fighting planes strafed and bombed troop columns and shot down anything that opposed them. The dive-bombers plowed through the flak to get at the big coastal guns and the A.A. batteries. Submarines were sighted on the surface heading south, presumably for Dakar. It seemed that the pack was assembling.' All that day's action had been covered in those few words but in many ways the day had been like the other two for the fellows who were taking part, with the sole exception that we had all gained a lot of experience. Harris, the Short Man, put it this way: 'One minute's actual fighting is better than three years' training.' I suppose we all felt that way, now we had started cooking with gas."

"I had had quite a busy day in spite of what might seem dull," said Tommy. "The squadron had had to be reorganized tactically, but it had worked pretty well. I was trying to convince myself that all the boys would be all right. We had heard of the Wildcat that had burst into flames when it hit the ground, but I knew it was not one of ours. Then Mac had reported from the ground. I knew Mac would be all right even if he turned up years after Hubie and Bus had done a good job of seeing him down. We had to account for Tag Grell, Mikronis, Shields, Chuck, and Spanky. There had not been any news of them. Tag was pretty sure to have been picked up by the fishing boats, but there was always a chance that they had not seen him, or been too scared to heave-to. Before going to my bunk I read the orders for the day ahead, Wednesday, November 11. The ship was to be ready to launch aircraft at 0530 and our reveille was at 0400. Reading those orders I couldn't help remarking to myself on the Navy morale and team spirit so prominent in this action."

The task force commander had sent a message: "Your continued efficiency and effective operations are an inspiration to all. Well done again, ship and ship's air group." Another was from one of our cruisers: "Congratulations on the splendid job yesterday and today, particularly the shellacking you gave the *Jean Bart.* The volume of traffic on your flight deck is something to observe. If opportunity offers we shall run interference for you with pleasure."

The Captain signaled back: "I am proud of the boys too. Now I hope we go to the South Pacific and would like to have you as our blocking back. It is like the old lacrosse days to have you behind me. Congratulations on your excellent work."

Durgin had captained the 1916 Navy lacrosse team. The cruiser captain had been his teammate at Annapolis. Those things help.

Chapter 8

NOVEMBER 11, the fourth day of the action, dawned bright and clear with good visibility. The first plane to leave the spacious flight deck, showing dimly in the half light, was a photographic reconnaissance fighter. The crewmen watched it go with tense anticipation. There had been rumors that Vichy wasn't going to fight any more. The plane had gone to find out. The pilot was soon back. He reported that he had been able to take photographs of the *Jean Bart* from as low as five thousand feet. There had been no anti-aircraft fire but a lot of smoke. The big battleship was showing her wounds plainly and the shambles in the dock area proved that it had taken severe punishment from the heavy bombing and from the bombardment by the U.S. battleships. The landings were still proceeding.

Shortly afterwards, the ship's fighter planes took off to clear the air for further attacks by the Dauntless scout bombers, each carrying a large bomb of the type that had been so effective the evening before.

"They had not been gone very long before we got the urgent message," said the Padre: "'Cease firing in the Casablanca area.' Ship relayed it to Embree. We waited. A silence! Then we heard him check back. Then he announced to his pilots, 'Boys, it's all over for now. Let's go back.' We knew then that the first stage of the Battle of Africa was over."

"It may be over out there," commented one of the crewmen, a lean, lanky Texan, "but it isn't over for us. We gotta get out of here. There are too many subs around for my liking."

The scouts returned, swooping out of the sky like dark homing pigeons. One by one, they jettisoned their bombs in the sea and landed. Overhead the Wildcats were circling the routine combat air patrol. "I had done three hours and seen nothing," said Woody. "I was coming down to land followed by Andy, when suddenly a U-boat surfaced inside the destroyer screen and fired three torpedoes at the ship from about three hundred feet—point-blank range. Miracle of miracles, they all missed us. One hit a ship near by, but it was a dud. Another passed under our stern ramp about three feet away, and the third went harmlessly away out to sea. That may have been our nearest escape, but the attacks continued all day as more submarines than ever before were detected."

Two pilots spotted a large black submarine surfaced and proceeding towards the carrier. They dived and attacked with machine-gun fire. The submarine went under hurriedly with the .50-caliber bullets bouncing from its hull.

"Armistice day was marked by constant submarine attack," said one of the ship's officers. "They seemed to be arriving in schools. We knew that we would have to fight every minute of daylight. The crew was very confident by this time, and the lookouts were doing a splendid job."

Almost every hour produced a submarine alarm or attack. The enemy was determined to get the carrier. All day the destroyers were circling and letting go depth charges while the planes droned overhead, reporting the presence of the undersea enemies, and attacking wherever possible.

"If the war was over on the land, it was certainly not with us," recalled Ed. "We were busy as ever, and the crew were still geared up to fighting pitch. I would say that it was one of the noisiest days of all with the depth charges and ship's guns going off at intervals. It is just an illustration that a carrier's work, like a woman's, is never done. Like other ships she has to combat action and weather. There never was any suggestion of less action or a letup after the news of the signing of the armistice. There may have been a slightly decreased activity in air operations, but the tension among the personnel increased.

"I know that some of the ship's crew couldn't understand why we were still in the vicinity. 'Let's get to hell outta here,' I heard some of them say after one sub attack. 'If we don't, there'll be no carrier to take back to the U.S.A.'"

There was a good bit of tension in the wardroom among the ship's officers. Where the aviators left off worrying, the officers' work began all over again. They were a part of the ship. They lived with her always, never leaving her except when she was in drydock.

They realized far more vividly than we did what a torpedoing meant—the loss of a ship to which they had been attached for so long a time, and a sense of defeat. The tension of that day was greatest for those whose battle stations were topside. They were right out in the open, keeping constant surveillance on the open water underneath which lurked the subs. Not for a single moment could they afford to relax their vigilance.

"It was a good thing everybody was on the alert," said Ed. "About noon, when the combat air patrol was being landed aboard, a submarine alarm was sounded. The ship went into a sharp turn, and a torpedo missed us by fifty feet. We saw it coming from our ready room. It was not a pleasant sight. To see a torpedo coming at your ship is a bit breathtaking. You wait, mentally holding your hands over your ears waiting for the explosion and sharp jolt as the torpedo hits the ship. This kind of thing happened once or twice and alarms were going all the time. One torpedo went across the bow shortly after. A fighter sighted a sub five thousand yards away and strafed the spot. One of the scout bombers let go a depth charge and simultaneously the ship's guns opened up at the periscope wake that was sighted. These five-inch guns made their peculiar *phrumpf* sound, which is more of a physical impact than a sound.

The Chicago pianos joined in and the twenty-millimeters—quite a symphony of war. This went on without a stop for three hours.

"When I took off on a combat patrol later in the day I had a good view of the battle between the destroyers and the wolf packs of submarines. A carrier's job is no easy one, because it has to remain in the same area all through the action to take on its planes, but it must be constantly on the move to dodge submarine attacks. While planes are being taken aboard the ship has to keep on the same course, and this is not good tactics because the submarines can get a good aim. Flying on combat patrol over your carrier you have one thought uppermost in your mind. If the ship is torpedoed you will have nowhere to land. It is not a pleasant thought, as you look down on what seems a very tiny piece of firm land on which you are accustomed to come down, and where warmth and comfort await you.

"I remember that morning circling, circling, circling in a wide circle at ten thousand feet above our ship and her escorts. They were going round, graceful slivers of steel, and although I was free in the air, I felt more than ever that I was attached to the ship.

"That kind of patrol brings up all kinds of emotions. You realize you are responsible for the safety of your ships. If you 'dope off,' you endanger their security, which is rather tenuous to say the least. And so you circle endlessly trying to keep a sharp lookout not only for planes above but also for subs below. The droning of the engine, the warmth of the cockpit, the smooth flight of the airplane, which you have trimmed to fly by itself, continue to give a false sense of security and tend to make you sleepy. 'Snap out of it!' you tell yourself suddenly. The very quietness up here is dangerous, false, disarming, absurd—absurd because we are fighting a war and the ships are still in danger. But there's not a bit of noise up here pertaining to war. If you sit in a plane for three hours doing nothing at ten thousand feet you lose touch with the world. Nothing happens—the scene of your ships moving about below is just like a silent film. The engine drone fades from your ears because of its repetition that first becomes monotonous, then boring. Won't *something* happen? You begin to ask.

"Every once in a while you can hear something coming in over the radio—nothing for you though, only routine conversation. Tommy's quiet, assured voice, Pete Bolt struggling with his Carolina accent and trying to make himself understood.

"Suddenly there was a break in the monotony. Our small brood of tiny ships below changed their course abruptly. I lost them beneath the wing and bent the plane around more sharply to get a view. I could see the two destroyers on the starboard side of the carrier churning up increased wake behind them as they darted to attack some submarine. They closed quickly to the point of contact. The first dropped a depth charge. From the air you cannot see the splash it makes as it goes over the side, but you see the circle of foam widen out behind as the charge is detonated, like a big white rose. You make a note of the time on your pad. Ten seconds later two more blobs of white circles appeared. The second destroyer cut across the path of the first to lay its own charges. In thirty seconds I counted seven white expanding circles, which must have meant death to a sub below them.

"You can't hear a thing. Depth charges go off below you and you see nothing but white blobs, hear nothing but the tiny regular click in your earphones which means that your generator is still controlling your prop speed.

"The drama is going on below you and you are an omniscient observer with his hands tied. The destroyers certainly churned up the water as they hurriedly maneuvered round the danger spot. The destroyers were our first line of defense because they were equipped with the devices, which gave them the best contacts with underwater craft. Our hopes were on these smoothly handled craft. If the carrier returned intact a lot of the credit should go to these babies.

"Occasionally my view was cut off as I passed over or through a wisp of cloud. I was impatient to get into the clear again to see what was going on. At any time a silent thunderous mountain of water might flare up from the side of one of the ships below as it got a torpedo. Whenever a cloud cut off the scene I got angry—and anxious.

"Sometimes I could see our Wildcats and dive-bombers going down to attack submarine wakes and remaining at a low altitude scudding along the surface like birds flying low in the storm. Sometimes a dive-bomber would plummet down like a hawk and the sea underneath would throw up a white plume as the depth charge exploded."

All the pilots were in action against the waves of subs during the day.

"We were called to Fedala to give a hand at protecting some battleships and anchored transports against subs," said Max. "There had been some trouble the night before. When we got there, there was a tremendous oil slick on the water and the life rafts were bobbing around. I could see some of the destroyers keeping a continual patrol to seaward of the ships. They were scouting around, cutting paths in the oil patch. Then they would stop and listen like dogs stopping to sniff. Those transports were beautiful torpedo bait. I could see two of the French ships lying there with the U.S. flag flying over the Tricolor. I flew over one of our destroyers and I could see that she'd been hit.

"There was one ship in Fedala Harbor, unloading. As I flew down, the soldiers looked up and waved. They had changed from khaki into fatigue blues. Jocko and I then cruised along the shore to take a look at Casablanca Harbor. On the way we noticed a scout sea-plane crumpled up on the sand. I figured it must have been the one we saw being shot down the day before. The sea had evidently washed it ashore. It was interesting to see Casablanca Harbor without having to look through a hail of tracer and stuff. The whole place had an atmosphere of calm and repose. I saw it rather as a picture or a movie set and it was a vivid contrast to what it had looked like when I last saw it. I could see the scars, of course—there were two destroyers lying on the beach, looking like big dead fish, and then the cruiser we had hit was burned out, looking extremely desolate. Then again, the harbor looked different. I got the impression that it was much smaller than it had seemed to be when we were fighting. There was a passenger ship moored against the Dock de Commerce. Then I went over to take a look at the great *Jean Bart* that had been our principal headache. I could see the gaping bomb hits, but she didn't look as bad as I had expected. I wanted to go aboard her and see what damage we had done, but it wasn't the moment. We then went over the anti-aircraft battery that I had hit on the Jetée Delure. I went down quite low. There were lots of people standing on the edge of the bomb crater, just as they do back home when men are digging a hole in the road. They could probably see much more than I could, so I followed Jocko out to the ship. A few minutes after we landed, a destroyer began dropping depth charges close off the starboard bow. A big air bubble came to the surface, and Ralph, who was doing anti-sub patrol, went down like a terrier after a rat—Ralph is certainly quick. He dropped his depth charge in the middle of the air bubble. I was standing on the flight deck, watching with a helpless feeling. If I had seen a periscope then, I think I'd have taken a pot shot at it with my pistol."

The war against the submarines continued all night as the carrier continued to navigate in the neighborhood while the armistice terms were being discussed. Every member of the ship's crew was braced to defeat the enemy.

In the wardroom the pilots gathered to discuss their action and swap stories. There were absent faces and vacant bunks. Information had been coming in through the day from the shore, as the American troops were making contact with the French, but there was no definite news of the fate of the pilots who were missing.

"We would have felt better if we could have gotten a report from Mac," said Tommy. "Mac is one officer who would be sure to report at once, but nothing had come through. We did hear, however, that Mikronis, or at least an American Navy pilot who answered his description, was in the hospital. I was hoping that we should be able to get news of all of them, but there was nothing doing."

The intelligence officers were again working overtime collecting and dispatching information. Only to the pilots did the first night of armistice bring any respite. Some went to bed early, others stayed up to discuss the war.

"One thing stood out above everything," said Prof Dowling. "All our pilots testified that they had been correctly informed on the political and military situation in the Casablanca area. Quite a tribute to our intelligence department and its sources of information. They had been told that the French Army and aviators would be inclined to offer little opposition. This was shown to be true by the number of airplanes that were destroyed on the ground. The French are not fools, and surprising as our attack may have been, many more of their planes could have been taken off the ground if the pilots had not preferred to see them destroyed, rather than avail themselves of the opportunity of resisting invaders whose aims were in sympathy with their own feelings. Again, our intelligence had told us that the French Navy would be more hostile than the Army. Our planes coming in with scars from anti-aircraft fire were evidence of this. All our pilots admitted that the fire from the harbor installations, particularly at Point El Hank, got deadlier every day. What was particularly satisfying to all of us was that this was an all-American expedition in which we had enough of everything, too much perhaps, and it succeeded through careful and painstaking organization and training that fused itself into brilliance."

The ship's news was carrying many interesting items that served to key the wardroom to concert pitch. Reports were coming through that Hitler was to take over the whole of Unoccupied France, and that the French fleet had left Toulon to join the United Nations forces. Pétain had left Vichy for an unknown destination. The Free

French in London were appealing to the French people to join the Free French. In Lille, Georges Claude, the distinguished French scientist, was warmly recommending Franco–German collaboration. "If France is to get on her feet again, the position we hold in the future will be as great as our courage."

The German radio announced that German troops had arrived in Vichy, and Hitler had announced that the German Navy had already sunk over twenty-four million tons of enemy shipping, twelve million more than in the last war. Germany had far more submarines than in 1918 and was building still more.

"And most of them are around here," laughed one of the ship's officers grimly. "But they won't put this ship's tonnage in their list."

"O.K.," said Hubie. "But be sure to wake me if a torpedo goes through torpedo heaven. I'd like to know."

"I slept well for the first time," added Woody. "Most of the action nights I had been too tired even to take my shoes off, but submarines or no submarines, sleep seemed the appropriate thing on the night of the eleventh—our little armistice day."

The next morning the carrier's Wildcats were out at dawn on anti-submarine patrol. "The sea was lousy with submarines," recounted Woody. "They had ganged up on us during the night. In a three-hour patrol we sighted so many that the total seems almost a fisherman's story."

The first submarine to make an attack appeared supported by two fishing vessels two miles off the ship's port quarter. One of the dive-bomber pilots sighted it and went into attack from 1,300 feet, while the ship was blazing away with antiaircraft guns small and large. "I could see what I thought was a submarine thirty feet below the water," he said. "I let go my depth charge when I was in a power glide from three hundred feet, and then fired on the fishing boats to drive them away. Shortly afterwards I noticed a scout circling the same spot and dropping a depth charge, and another went in to strafe with his guns. That U-boat certainly got itself a lot of trouble."

"I saw oil slicks on the starboard bow, quite close in," said Hank, "but could not ascertain whether they were the result of a submarine having been attacked or not. A minute later, however, the ship opened fire on a feather wake halfway between my position off the starboard bow and the ship. I went down and strafed it, as another plane dropped a depth charge. We saw no result, however, but a short time afterwards another wake appeared five hundred yards from the ship, and simultaneously Woody called my attention to the conning tower of a submarine on the port quarter about one mile away from the ship. I saw him dive on it, and he seemed to register hits with all six guns. The conning tower disappeared, and I saw a destroyer dropping depth charges, after which an oil slick was seen. The submarines were getting very little chance that day."

The strangest thing that happened during "Torpedo Day," as some of the pilots called this, was when a submarine actually jumped out of the water as it was attacked by a depth charge. "It surfaced like a porpoise, and then went under again immediately with depth charges bursting all round it," said Woody. "Something to see."

All through the action two trawlers with no fishing gear visible were following the formation. "They seemed to be cutting corners to do so," said Ed. "It may have been that our ships were taking an irregular course, which gave that illusion, but we were certainly having anxious times."

As the day wore on it seemed that every submarine the enemy could muster was being concentrated on the ship. The bridge warned all pilots to be particularly alert. Shortly before eleven in the morning, two U-boats appeared simultaneously, one off the starboard bow, and another off the port quarters.

"I was on submarine patrol," recalled Embree. "I could see a destroyer on the port quarter dropping depth charges, but I could see nothing in the water.

"I started to fly around the ship's stern counter-clockwise, and about half a mile away I saw this destroyer dropping more depth charges. I saw the shock wave, and a few seconds later the black bubbling disturbance of a submarine disintegrating in the water. Then I saw a large white bubble of air and foam come to the surface. I knew it must be air from the submarine. I circled around the white patch, and dropped my depth charge right on the patch. This bubble area was about thirty feet in diameter. I then heard the ship call 'Submarine on the starboard bow.' As I pulled out of my dive, I saw the charge explode, throwing up its fan-shaped spray. The ship was all the time keeping up a constant fire of tracer bullets.

"I then climbed to one thousand feet. As I came back to the ship I saw an object in the water, a light green object about the size and shape of a rowboat upside down. I told my radio gunner to throw out a smoke light. Then I wiggled my wings and went down to the spot. On the way down, two other fighters passed me in steeper dives. Each strafed the same spot. The smoke light worked and was smoking as I pulled out of my dive. Immediately the destroyer on our port quarter was circling around dropping depth charges. An hour later, another scout sighted a submarine two miles from the ship but no result could be checked."

Shortly after three o'clock, another oil slick was seen and attacked, but no result was known.

And so the ship with its escorting vessels headed towards home waters, thus closing this phase of the battle for Africa.

On the ship's communique appeared a two-word message from the commander of the task force: WELL DONE.

The next day Captain Durgin addressed the crew, still alert, still at their action stations. The skipper was smiling and genial with the tang of victory in his voice.

"At long last our carrier has had its first taste of battle and has come out with flying colors. You have done well. There is no doubt that if Capt. John Paul Jones, our most famous naval hero, were here, he too would say 'Well done.'

"We all know that our pilots were the spearhead of our attack. With great courage and skill, in the midst of heavy anti-aircraft fire and fighter-plane opposition, they performed their attack missions with deadly accuracy. I firmly believe that their superb flying, shooting, and bombing were the major reason for the early capitulation of Casablanca and the adjacent cities.

"But the aviators are not entitled to all the credit by a great deal. Every one of you contributed to their success. I cannot even begin to give the credit to everyone to whom credit is due. It is due to the flight and hangar deck crews and the ordnance gang whose speed and untiring efforts enabled us to launch flight after flight in rapid succession; to the boiler room gang who kicked in the extra burners that gave us that spurt of speed we needed so badly; to the engine room detail that answered so promptly our emergency calls for every turn they would make; to the cooks and bakers who worked night and day to enable you to have hot meals at any time you desired; and to the lookouts and gun crews who kept the submarines from putting torpedoes in our sides, and to everyone else aboard who did his bit no matter how big or little.

"It was a wonderful exhibition of a well-trained crew doing its job in a smooth and efficient manner.

I should like to pat you on the back and say, 'I'm glad that I am shipmate with you.'

"Unfortunately all of our shipmates are not here to rejoice with us. Two we know have made the supreme sacrifice for their country and others are still missing. We are afraid that some of them will not return. This is the fortune of war and we must continue to carry on—they would expect us to do so.

"As we assemble all the details of the results of our attacks and obtain more information from the high command we will give it to you in one of the communiques.

"One thing more—and I want you to remember this—while we have good reason to rejoice we must not for one moment relax our vigilance and our efforts. We must keep the ship afloat to fight again another day.

"Now here is a final bit of information you have been waiting to hear: Just a short time ago we received orders to proceed to the States, and we are now heading for that point. With favorable weather we should be at the pier for Thanksgiving Day."

The men cheered—we felt good. When a man like Captain Durgin hands it out he means it—and we were still afloat and heading out of danger.

The engineering officer unloaded himself to his men thus:

If ye win through an African Jungle,
Unmentioned at home in the press,

Heed it not. No man seeth the turbine
But it driveth the ship none the less.

"The Captain has stated that he is extremely
pleased with the manner in which the Engineering Department performed during the time ship
was in 'Battle Condition.' The high speed maintained and the extremely rapid acceleration obtained when 'Emergency Ahead' was called for
contributed materially to the safety of the ship
when in submarine waters.

"I wish to congratulate you on the cheerful
and efficient manner in which you stood many
long hours of watches both to get the ship to and
from the scene of action, and during the action days.

"This splendid performance is the result of
every man knowing and doing his particular job
in the engineering team.

"I am proud to be the 'Chief' of a department
that has contributed so materially to the opening
of that all-important Second Front."

"We were homeward bound and having regular meals again," said Ed. "But it would be a
strange homecoming after our first action. There
would be the usual rush to the pier by wives and
relatives with their cars. Somehow I hoped that
the wives and girlfriends of the boys who were
missing would not come down to meet us. Those
of us who were going home ready for the next
show were very lucky. I allowed myself to think
of New York and of Princeton again because that
seemed the right thing to do."

We spent the rest of the voyage on paper work, filling out forms and writing suggestions based on our experiences. On two things we all agreed—that our Grummans are good planes for the job and that our few hours' fighting experience was worth many hours of training—we were talking about being blooded veterans.

Now all we wanted was another show—some more cooking with gas—but with more gas.

I was thinking that when the Padre came in: "Here it is . . ." Immediately I was back at Casablanca ready to dash to the flight deck, but it was just that we were going to refuel—in really heavy weather this time.

We were going home, even if Tag and Chuck were not in evidence writing endless letters. "They'll be back—waiting for us," said Hubie. "They probably flew with Doolittle."

We all hoped so—if we didn't say anything.

Chapter 9

"HAVING LANDED so unexpectedly in Africa," smiled Mac, "I felt extremely grateful but also extremely chagrined! I hadn't done a particularly salubrious job. Imagine being shot down on the first hop of the first day in the first engagement. Too many firsts!

"As I sat back in my seat unbuckling the straps, I began figuring out what the next step would be. I prepared to salvage what gear I would need to make my way to Fedala and abandon the rest. I hastened to destroy my confidential gear because many natives were running towards me. Some of the younger ones wore fezzes over European dress and some of the older ones wore white Arab Jeballahs. One of them picked up a stone, but he didn't throw it. He just stood there jabbering at me at a safe distance with the others crowding around him. I had my pistol, of course. Standing in the cockpit, I waited to see if any of them were armed. They were not. I called out *'Americano'* at the top of my voice, and tried to talk to them in French. They stopped chattering, gaped at me in awe, and moved back a bit.

"I had won that round. I knew that I wouldn't have much time to do what I'd have to do to the plane, so I got busy carrying out the usual routine. I cut away the canvas bag containing food, water, and necessary items. I also grabbed my standard escape kit and emptied the chart board. I stuffed the papers in my pocket, including that fabulous passport and the fifty dollars. I got out of the cockpit.

"As I began to take off my flying gear, the natives crept up on me. Soon I was surrounded by quite a mob of them. They were staring at me just as Americans do when they see a hole in the road. I took no notice of them but went on deliberately with the job. I threw my life jacket and radio microphone back in the cockpit and secured the battery switch. I closed and locked the hood so that nobody would tamper with the switches.

"Then I felt someone touching me from behind. I swung around sharply. It was an old Arab, who was fingering the fabric of my uniform blouse. He probably wanted to buy it. He was grinning all over his face and muttering *'Inglesia.'* I replied, 'No, *Americana,'* but he kept on saying *'Inglesia-tauriste.'* Some tourist, I reflected to myself. I suppose I smiled, because that set them all to chattering and laughing.

"Suddenly there was much excitement and chatter. A shell had landed over in the corner of the field. It was either from our own or some French guns shelling the place. I had to get out of there, and I was forced to decide at once what I should do with my Wildcat. You know it is all very well talking about planes being expendable, but a man wouldn't be human if he hadn't some affection for his aircraft. Also, the damage was so slight that it seemed a shame to destroy Uncle Sam's property. How long it would remain our property I didn't know, but there it was, almost intact. If the operations at Fedala were proceeding according to plan, it would be a matter of only a few hours before the plane and all this area were in the hands of the Americans anyway. I hadn't the heart to set fire to my Wildcat, especially with a chance of salvaging it.

"The oddest things come into your mind in moments like that. As I was gazing at that plane, I remembered that my lucky number was seven. I think I liked the plane for the reason that its number was 11707. Then I remembered that I had taken off at 0707 and that my watch had shown 0827 when I had landed. Now it only needed Snow White and the Seven Dwarfs to come along and rescue me, and I would be superstitious.

"Someone in the back called out—'Cigarette, you give me cigarette.' As I don't smoke they were out of luck. It was no good my staying there, so I decided to move away, either to escape or to get captured. I looked round the mob, which was still chattering like a flock of geese, to see if there was anybody who looked intelligent enough. There was one man, a great big ox of a fellow with a serious dark brown face. He had been standing there, head and shoulders above the others, and not saying anything. When I hailed him, he brushed his way through the others and came quite near me. I began to jabber some French at him, telling him to guard the plane and not let anybody get near it. To my surprise, he understood, because he immediately picked up a stick and began to wave it at the others. They backed away.

"Before I went, I suddenly felt an urge to have another look at the damage. There were plenty of bullet holds in the left wing, the left side of the fuselage, and the tail section. Otherwise, she was in pretty good shape. I was more determined than ever that she should be salvaged. I started to give the guard a dollar bill but decided against the wisdom of displaying money to that mob. I headed towards Fedala. They followed. I shooed them away once—but they came on. With that kind of publicity, I wasn't likely to be able to miss being picked up by the Vichy soldiers who must have seen my plane come down. We hadn't gone far before there was a whiz, followed by a loud explosion. Another shell had landed quite close at the right. The natives screamed and scattered. I found that I had been hit in the left leg, which didn't increase my comfort and made me all the more determined to get the hell out of this place. I walked pretty fast, the natives again after me. As I looked back towards the plane, some of them were lying on the ground, as if they had been hit. The others were taking no notice at all but were more absorbed in pursuing their center of interest. We continued on across the field, heading for a little stucco building with big wooden shutter doors that were open. I intended to go there to dress my wound before infection set in. This building proved to be a wine shop at the fork of the road to our left. The proprietor came out from the little room at the back of the shop. He was a short, fat old fellow with sparkling eyes and a considerable stomach swathed by a dirty blue apron. He just stood looking at me. I told him that I was American. He answered *'Bon,'* just as if I had arrived on a holiday trip. Then he scratched his head and asked, *'Soldat?'* I said I was a flier. He grunted, not unpleasantly, and then remarked that I was wounded. I remembered that, and to be on the safe side, I immediately broke out my sulfanilamide and began to dress the wound. He proceeded to disperse the mob, but they only went a short distance away. The wound wasn't serious, it didn't hurt much, but it began to bleed copiously as I cleaned it out. The old man ordered his wife to get me a bowl of water, but I told him everything was all right. After putting on a sterilized bandage, I swallowed some sulfa pills and sat down. I saw then that he was grinning at me. Good, I thought, this guy was friendly. From behind one of the big barrels, he produced a bottle from which he filled a glass and handed it to me. I toasted him with *'Vive la France.'* He replied, *'Vive l'Amérique.'* It was rum, and good, too. I felt better, thanked my benefactor, and decided that I had best get on towards Fedala.

"I had scarcely reached the door when I saw a group of native cavalrymen coming up the road from Fedala. I knew they were the Spahis, the French Colonial troops, because of the glitter from their crossed bandolier belts. I doubled back inside the shop, and appealed to the first *friend* I had found in Africa.

"'Monsieur, I want to hide! There are some soldiers coming and I don't want them to see me. If you protect me, you will be rewarded.'

"He looked a bit doubtful and just stood scratching his head. He ushered me into the little back room, saying I would be safe there—nobody would come. My luck was out, though! The news of my arrival in that little place had spread around the countryside, and twenty or thirty natives were clustering and jabbering around the door. Presently, a native corporal came in.

"He had a rifle in his hand, but he just stood looking at me as if he didn't know whether to shoot me or to have a drink with me. We stood grinning at each other till I did my stuff, telling him that I was an American officer. He shook his head and showed a lot of white teeth. I didn't know whether he understood my French, which I hadn't used for some time, so I fished out the passport and showed it to him. His eyes went very round. He read the message, whether it was the Arabic or the French I couldn't know, but he seemed to be in complete control of the situation and asked me for my pistol and said, *'Prisonnier.'* I didn't want to give up the pistol, but as the outer room

was now so full of his men, I thought it was un-
wise to argue. I unloaded it and handed it to him.
'You've got to give me a receipt for this,' I said.
He agreed, quite cheerfully. So the old proprietor
produced a billhead and wrote out a receipt, which
he put in front of the corporal. The fellow looked
at it, grinned, and shook his head. He took it back
outside, and I could hear them confabbing. He
came back again to say that he couldn't write but
that he would sign the receipt with his fingerprint.
He probably signed for his pay that way. I watched
him lick his thumb, put it on the top of the not too
clean table and make his print. Then he stored the
pistol away in his pocket and asked me for the
ammunition. 'No,' I said, 'I'm keeping that. The
pistol is no good without the other.' He went back
outside to his pals and repeated what I had said.
My logic must have appealed to them because they
all agreed, and so I had my ammunition.

"The corporal then posted a guard on the door,
one of his biggest men, and went away with my pistol.

"'*Voilà,*' said the old man, 'so that is it. They
will come back and take Monsieur away.' To
which I concurred.

"Then he had a bright idea. Was I hungry? I
wasn't, but, as I didn't know when I was going to
get my next meal, I thought it might be a good
idea to fill my stomach. He dispatched his wife to
kill a goose and prepare the meal. While she was
busy doing this, he offered more wine and proceeded to talk. He made a few derogatory remarks
about the war and the Boche and life in general.

I must admit that he didn't look as if he had suffered very much. If all the French in Morocco were as well covered as he, they must have been spared the privations of war.

"He told me that there had been very few Germans there but they expected them at any minute and that Casablanca was full of them, especially the hotels. They had nothing but the best and a lot of money, he assured me. Then he really started to cuss. They were shelling, and the old man cursed. I hoped that I wasn't going to attract the shells as I had done before.

"Presently some French neighbors came in. They were all pretty scared, and this was their idea of taking cover. They began chattering, as Frenchmen always do. I could see that many of them were middle-class business men, one of them was wearing a derby hat with a high collar and a most fantastic tie. It wasn't difficult to see that they didn't like me. A little fellow with about four days' growth of beard tried to push past the guard. He said something to me that I couldn't understand, but the proprietor of the shop told him, in what sounded like extremely forcible argot, to mind his own business. He came back muttering *'Salaud,'* and when a Frenchman says that, he means something. Another Frenchman handed me one of President Roosevelt's leaflets that had been dropped from the air. He gave it to me only after he had made a copy to keep for himself. He was immensely proud of this and asked me if I would autograph it, which I did. After scrutinizing it for a few seconds, he then asked me to put *'aviateur americain'* after it. That won him completely. He was immediately an ally and returned to speak to the others. What he said I didn't hear, but they quieted down, and I had a chance to study the leaflet. It came to me then that our propaganda was much too mild for the situation. The Frenchmen were used to the bolder, stronger, German type. I discussed this with the proprietor and he shrugged his shoulders and quite agreed that it hadn't said very much.

"The man with the leaflet asked me if I would like to come and talk to some of his friends. We went over to the bar, and I attempted a little good American propaganda. What did I think of Pétain, they wanted to know, so I smiled and said, 'Well, Pétain must be doing his best, but it was France that mattered.' That hit the spot. They all stood up and filled their glasses and cried, *'Vive la France! Vive l'Amérique!'* There was quite a lot of health drinking and toasting.

"When the corporal came back with another Spahi, he announced that I was to go to Casablanca. The proprietor told him that he would have to wait, as there was a goose cooking for me. He tactfully poured out some wine for the soldiers. The corporal said that was quite all right, as long as we got to Casablanca. Soon I was busily engaged eating the meal which the proprietor's wife and young daughter had prepared. The goose was excellent. I began to give away the various items of my kit that I wouldn't need for the trip to come. There were fishhooks, goggles, a jackknife, and the escape kit itself. I put some condensed food, some medicine, and the compass in my pockets. I signed a few autographs, burned the rest of my papers, said fond farewells to my French friends and proceeded to depart.

"There were two horses, one for each of my guards. They intended me to walk between them. I shook my head. 'I'm an officer and I am wounded. You can't do that—it will never do.' That set off a discussion. Finally it was decided that I was to ride and one of them was to walk, but immediately I got on the horse the man to whom it belonged began to protest furiously. He probably felt it was no good being a cavalry man if you had to walk, even with a prisoner. They conferenced and the procedure was to be changed—he was to ride the horse and I was to set astride its rump, pillion fashion.

"We set off with the corporal leading. Some guns started shelling again and the Spahis began to get nervous. They stuck their spurs into their horses. Oh boy, I've spent some pleasant moments in the saddle, but that trip will never be included. I remember that I had always wanted to ride an Arab horse, but this was awful. They hit it up like mad, and soon I was in great pain. I yelled for them to stop and explained to the corporal that my wound was hurting me. He didn't seem to care about that at all, but I told him that they must walk the horses and yelled at him that I was an officer. That impressed him not at all. They were heading towards the plane. It was still there with the big native guarding it, but he hadn't done a very good job because I noticed the lifeboat and the parachute had been taken, as well as my safety straps. The Spahis added to the job of pilfering. They took radio cords, the life jacket, and anything else they could find, each grabbing one article. One of them got the signal pistol. I don't think he had ever seen such a thing. He looked at it, inspecting the muzzle, the firing pin, and then showed it to his friend. They probably thought it was a heavy-caliber revolver because they uttered exclamations of surprise.

"The last of the journey was along the main road to Casablanca. My leg began to bleed again so I asked to be allowed to walk. The corporal agreed. The shelling had made them nervous or else they were hungry. Every now and then, the man on the horse would make me get up and ride for a while till I hollered to get down. As we proceeded, I recognized off to the south what was supposed to have been our rendezvous, 'Saddle Rock.' Ironically enough, I was to see it from a horse.

"All the while I was playing for time, because I thought that by the time we got to wherever we were going, Casablanca would have surrendered. We were jogging along when the corporal announced a bright idea. They hadn't searched me. There was more plunder. They went through everything. I objected strenuously but the corporal just smiled and said everything would be given back and wagged his finger to intimate that he had given a receipt. Everything went—my rations, the money, my watch, and my shark knife. The man who found that grabbed it and snarled, as if he thought that I might have been going to make a secret attack. He kept on saying *'Officier,'* which I presume meant that he was going to tell the officer that I had a concealed weapon. I supplied the information that it was for *poisson,* having temporarily forgotten the French word for 'shark,' which only made him more angry because he probably thought I was calling him a poor fish.

"Resuming our journey, I noticed we were nearing the zoo not far from Casablanca. Farther to the right and below the highway was the blue water of the outer harbor, of which I had an excellent view. This was one happy aspect of the ride—I was getting a bird's-eye view, or a horse's-rump view, of a naval battle, in which the Spahis were not in the least bit interested.

"Close in, there were three large French destroyers, two on fire, all taking an awful lacing from two of our cruisers and a few supporting destroyers. The fall of shot was beautiful, with colored dye of the shells showing from which of our ships the various shells came. But too many of the shots were not close enough to suit me. The French destroyers wiggled and squirmed but all in vain.

"The Spahis hardly looked at the naval battle. It was obviously no concern of theirs. I had just gotten on the horse again when four of our Wildcats passed low overhead and turned seawards in a sharp right-hand circle. They were so low that I could almost read their numbers. I waved my helmet and shouted like mad. I thought they were Red Rippers. The pilots were watching the ship engagements and did not see me. I hung back looking at that glorious sight like a kid having a first look at a circus.

"Everything was going well. The French destroyers were gradually being forced in towards the coast just north of the Roches Noires. One of them looked as if it was already aground. Two others were on fire. The one I had noticed burning aft was now burning in the bow, the other was down by the stern. I don't suppose anybody could have had a better view of a naval battle on its receiving end, and those ships certainly were taking it. It was like a movie. As we neared the villa-lined suburban road leading to Casablanca, I managed to make another halt. One of the cruisers had started firing at our ships. That was the fellow that probably straddled one of our cruisers earlier.

"The guards were getting impatient. One touched the butt of his rifle ominously, his way of telling me to get on. 'O.K.,' I said, 'let's go.' The last thing I saw of the naval battle was that two of the destroyers were apparently beached to the southwest and burning. All the firing had ceased.

"We were soon on the outskirts of Casablanca. I was sorry that my ingenuity had failed to delay my entry. On the outskirts, which I judged were residential suburbs—mostly with good-class white-façaded villas and lush green gardens with pretty trees and flower shrubs—we came across the first signs of French resistance that had obviously been hurriedly prepared. There were broken blocks of concrete, improvised machine-gun emplacements, and disused motor trucks piled against each other.

"Along the sides of the road and dispersed along some narrow dirt tracks were concentrations of French troops. They seemed mostly natives—some of them almost white, others the inky-black Senegalese. I could see other native infantry units camped at some distance from the road. There were guards on all the bridges and railway tracks. The men were strangely unperturbed, smoking and laughing over cards. Many were squatting by the roadside with their rifles stacked. When a shell whizzed over, they didn't seem to be in the least alarmed.

"As we came nearer to the city, I got the impression that the French had been caught unawares. Their transportation system was bad. Occasionally we had to pick our way between broken-down mechanized vehicles with their hoods up and with flats. There had been no shelling or bombing in the town, because our task force commander had given strict instructions to the contrary.

"My arrival naturally caused a considerable stir amongst the population. A pack of Arab children began to follow our little cortege, yelling out *'Americano!'* and a few French, including one pretty girl in a red sweater, attached themselves.

She wanted to know if we had come to rescue France—and also if I would autograph one of the Roosevelt pamphlets. The Hollywood system has struck deep even in Casablanca. There was no time for such luxury, however.

"It occurred to me that as I was an unofficial and unwilling ambassador of the good old USA, I ought to do my best to be sociable. I greeted everybody in my best French and answered the questions as well as I could. Rumor had been busy. I was supposed to be the sole survivor of a submarine. I was a parachutist and probably many other things.

"The trip soon began to take on somewhat of a comic aspect, supplied by a stout old lady who kept wobbling along beside the horse and shouting at me. At first I thought she was hostile. Then I found that she had a sister in Detroit, and she wanted to know if Marie was all right. I told her that everyone was all right in America. 'I hope she has enough to eat,' she called, ending with the inevitable French *'Il faut manger.'* How many more times I was to hear that!

"I soon began to feel like Don Quixote, with the Spahi guard as my Sancho Panza. He didn't completely look the part, but it was easy to see that he was immensely proud of having taken a prisoner and therefore felt the position demanded a great show of dignity. He was as delighted as a child with a new toy, and now that he had an audience, he kept turning back and grinning at me, then sticking up his thumb in a manner that I feel sure would have delighted the heart of Winston

Churchill. I wonder why Vichy had not forbidden the sign.

"All the time I was expecting to meet crowds of terrified refugees, because the docks should have been taking a sizable pounding from our ships and dive bombers, but instead there were a few people driving automobiles as if they were making a trip into the country. They were proceeding quite leisurely. The cops were waving them on or bawling them out, just as French cops always do.

"When we got to the south of the city, we turned off what appeared to be the main road to Settat and went down a dirt road near the railroad tracks. There were some shells whistling overhead—where they were falling, I couldn't see. They may have been ricochets from our own guns, which were shelling the port, or they may have been headed the other way.

"The corporal pointed out a pair of high doors set in a stone façade in the distance, and told me that was where we were going, saying 'Cavalerie.' Before we got to the doors, which were guarded by dismounted troops in khaki greatcoats, we passed a large and very dirty-looking encampment, which was crowded with black troops in red fezzes. Many of them were squatting on the ground outside of their depressing-looking huts, and I could distinctly smell the refuse heaps that were everywhere.

"I dismounted a little painfully—it had been a long ride—and because my wound was hurting, I waited with the guards on each side. A young

French officer came out. The first impression that I got was that he was extremely well turned out, with his khaki uniform and highly polished boots, and a glittering Sam Browne belt. He took not the slightest notice of me, but received the report and went inside.

"I was kept waiting outside, while the corporal took my effects into the office. They were apparently examining the effects that were removed from my plane; however, my money and other personal things were never introduced. In the meantime, many French enlisted men were openly curious and made signs of being friendly to me. Whenever an officer saw this, he would order them away. They went with good-natured reluctance—smiling and giving me high signs of encouragement.

"Presently, one of the officers came out accompanied by my corporal and ordered me to follow them. They walked me to the main entrance where a small black Renault automobile was waiting with a civilian driver. The corporal and I sat in the back of the car at the officer's orders. The officer gave some orders to our driver and we left for town. We were heading towards the center of town. Many people were on the streets and many shops and cafés appeared to be open.

"We went on to what seemed to be the military headquarters in Casablanca, in a typical gray stucco military building, with the Tricolor over the door. It was Sunday, so there were very few officers and scarcely any enlisted men. It became more obvious every minute that the French were not ready for the attack.

"I waited in the corridor for a short time, while the corporal reported me to the Commandant. I was still standing in the corridor when an officer came out and introduced himself. This was Adjudant-Chief Courvilliers, who took me upstairs to the 4th Bureau office where there were quite a few officers and what seemed to be noncommissioned officers sitting at tables and standing around. 'Messieurs, here is an American officer who has invaded our country and is a prisoner of war. He will be entertained.'

"They stood around rather like well-dressed wax figures for a few minutes, and then relaxed and began to talk excitedly. I noticed that the older officers (and there were quite a few, with many rows of brightly colored decorations) turned away. 'You'll take a glass of wine with us, I'm sure,' said Courvilliers. 'If you will give me your name, I will introduce you to my comrades.' I gave him my name and rank, and he introduced me all around. They made no attempt to question me about myself. There were a few remarks about the weather, nothing about the war.

"Courvilliers was quite a man—a dark, dapper, soldierly Frenchman. He confided to me that he loathed the Germans. It was easy to sense his emotion from the contempt and scorn with which he edged his voice. Before the war, he had had a chateau in Alsace-Lorraine, which had been taken over by the German staff, and he had had no news of his wife and daughter since. When he had finished that, he whispered to me, 'My friend, I will help you. America is the best friend of France and always will be. Anything you want, you have only to ask me.' That was worth knowing, I thought.

"Occasionally a shell burst shook the windows, and one of the officers made a wry grimace at me. To get conversation going, I began to ask them questions. No one spoke English, but my French blossomed a bit, and immediately they realized I could talk their language, they thawed considerably, especially the younger ones. I was conscious all the time of the older officers standing at the rear of the little circle, ignoring me, but probably straining their ears to hear what was going on. I asked the young Frenchmen, who might have been American college boys except for their uniforms, how they felt about America. 'But are the British attacking?' they countered. 'You are an American, perhaps, but the British are invading our country to steal it just as they stole half the world.'

"'We are Americans,' I replied. 'You know, we've come to help you beat the Germans.' 'Huh—so you say,' replied one of them. 'It is all the same, American or British. This is the last piece of land that France can call her own.' Another reproved him. 'No, the Americans are a *brave* people. They have come to fight the Germans. It is a pity that we have to fight them. *Nom du chien!* It seems that we must fight anyone but the Boches!'

"I could see then that I had thawed them, and

so I set out to become a one-man propaganda agent for America. I began on the debt America owed Lafayette. They were immensely interested—these youngsters. I sold Lafayette over and over again until I myself could hardly remember anybody else in the American Revolution.

"When the Commandant came in, I found myself telling him the same reason why America was so close to the French. It was Lafayette, nothing but Lafayette. He smiled a bit cynically and still didn't ask me any questions.

"Never in my life have I been so grateful for knowledge of a language. In those few hours, my French improved so much that it was better than it had been when I stood interpreter watch on my midshipman cruise to Villefranche on the French Riviera.

"It was getting late when one of the officers said, 'You must eat'—the same old story, *Il faut manger.* I was too tired then and feeling a little sore and sick. 'What, you don't want to eat?'

"'No, I want to turn in. I want to sleep.' No one had thought of that. They seemed to have no instructions about me at all. I was there in the office, talking to the officers, but the higher-ups just didn't worry. Presently one of the young officers said he would obtain my guard. Within a few minutes, a young Army private shouldering a rifle appeared on the scene. The officer introduced him to me as Jean. He couldn't have been more than twenty. His clear features reminded me of the young men I met during my last trip to France.

We found many things in common, particularly places we had both been to. This was his way of introducing himself socially. He wanted to make his job of guarding me as pleasant as possible for both of us. He said that I could not leave the building, but they would try to fix me up with a bed. He looked at me a little doubtfully and said, 'Monsieur will not attempt to escape. I am responsible.' I said he needn't worry about that, and he went away and presently returned with a rather shabby-looking mattress, which he put on the floor of the office. 'It is the best I can do,' he apologized, 'and it doesn't belong to me. The poor *diable* who sleeps there will sleep hard tonight.' 'No blanket?' I asked. He later procured one for me.

"I suddenly realized I couldn't sleep even if it had been possible. There was a lot of heavy gunfire going on that shook the building and rattled the windows. Then the French Army took over. Men appeared and settled down at the desks and began writing up orders, making requisitions, and typewriting. It was as if they had suddenly decided to fight. I could hear them ordering ammunition and supplies. Some of them cracked jokes to each other over the telephone and others were grumbling and cursing.

"I lay back and tried to watch it all without being conspicuous. All at once I felt horribly, disgustingly depressed. That alarmed me. I had a long way to go, and my morale must not crack. It is difficult at times like this, when you are aching all over, to keep in tip-top form. I consoled myself with thinking that I had been up since three o'clock and that I had been wounded. Even the most normal person would feel tired. My thoughts ran to the squadron, to home, and to everything that I held dear. There was time for reflection now. I would, I supposed, be reported missing. Andy, Bus, and Hubie had seen me go down, so they would know I was alive, but my wife Ruth would get one of those Navy Department telegrams reporting me missing if I didn't get back with the gang. I began to think of the children, too. My apartment seemed very remote and desirable. Although Ruth isn't the type to worry, I knew it would be upsetting. Between her and the Navy—and to her I am part of the Navy—there has grown a spirit of quiet and steady confidence. We never talked very much about what could happen, because we feel that those things take care of themselves. She always had a great deal of faith in my chances of getting back. I never gave her any reason to change that. I earnestly thanked God that I was still alive and not seriously hurt.

"Navy fliers seldom talk about religion, but most of us carry it deep in our hearts, even if we screen it from the scrutiny of our fellows by a wrapping of banter. I would say that flying alone has a very definite influence on a man's character. Difficult to describe what—but it is there, a reverence for the Unseen, for the Almighty—or what you will. It is the same conviction that grows in the hearts of sailors. It comes to most pilots as they fly in the upper skies. The loneliness and the

sense of vastness imbue them with a consciousness of things past, present, and eternal. This may
be even more emphasized because when we land
on the carrier, we are still on the sea, which in
wartime can produce so many varied hazards in a
matter of seconds.

"Finding sleep impossible, I told Jean, who
was lying on a table near me, that I was going to
walk out on the terrace to shake my thoughts. He
accompanied me.

"The night air was pleasantly soothing. The
stars were bright, and there was a pleasant tonic
from the smell of the garden.

"Earlier that evening, from this terrace, we
had watched the sunset out over the airport and
had seen a large transport plane sneak out of there
just before dark. 'That was one of those German
machines, saving their own skins,' said Jean.
'They have got us into this mess, and now they
are leaving us, the rats!'

"We paced the terrace for some time. I didn't
say much. Jean began to whistle and then stopped,
as if he felt it had been indelicate. 'Don't worry,'
he said, 'everything will be all right. No one will
hurt you, and you can fool them all. Americans are
smart.' That was nice to hear, anyway, but I wasn't
feeling so good. I was suddenly very tired and so I
turned in. I think Jean was very relieved. I noticed then that my bed was right in the track of
some kind of routine office activity. I had just got
down to bed when a man walked right over me.

"My leg hurt during the night and was very

stiff, but I managed to nap a little. It was day-break when I woke up. The gunfire outside had ceased, and the office was practically empty except for Jean, who was sitting on a chair and looking a bit green from fatigue. I lay there for a while, and then I was aware of men coming in to work, and as it didn't seem exactly conventional that I should be lying in bed under such circumstances, I contrived to get up and persuade my escort to take me somewhere where I could wash.

"'Now you will eat,' insisted Jean. 'We have not for you bacon and eggs, or what you eat in America, but we have something.' The 'something' consisted of a piece of French bread without butter and some ersatz coffee, without sugar or milk. The coffee was welcome to me because it was warm, but I cannot imagine that the great American public would appreciate it. Jean explained to me that it had been made of barley and was about the best they could get. He told me that the Commandant wanted to see me as soon as he arrived at the office. I was glad about that, because I felt that I was being ignored, and after all, if I was to be a prisoner, I might as well know what lay in store for me.

"The Commandant was bored with the procedure. Our meeting was limited to formalities. After he had asked me a few questions, he turned to one of his aides and said, 'This man has not been interviewed before? Why?' Then he got angry. It seemed that his interview was merely to satisfy his curiosity and not to get information.

While he was confabbing with some of the others, I had a chance to look out of the window. We were apparently in 'The General's Garden,' a cool, green oasis with beautiful palms and colorful, flowering trees like those I'd seen on my way in.

"The Commandant turned to me with a rather sour expression and said something in French, which I didn't get. I told him so in my French, and that didn't get across either. So we stared at each other for a while and tried again. It was no use. Then to my joy and surprise, Jean, my guard, produced some English, which wasn't so bad. I suppose the Commandant and I had passed a quarter of an hour staring at each other. I gave him the usual answers to questions, none of which were embarrassing, and then—because he didn't ask me anything important—I decided I should open up my own offensive. Flying training teaches you that offensive methods are the best defense, and I was beginning to get rather hot under the collar at their seeming half-heartedness at everything that was going on. It was wrong, of course, to judge the French, seeing that they were in a difficult spot, but the uncertainty of my position bothered me.

"I stood up and told him that I wasn't contented with my treatment, that all my personal belongings had been stolen, that I needed above anything else some soap, a toothbrush, a bath, and medical care.

"'So you were wounded,' he supplied—'by your own shells, I suppose?' I didn't answer that. I said that I wanted medical care and also some fresh air. He told Jean to look after the matter, and I went back where I had come from.

"There were three very pretty girls sitting at the desks, and one of them threw me the kind of glance that showed quite definitely that she was not mad at the Americans—I can't imagine there was any other reason for it. She produced a package of cigarettes from her pocketbook and held them up, but as I don't smoke I refused with a smile. Jean came back and shrugged, 'I'm sorry, *mon vieux,* but there is no doctor. They eatall too busy patching up our own wounded. I may be able to get a nurse for you.' I then told him that I must have some fresh air. He took me up two floors to the roof, and from that moment I forgot my wounds and the discomfort I had undergone.

"Casablanca is a beautiful city. It is a blend of old and new with domes, minarets, spires and white-faced houses, wide streets, parks, and gardens. The building had a lovely view over the center of the city. Right near by was the city hall with a tall clock tower set on Vichy time. On the top of the tower was what seemed to be an exceptionally well-equipped air-raid precaution center with acoustic listening posts and machine-guns. I could see French officers and men crowding that area all day long. It obviously had a commanding view of the city and of the waterfront.

"I sat there listening to the guns that had been firing again and weighing up the situation. The weather was warm and bright, as the sun—which was exceedingly cheering—burned away a heavy morning haze, which had hung over the city. Below us, a few civilians were leisurely going about their daily tasks, although occasionally policemen were warning them to keep off the streets. Occasionally a shell would *wang* over, and I heard the noise of aircraft in the distance. Immediately this happened, French anti-aircraft guns would blaze off, never seeming to hit or aim at anything.

"About noon, I saw what looked to me like a salmon-colored Spitfire. He came in low over the city, flying faster than I have ever seen a plane fly before, and disappeared in the west. I got the impression that many guns were firing at him, but I seriously doubt that he was hit. He was probably taking pictures. The British had been doing quite a lot of reconnaissance for us.

"Jean, my guard, was rapidly becoming friendly. He was an engaging young man whose home was just south of Paris. I soon became adept at listening to whatever he had to say and telling him nothing very much. This particular morning he was bubbling with rumor. It appeared that General Bethouart, who had his quarters in the building where he lived with his family, had been visited by a colonel in the American Army who had been a classmate of his at Saint-Cyr. The interview had taken place in an automobile sent from the American Consulate on Sunday morning during the first attack. That evening, the General had not returned to his headquarters, although his wife and daughter were still there.

"The current rumor was that General Bethouart

had gone to Fedala to join the American forces. My cautious mood urged me to take it with a grain of salt. It seemed to me that it probably was a come-on to get me to talk.

"Then Jean waxed indignant. Most of the Germans had flown out of Cazes airport on Sunday evening in transport planes. 'Our fellows fired on the Boches, but they got away,' he lamented. 'You see how they leave us in our troubles. But we are well rid of them.'

"I learned later that Jean must have been telling me the truth. General Desré had been appointed the new commandant of the subdivision of Casablanca. Apparently General Bethouart's family had been taken away by motor during the night, and the new general had moved in. Jean himself was rather serious when he told me that the Americans had moved up nearly to the outskirts of Casablanca. 'Good,' I thought, 'they will at least stop my airplane from being stripped by the natives.' I was still thinking rather affectionately about the Wildcat I had left out there.

"After lunch, which consisted of hard bread, a hard-boiled egg, and more of the native wine, Jean brought me in a newspaper. It was printed in French, but it was so pro-German that I could see pretty clearly how completely the Nazi element was controlling the press. The headlines revealed that the Allies were being beaten back with heavy losses, and that the situation was certainly under control.

"Shortly after two o'clock, I was hailed for a formal interview, with Captain Le Vaçon, head of the 4th Bureau and an intelligence officer. The interpreter was Monsieur Fonde, who had been an English teacher at L'Ecole Industrielle.

"Monsieur Fonde, who looked rather like Caspar Milquetoast, had previously taken me aside and rather astonished me by saying, 'My friend, you don't have to say anything you don't want to. Just don't answer if I ask you a question that is embarrassing. You understand?' From the expression on his face, I could see that he was distinctly friendly, probably because of his relations with the British and Americans before these unhappy days. The stock questions were asked again, and I answered them because I felt that they were better propaganda than I could originate myself. I certainly disclosed nothing of value and did my best to keep the interview on a cheerful note.

"During a lull in the proceedings, in which the Captain began to look exceedingly frigid, I decided to strike a mild blow for my own comfort. 'M. Fonde,' I began, 'I'm surprised that an American officer is treated so badly. I have been wounded, and last night I was promised a doctor. He has not come. I have had no soap. I have not been allowed to shave and there is not even a toothbrush. What does this mean?' The poor chap was most embarrassed. He seemed rather afraid to tell the Captain what I was saying, but the Captain, detecting a new note in my voice, insisted on knowing.

"They went on arguing and chattering, and finally I heard the Captain instruct the interpreter to tell me that he would get my things back. He would make himself personally responsible. He then began to tell me why it was necessary for the French to resist. He said that their families back in France would be mistreated by the Germans, as well as the fact that they received their orders from the local officials, which came from Marshal Pétain and various pro-German officials. I could detect a note of disunity here, but did not press it. I felt sincerely sorry for these officers torn between a love for an old friendship with America and their loyalty to the Vichy order that gave them their living.

"I walked upstairs to my rooftop seat, with a feeling of relief. I had survived another interview, and there was a good chance that I was going to get some comfort. Jean joined me with suppressed excitement. His news was that I was going to have a good dinner prepared by the General's own cook. When it arrived, it was cooked lentils, uncooked sausage, and red wine—altogether quite acceptable.

"I don't know whether it was the fact that I had been allowed to share the General's *chaouch* (cook) or whether it was just that the French officers had decided to become friendly, but when I went back to my room after dinner, many new faces came to call on me. They were, most of them, middle-aged men with numerous multicolored decorations. Some of them had wound stripes. I didn't have to guess they were veterans, because they soon made that clear. I wondered what had happened to them. It came to me momentarily that the American success had revived the spirit of France, or was it that they wanted to be on the right side? Their anxiety is easily understandable. They went about the job of making themselves pleasant to me with astonishing thoroughness. Each one insisted on introducing himself and telling me of the part he had played in the early defense of France. One question presented itself repeatedly: 'What did the Americans think of Pétain?'

"I was becoming quite French by this time, so I shrugged my shoulders and smiled and said that Pétain was a great soldier, and that Roosevelt was a great president. That worked like magic, and they all began to drink toasts, plying me with further questions as to why the Americans had come all this way to invade French territory. This was a good chance to deliver some propaganda. I felt it was needed here. I was inspired to lend hope to these fellows because they were most responsive. New light appeared in their eyes when I mentioned that this was the beginning of the end for the Germans. They had thoughts of the liberation of France. They seemed happy when they left that evening.

"I was still supposed to sleep in the office, which wasn't comfortable, and so I resigned myself to lying and listening. The place rapidly filled up with enlisted men and officers. Some of the civilians who had been working there all day lingered. (Probably because they felt safer.) The enlisted men and officers were trying to do the work, but they seemed irritable from lack of sleep. Many of them had bottles of wine, from which they took long drinks. Occasionally some of them left for the front. Others were coming in with gestures of weariness and exclamations of anger and disgust and commiseration. It was good practice for my knowledge of French to be able to piece together the bits of information that were passing from one to the other.

"The Americans were definitely encircling the city. General Desré's Chief of Staff had been wounded, and the General himself had wanted to surrender to the Americans. *'Mon Dieu,'* said the young officers who brought this news. 'But the Vice-Admiral was there, and the old *cochon* would not allow such a thing. They say that he sent for the General and ordered him to continue the resistance.' The General had replied, *'Mon ami,* you give me men and arms and gasoline, and I will continue.' The Admiral just thundered at him and told him to fight.

"With this kind of thing going on around me, I gave up trying to sleep, so I began to figure out the whole setup. It seemed to me that the whole show was very confusing. There was no unity, no cooperation. The Army wanted to do one thing, the Navy another, and of course I had no information on the Air Force. If ever there was a striking example of the need for a unified command, here it was. Perhaps this was just fanciful dreaming from being too tired, but listening to these Frenchmen milling around and jabbering and grumbling and going down to inevitable defeat seemed to me enough justification for those thoughts.

"The night suddenly got cold again, so I got up to walk around. Jean proceeded to get me a leather coat that belonged to a tank officer who was at the front. He handed it to me, saying, 'Poor devil, he may not need it again.'

"There was such bedlam in that office that I walked out on the terrace to see what was going on. Everything was quiet, but the city, strangely enough, was only blacked out in certain sections. Occasionally I could see a searchlight flickering, and I could hear voices in the streets below.

"I admit I was feeling depressed as I paced up and down that narrow terrace. I was so tired, too, that the cool evening air nearly knocked me out. In moments like that you snatch at any kind of straw for consolation. I was using a ruler that I had taken from the French office as a swagger stick. I always carried it—it bolstered my morale immensely.

"I went inside again to consider whether I could sleep or not, and there I found a friendly face. It was Adjudant Courvilliers. He had seemed very friendly from the first. He stood there smiling a little anxiously. 'Have you everything you want, my friend?' he asked. 'Is there anything I can do?'

"I immediately unloaded my troubles on him. I told him that I had not seen a doctor, that my wound was sore, and that I couldn't sleep in this infernal place. 'You leave everything to me. I will do what I can,' he said.

"I went upstairs to the roof, hoping to see something. There was nothing. The night was quiet and still. Then I went down and lay on my mattress on the cement floor of the office. I was beginning to get the impression that the place was not too clean, because I was itching all over, and the noise that the men made all night was terrific. My bed was quite near where the codebooks were kept. Every time a coded message was received, a French enlisted man would step over me to the safe and consult a book. It seemed to take them a considerable time to decode their messages, and many were grumbling at having to work at night.

"I believe I dozed some time in the early morning. Then, after having had the usual ersatz coffee, I tackled Jean about getting a doctor for me. My leg was getting very painful indeed, and walking was difficult. It seemed to me that I might have some kind of infection. I hadn't washed, shaved, or cleaned my teeth. The lad, who spoke English with an Oxford accent that he had picked up from an English tutor, was distressed about the whole affair. 'I'm only the guard, you know, but I will do my best.'

"About nine o'clock, I was taken up for interrogation. More silly questions were asked. I could see M. Fonde was a little nervous about this. Where had I come from? snapped the Captain. M. Fonde said in careful high-school English, 'Where 'ave you come from?' He could speak English much better than that, but he seemed to be putting on an act to convince his superiors. He had obviously been conscripted along with the rest of the civilians for any possible duties. I told them that I came from America.

"What was I flying? 'An airplane.'

"How many troops had we? I shrugged my shoulders.

"How fast did my plane go? 'Oh, very fast!' That definitely impressed the Captain. I think he rather disapproved of airplanes. For a while poor M. Fonde stumbled along. Had I a wife? 'Yes.'

"At that the interview broke down, and we sat there looking at each other, until I said, 'You know well, I can't tell you anything.' He translated this in his clipped Parisian French. I smiled, and they smiled, and the Captain put on an act to let on that he didn't care much one way or the other whether I answered his questions. The interview came to an end when the electric power went off. That caused a bit of commotion. Everyone immediately lost interest in me, and rumor reported that the Americans had taken the electric plant near Roches Noires and were advancing towards the city. I felt better. I was wondering whether the officers and men around me were going to get ready to fight or evacuate. But they continued quietly as if they were not very interested.

Later, the power came on again but failed shortly afterwards.

"I went up to the roof. At least, if I couldn't get a wash or shave or clean my teeth, I could get some sun and fresh air, which was free. I remember opening my mouth with some idea in my mind of the sun's rays being good. There were occasional showers, but I endured them so that I could get as much of this blessed sun as possible.

"About noon, things began to look up. A formation of glide bombers came over, to make a glide-bombing attack on what appeared to be the area west of the main docks. I couldn't see very much, but it must have been a good show. Everyone who could seemed to be out on the roof tops watching. I could hear the Frenchmen whooping excitedly as every bomb went off. My only observation was that some of the bombers pulled out too soon, but conditions were very difficult.

"The planes had been gone a few minutes when I saw that the ambulances parked in the square opposite were setting off towards the docks. Most of them were old, broken-down affairs. Some of the wounded were coming from the docks in covered trucks. There were a few people in the streets, and occasionally an automobile would stagger by with family furniture strapped on the hood—mattresses, chairs, and washbowls. Other civilians were pushing handcarts similarly adorned.

"I soon found that my friend Courvilliers was a genius. Jean came up at one o'clock. 'Voilá, here is a doctor.' The doctor looked at my leg and dressed it, and said that it would be attended to each day, that there was nothing to worry about and that I was in good shape. From that moment, I could tell things were looking up for me. The Americans were moving and everyone was determined to do as much as possible. Later, when I

was sitting on the terrace, a formation of Wildcats came over the city and made what seemed to
me a perfect strafing attack on the port, followed
closely by a dive-bombing attack on the port area.
They opened up from over the Hotel de Ville, diving in at high speed. I was disturbed by an excited French officer who came up to me, his eyes
blazing. 'You see,' he said, 'the Americans are
shooting people in the streets.' I was amused by
this at first, because I knew that every one of our
fellows had been given instructions that we were
not to bomb or machine-gun the populated areas.
The boys had discussed this many times on the
journey over. We just wouldn't do that kind of
thing.

"Other officers came in. 'It's true. Many
people have been wounded already. They are lying in the streets.' I found time to be angry, and I
felt I could afford to be. I said, 'Nuts! Americans
don't do things like that.'"Presently one of the officers came up with a piece of metal in his hand.
It was one of the links of a .50-caliber ammunition belt. As our guns fire, the belts disintegrate
and fall out. The people had heard these clattering on the roofs and streets, and that, combined
with the psychological effect of hearing the .50-
caliber guns popping off, had convinced them that
murder was in the air.

"'You see,' I said, 'I knew that our fellows
wouldn't machine-gun a civilian population. We
had special instructions, and,' I added, 'we are not
the Boches.' That crack registered.

"My stock was rising. My good friend Courvilliers came along all smiles. 'My friend,' he said, 'everything is arranged. You are going to have a bath.'

"'A bath!' I believe I stared at him as if he were a man from Mars. 'A bath! But where?' He waved his expressive hands as dramatically as the Wizard of Oz. 'In the bathroom of the General!' Gosh, I certainly was making progress!

"And so there I was a few minutes later, splashing, sniffing, soaping myself, and wallowing in a real hot bath, in a bathroom with modern plumbing. There were even clean towels, assorted soaps, talcum powder, and everything the well-dressed Frenchman uses in his ablutions. I have never enjoyed a bath so much in all my life, and the hot water was so tempting that I took the opportunity of washing my socks and skivvies. It may have been sacrilege, but it was an excellent opportunity. I was hanging these out to dry on the terrace when out of the sun came another coordinated attack by the Dauntless dive bombers and the Grumman Wildcats. I was elated to see those fighters—Red Rippers, I hoped. It was the most beautiful sight I could ask for—their square-cut wings sharply outlined against the sky as they went over at a terrific speed.

"The fighters were strafing, and the empties began to pour down beside me. I got wild then. I was so excited I began to cheer, and when the bombers dropped their loads, the explosions made a terrific noise. From the area of the dock great columns of smoke shot up and dirt and debris flew into the air.

"I remember yelling 'Bravo,' although quite a number of the French officers had come up to watch. Their faces were a bit sour, although they seemed to treat the affair rather as a sideshow, passing around cigarettes and commenting excitedly. Once or twice one of them looked over at me with a queer, hostile look on his face. I quieted myself then, because cheering didn't seem quite the thing to do. The French guns were putting up a barrage, but it was exceedingly ineffective. Many of the shells detonated almost as soon as they left the guns. The greatest danger was from the shrapnel of their shells, which was flying everywhere. One nose cap of a shell that had burst prematurely whizzed past our terrace, missing it by a foot, and hit the lower roof.

"After the attack was over, I could see that two good fires were burning in the port area—one to the west and one in the center. As there was practically no wind, the heavy black smoke that began to show a pink-orange tinge as the evening approached went straight up in the air.

"The street below sprang into activity. Again ambulances and trucks were heading towards the docks. The morning newspapers had ordered that every civilian be mobilized, and it seemed as if they had obeyed the call. There were Boy Scouts manning some of the ambulances and Girl Guides marching behind Red Cross flags with hand trucks carrying medical supplies. The only other traffic seemed to be a few civilians riding on bicycles and French motorcyclists with rifles on their backs, probably dispatch carriers, were roaring up and down the streets.

"That evening when I sat in the inner office having some food, the French were quite free with their information. 'Your bombs killed five hundred sailors on the *Jean Bart*,' said one. 'You have ruined France's most beautiful ship. It is a tragedy.' He was lamenting rather than resenting. Another volunteered that the Commandant of Casablanca had been wounded. A young Army officer, battle-stained and weary, burst in dramatically. 'Our men are surrendering,' he said, 'we have nothing left to fight with. Damn those Boches to hell. They caused all this. France will pay them back.' He began to weep. 'The dirty dogs—the filthy *cochons*—they have betrayed us. We were betrayed, we never had a chance to fight.' He buried his face in his hands dramatically and sobbed. One of the others came and touched him on the shoulder. The youngster, who I noticed was bleeding in the face, stood up and shouted, 'I don't care. I hate the Germans. I always did. This whole affair has been a sell-out.'

"These Frenchmen were tired. Many had been in the action and were coming back into headquarters. They began to drink their wine and that made them talk. I learned all kinds of things that gave an insight into what had been going on behind the veils of the German propaganda drawn over Vichy.

"One young officer, who spoke with considerable authority, assured me that the French knew all along that we were going to attack that Sunday, but that nobody was prepared to do anything about it at all. He made it clear that this should have been taken care of by the Navy. The more they drank the more friendly they got and the more they told me how disgusted they were with the Germans.

"'Pétain is all right,' said one of them. 'He is a soldier, at least he was a soldier, but he's an old, old man with his eyes in heaven. He doesn't know. We could have fought—Frenchmen will always fight. But the politicians at home have betrayed us.' I was very careful not to give them any idea that I was not impressed by the old Marshal.

"It was late that evening when my friend Courvilliers came to see me. 'Old man,' he said, 'there is a conference going on below. A very important conference. I think that we are going to have an armistice. Listen, those are probably your guns.' Through the window came the sound of what I took to be tank gunfire.

"When I was taken back to my bed the French enlisted men were running in and out of the office like bees out of a hive. They were stepping over me to get to their codebooks and arguing fiercely. There was no sleep. I almost sat straight up when I heard an American voice, with a Tennessee accent. The French had just brought in an American private from Memphis. It appeared that he had become lost from his unit and was picked up by the Frenchmen. He did not see me at first, and as they were giving him the works I lay down listening.

"My old friend, M. Fonde, had come in to do the interrogation with the examining officers. He looked more like Caspar Milquetoast than ever. I could see him nervously wiping his glasses and peering at the American soldier. I wondered if M. Fonde was anxious about his future. The Memphis boy was very much lost, but quite articulate. I heard him begin to talk about his hometown and his unit, but his accent baffled them. I saw M. Fonde looking very worried. You could cut that soldier's accent with a knife. The interrogators were talking with their backs to me.

"I could make signs to the doughboy, who was facing me, but the French couldn't see. It was a queer situation, like a movie. He kept looking at me whenever they fired a question and I would put my hand to my nose and sign him to say nothing. He caught on very quickly and winked at me. Whether the French saw it, I don't know, but they didn't take any notice. I lay there, propping myself on my elbow, and watched. I could see the lad was tired. He probably felt better to find there was an American officer at hand, even though I was in bed. I could see from where I was that he could hardly keep standing up, but he managed, and whenever they fired a question and he saw my hand going up, he just shook his head and grinned at them in a pretty sickly way. The officer in charge was getting mad at this and he turned and had a long confab with Caspar Milquetoast. The little man rubbed his spectacles nervously and went at it again. The private just looked at him and then he looked at me. Then he quit talking and simply stood there staring at his questioners. He looked as tired as a ghost, but he held up.

"'But you know the armistice has been signed,' said Fonde. I knew that they were trying to put him at ease so I assured him in my own particular sign language that that was a lot of baloney and so he didn't answer. He just sort of chuckled in good American style. Then they asked him if he was one of the two hundred thousand who had landed at Fedala, to which he answered that he had come alone. In the end they got nothing 'very much from him and so they gave up.' They asked him for an armband he was wearing which showed the American flag. The captain wanted it for a souvenir.

"Immediately that doughboy stiffened up. I could see that he wasn't going to give away any of Uncle Sam's property. He shook his head, but the captain gave him a rather wistful little smile. I understood immediately that he was merely looking for something to show his wife and children that he had been in contact with the first American troops. On the surface of it, it seemed such a little request. I signaled a green light sign and immediately the soldier burst into a really hearty smile. 'O.K., bud,' he exclaimed in that drawling Tennessee blur. 'If you want it that way, it's yours, and it's a pleasure.' I admired his spirit. The poor lad must have had a hell of a time. I figured that he had been all alone and that they had been giving him the third degree, but he was game. He took off the brassard and gave it to the officer and then they shook hands. It seemed to me a happy gesture, cementing what might be a valuable new friendship. The officer was delighted with his treasure. He called an orderly, who presently came back with a glass of wine. The Tennessee boy eyed me for my yes. I gave it to him, and that was that.

"I settled down to try to sleep, but I was soon disturbed by Jean, who came in with the news that an armistice had been signed. I was a little suspicious and said that I was very glad because we could really be friends. Again I tried to go to sleep but there was no hope, because people were streaming in and out of the office all the time. I lay there dozing and counting my blessings—the bath, the fact that I had seen a doctor and that I was alive. All kinds of things went through my head, including a squadron song we had worked out to the melody of the Strip Polka that Hubie played on his jukebox. Naturally, it was dedicated to our own 'Queenie.' I couldn't help wondering where 'the round man' was. And all the gang? With an armistice—Were they ready yet? I never realized until then, perhaps, the attachment you get to a squadron. These boys were part of my daily life. Their chatter and gags and their little idiosyncrasies—I remember them all. I realized, too, how much everyone contributes to a fighting squadron. Each one is a type, each one is an individual with his own peculiar way of doing the same thing that everyone else does."

Chapter 10

"THINGS BECAME quiet all at once," went on Mac.

"Jean had fallen asleep. I thought it would be a good idea if I followed. The room, however, seemed to have taken on a cold and eerie aspect. I could just see the shape of an infantryman standing by the window. He was perfectly immobile. The atmosphere of the place was quite different, and I felt as if I wanted to shiver. To keep my mind busy, I began to think how lucky I was to be here even if I had been through some uncomfortable moments.

"Supposing there really was going to be an armistice. That would mean that the Americans had the situation in hand, and I would soon be free again. I suddenly found myself getting quite excited, so excited that sleep seemed out of the question. Then I decided that this was no time to be excited. I had been waiting so long for something to happen that I might just as well wait and get the truth. Heck, I thought, I'll know something in the morning.

"After that, I must have joined Jean. Before I dozed off, I noticed the guard was sleeping standing up, and snoring as well.

"I was up early the next morning to be greeted by a completely different atmosphere from that of the previous day. The little reserve towards me that had remained the night before was completely gone. As I was rubbing my eyes and stretching, I was aware of Jean's outline standing over me impatiently. Even he seemed different. He was bubbling to tell me of something.

"'What is the news?' I asked. 'Is the war over?'

"'Yes,' he said. 'The armistice is certain now. Everything is arranged.'

"He went on excitedly pouring out all the news. 'And now, my friend, we can go at the Germans together,' he said. 'I have always wanted that. The Americans and the French can lick the world!'

"I felt happy about the whole affair and thought the situation merited that I should pat him on the back and say, 'Yes, Jean, we'll do it together, but there are many problems ahead. It won't be easy going.'

"He looked at me as if I was mad when I said that. I was too busy making plans about what I should do to argue with him. I should have to get in touch with my carrier as quickly as possible. Tommy and the others would be worrying about me. And Ruth would probably have got a telegram saying I was ill. It would be good to hear an American voice again. I hadn't spoken to a single American since I had been a prisoner.

"Many of the French officers were already on deck. They crowded round me to express their joy.

They seemed sincerely happy. I could see it was such a feeling of relief to all of them. 'It is the end of stupid and useless sacrifice of men and equipment,' said a grizzled major of the Foreign Legion. '*Dieu*—we can fight the Boches but we will not fight for them—Pétain or no Pétain.' They were very excited, but it was an excitement that quickly subsided into a kind of hilarious calm. Everything was over as far as they were concerned, and they were delighted. I myself didn't have to be convinced now that the armistice had been signed. They showed it clearly enough. Those who had been friendly before were even more friendly now, and many of the others who had been only lukewarm before were simply swamping me with friendliness and questions.

"That amazed me. It helped explain why the Germans were able to hold control as long as they did. It was difficult not to become elated at the way things were going, but I was still able to discern who was who, so I kept my mouth shut, although they themselves began to tell me far more than I had ever expected.

"There had been many internal disputes over the defenses. Many officers had lost their commissions because they refused to fight the Americans. Others had surrendered with their men without a struggle. I began to see in a glance the turmoil, trouble, and schism that had been destroying the morale of the French for many years. These officers and men had suffered because there had been no cooperation between the services and no unity of purpose. Watching them then, I began to realize the good fortune of being an American.

"The good news came fast.

"I was in the middle of my ersatz coffee—and it tasted extra good—when Jean came up. 'Mac, there are some Americans downstairs and they have come to fetch you!' I whistled to myself. Talk about good old American efficiency. If they had come for me already, everything was fine. I was taken down to the Commandant's office, which was serving as a reception office.

"There, surrounded by French soldiers and civilians, and framed against a gigantic picture of Pétain, were the last people in the world I had expected to see—Spanky Carter, Chuck August, Windy Shields, and another character, an American Navy flier whom I had never seen before. They looked like men from the backwoods, bearded and dirty and a bit tattered.

"'We didn't know they had got you too, Mac,' Spanky said. 'Well, well, Mac.'

"Spanky, I should say," went on Mac, "was looking decidedly unlike his real self, Spanky being one of those neat, meticulous men who like everything in order. I had to rib them a bit.

"It took me quite a moment to appreciate that all these fellows must have been shot down as well as myself. There was some consolation in that, but I began to wonder what the squadron had really been doing. I remembered then that while I was clean and shaven and comparatively comfortable, they were bedraggled and unkempt. Even our debonair Chuck August was not his usual self, although I did notice that Chuck was wearing a tie and a cap. His mustache was still there and augmented by a beard. He certainly looked ferocious as well as handsome.

"Windy had a cold, but it didn't keep him from talking.

"'Those characters had been keeping me locked up in a cell,' Windy complained. 'I'd been having a hell of a time, temperature about 110 degrees. No medicine. Thought I was going to die.'

"It was the old Windy, bursting to talk, and full of his own adventures," reminisced Mac. "He over-whelmed me and I enjoyed it.

"We all stood there, shaking hands with each other, smacking backs, laughing and ribbing each other. 'You might as well meet Tommy,' said Spanky. 'He's been with us through most of our troubles.'

"Tommy Dougherty had been spotting the gun-fire for one of the battleships when a Vichy Curtiss Hawk knocked him down early the first morning. He didn't know what had happened to his radioman who had been badly hit.

"'They brought us here to see General Eagles,' said Spanky, 'but nobody's shown up.' He looked at me a bit wistfully. 'Mac, you look pretty good. What can you do in the way of getting us a wash? I feel like hell.'"

"I was that way too,' interposed Chuck, laughing. 'I wanted more than a wash. A good delousing.'

"Spanky said a wash would be sufficient for

him," said Mac, "and asked me if I could fix it.

"'Of course I can,' I laughed cheerfully, 'everybody here is my buddy now. I'll see if you can't use the General's bathroom.' That might have been bluff if I hadn't seen my old friend Courvilliers coming along. The usual salute and the click of the heels and he was saying, 'You see, old man, everything is all right now. We're real friends—France and America. Now we can fight the Boche together.'

"'Splendid,' I said. 'Courvilliers, these are American officers, friends of mine—they want to wash up to see our General. What about the General's bathroom?' Courvilliers vanished. He came back and smiling genially and said that we could go to the General's bathroom in pairs. My stock as a 'fixer' soared. You can imagine how the fellows felt. They needed a wash far more than I ever had. My life had been luxurious compared with theirs.

"Spanky and Chuck went up first to wash while I extracted bits of information as quietly as Windy would permit on what had happened to them.

"'They had us clanked in the Bastille,' began Windy indignantly, 'and the night before that, we had slept in a donkey stable.'

"'Well, let it wait, Windy,' I advised, nodding my head at the corner of the room. 'We have company. We'd better not talk here.' Two Frenchmen dressed in civilian clothes were copying down news coming in on a short-wave radio set. We listened to that awhile. The Germans were moving into Vichy France. Rommel was still moving to the west quite rapidly.

"I soon went up with Windy and Tom as they washed. While we were up in the bathroom, General Eagles arrived. When we came down, Spanky said that the General had told him we were going to be released as soon as possible. The General, of course, had a lot on his mind, so he could not give any details.

"Jean came up bubbling with excitement. 'My friend,' he said, 'an American general has been here, and we are going to fight the Germans—all the French Army is. Liberation is in sight. Isn't it wonderful? You will soon be free as well.'

"That was good news, but half an hour later we were still hanging around in that reception room. Chuck was making the best of the time by chatting to some girl. I don't know how the conversation was progressing, but I imagine it was limited to Chuck's smile.

"Courvilliers bustled in to announce that a car was ready to take us to a place where we would be turned over to American Army officers. I shook hands with Jean and Courvilliers—they were sorry to see us leave. They had been most helpful to me. I wished them well, and we all promised to meet in Berlin.

"The car was driving away when suddenly I realized that I was wearing the leather coat Jean had procured for me. I yelled that I would get it back to him soon. He made a gesture of his hand to say he wasn't worrying.

"I could not help reflecting as we drove that this second auto trip in Casablanca was slightly more pleasant than the first. The streets were crowded now. Many of the people waved and cheered when we passed. Some advanced American Army units began filtering in, and the French troops had disappeared. They were being held in barracks while the armistice terms were being arranged.

"The car came to a stop on the outskirts of the city in what appeared to be a rather shabby section. However, the boys were remarking about certain landmarks they had seen before. We all got out of the car and headed toward a crowd of people assembled outside a big gate. We had only walked a few yards when Windy exclaimed, 'So, we are back at our home again. Mac, allow me to welcome you to the world-famous Hippodrome. The home of bigger and better lice, cooties, and cockroaches.'

"'So this is your villa in the suburbs,' I ribbed. 'This is going to be a treat!' Spread before us was the local racetrack—as delightful a mud hole as you could ask for. The ground had been well mired by hoofs and dung of many horses in the past few days.

"The buildings of the Hippodrome looked damp and foreboding. We decided to stay in the sunshine near the street—if no one objected—and no one did.

"We stood around for a while," proceeded Mac in that even, unruffled way of his. "The civilians came crowding in and asking us questions. Then I saw through the arch of the entrance some familiar uniforms, and more unshaven faces.

American soldiers!

"Windy told me there were quite a lot of them—also some British pilots, a Pole, and a few British civilians. They wouldn't take an oath of allegiance to Vichy so they clapped them in there. Windy was boiling. 'It's a foul place,' he kept saying.

"It certainly was. We walked in to have a look—at least it was a look for me. The American soldiers were tired and dirty. The British pilots were cheery. Poor devils, they had been through a hell of a time, but they were still cheerful and tremendously enthusiastic about the whole show. Many of them seemed to be just kids, but they had the air of veterans. Some of them had been through the hottest days of the battle of Malta, but they showed no signs of stress. They were the most cheery bunch of men you could imagine and greeted us like old friends. They told me that they were due for leave from Malta, and their ship had been torpedoed off Dakar, where they had been taken prisoners by the French.

"'I suppose we'll get our spot of leave now,' said one of them, a fair-haired young Londoner who looked as if he still should be at college, 'but I'm not really keen at the moment because if this show is going to continue, we might just as well stay and have another crack at the Hun.' I asked them what the conditions had been like with the French. 'Oh, forget it,' he said, 'it probably would have been worse with the Huns.' The poor kids were full of lice and bugs and scratching continually, but they seemed to worry very little about it.

I suppose you get used to that kind of thing after awhile.

"The most interesting fellow was a hefty, red-faced young Polish pilot. He told me he had fought against the Germans in Russia, against the Russians in Poland, against the Germans in France and Syria, and in the air over Malta. 'Now I got to have a slap at them Goddamned beasts anywhere,' he said, scratching himself pitifully. It was hard to see those chaps in such a state, with every kind of vermin all over them. These British flying officers were showing the signs of privation. Our boys were just tired.

"Immediately after the news came that an armistice had been signed the French civilian population, especially the girls, had come out in force to have a look at us and to cement the new friendship. The French officers in charge of the racetrack, however, were determined that there was to be no fraternization and so they ordered the soldiers to make a barrier between us and our visitors. It was particularly hard on Chuck. I will admit that I didn't like it, either, because some of the girls were exceedingly attractive and friendly.

"Even the soldiers' bayonets did not entirely restrain the Americans. They began to toss banter across to the civilians, whose main interest was in begging American cigarettes. I saw one fellow throw over something that looked suspiciously like a stick of chewing gum. As such a practice might cause injury amongst the people scrambling for it, I told him not to do it again.

"Just then through the entrance came a large number of foot soldiers. They were battle-scarred and bandaged, dressed in long, dark gray cloaks with black vertical stripings. A French officer volunteered the view that they were a crack regiment and had been hidden from the Germans in Casablanca.

"I tried to give the boys the story of how I was shot down and, as near as possible, the chronological order of events. Their only comment was, in unison, 'Damned lucky.'

"Windy came in to tell us that something was moving outside. The native soldiers who had just arrived were busy with hammers and ropes. We went over to see what was cooking. They were erecting two vertical poles."

"It looked as if they were going to hang out their washing or something," laughed Tom Dougherty. "They were getting very excited about the whole thing, and the noncoms were cussing and fussing."

"I thought it was for a radio aerial," said Spanky. "In between my scratching, I was thinking sometimes."

"I was willing to bet it was a sheet for a screen for roadside movies," volunteered Chuck. "It was a good idea anyway. What could be better than seeing Betty Grable again in darkest Africa?"

"We'll tell you about Chuck later," resumed Mac. "This business was the real thing. In a few minutes the poles were up side by side.

"Then a jeep came in and stopped beside the two flagpoles. Out jumped two soldiers carrying a waterproof sack. They opened it and attached what they took out to the pole and to the ropes. Up went a tiny multicolored bundle, which suddenly burst into the breeze and revealed itself as the Stars and Stripes. We all stood to attention. I looked at the crowd of Frenchmen. Their faces were very cold. I knew how they felt, facing the emblem of the new invader. Then another flag went up on the other flagpole. This broke, too, in the breeze, the Tricolor of France, but it seemed to be flying at half mast. I saw an old French officer with his hand at the salute. Tears were streaming down his face. A French private said brokenly, 'It's better than the Swastika.'

"We stood there, wondering what to do. There was nothing really one could say. The chilling effect of this demonstration of occupation seemed to have struck these Frenchmen. They looked so pathetic. Then we saw that the French Tricolor was still going up. It had opened too soon and stuck halfway. It seemed to climb slowly and surely. It came to a halt side by side with Old Glory. We cheered. The French stood to attention and saluted! This was not a conqueror who had raised her flag but an ally raising the standard of a weaker ally to equal status.

"We went back to our place outside the stable and began to discuss how best we could make contact with the ship," continued Mac. "I tried as hard as I could to get someone to take a message to the outside, but there was no one available. I lost Jean, and Courvilliers, of course, had gone back to his base. In a way I was worse off than before in regard to quarters, but it was better at least to be with the boys you know. Windy had heard that Mikronis was in hospital at Casa, pretty badly knocked up. Windy had seen him shot down just before they got him. We would have to take him up before we left. I wasn't going to leave this place while there were any of the squadron around.

"We began to reminisce on what we each had seen. Windy had a great yarn. He had seen a burning Wildcat come down out of control during his dogfight. Spanky said that he had seen another. They must be some of our gang, I guessed, and began to wonder if any of the boys had been killed and who.

"'I came right down on the edge of Cazes airfield that first day,' explained Windy. 'After I had bailed out a French pilot came straight at me. I thought he was going to shoot me, but instead he wagged his wings and went off. I hadn't got down very far before someone started opening fire on me with a rifle. Hell, I thought, if that is the game I can play it too, so I yanked out my automatic and started returning their fire.'

"'That must have scared them quite a lot,' chipped in Chuck. 'What did they do?'

"'They stopped! I figured that they were Germans. I don't think the French would do that. Then I landed on a barbed-wire fence. I tore the back out of my pants. Look.'

"Windy's pants were certainly evidence of some efficient work on the barbed wire," laughed

Mac. "The squadron boar couldn't have done a better job on them."

"It may be funny now but it wasn't then," recalled Windy. "I found that I had landed on the French side of the airfield. I waited for a while and nobody came to see me at all. Presently, three Heinkel bombers came out on the airfield followed by a Junkers transport. A group of Germans began to pile into the planes. Then I saw what must have been a German staff car bringing a big shot. When he had got in, as many as possible crowded in after him and off they went.

"There wasn't anybody to stop them. I wish I had been in the air then with my Wildcat. We might have caught most of that darned armistice commission. I was so mad at the French for not trying to keep them. After a while, I thought the best thing I could do was to give myself up, so I set off, walking to the military side of the airport. I hadn't gone many steps before I passed a couple of Germans. They took not the slightest notice of me, so I went on and presently an enlisted man came up with a rifle. I told him that I was an American.

"'Ha,' he said, 'prisoner.'

"'Mebbe,' I said and I beckoned him to follow me. I wanted to see what had happened to my plane, so I set off to the edge of the airfield. I had hurt myself when I fell down but it wasn't serious. I was just a little stiff. I was so anxious to have a look at the aircraft that I forgot my torn pants and the scratches. My Wildcat had fallen on the other side of the hill flanking the south of the airport and crashed so badly that it wasn't flyable. It was already surrounded by natives and a few soldiers. One of the crowd was a German in uniform. Directly he saw me, he turned and walked away. I clambered up and managed to get hold of the chart board and destroy it. The French soldier with me did not object. He kept on asking me questions, which I could not understand but I kept telling him I was an officer. Finally he took me to what I thought must be the officers' mess. Immediately, all kinds of French officers came out to see me. Some were Navy, some were Army, and some were L'Armee de l'Air. They were cheerful and exceedingly friendly, even though we had smashed up their airport. They invited me into what I imagined was the clubroom, and gave me a drink, some kind of brandy. It tasted good, I can tell you.

"No one asked me any questions in particular. There was no intelligence officer, no interpreter, only a little guy who had been in New Orleans and had a sister in Wisconsin. He seemed a bit disappointed that I didn't know the sister, but I told him that America was a very big place, which he already knew. Then a captain who could speak a little English arrived and told me that I was to be taken to Casa. He was a bit sour about something.

"'You are a prisoner of the French Navy,' he said. 'They will look after you. They'll be pleased to I'm sure.' They took me in a car to a big building in the middle of Casablanca.

"This they told me was the French Navy Maritime Prison adjoining the admiralty building in Casablanca.

"The accommodation was far from good—just a cell, and small at that. It was bitterly cold, and as I had a cold, I felt it all the more. I banged on the door, and told them I was sick and must have a doctor. A French sailor told me in no uncertain terms to *shut up,* so I bawled him out, and presently he brought a young officer along, who seemed to be quite friendly. 'Just like an American man,' he said. 'Want something quickly, and make a noise.' He said it quite nicely, though, and I took it the right way. He came back with another, who said they would get a doctor as soon as possible.

"Five minutes later, I was taken into a big sunny room to be interviewed by a tall, fair man of about fifty who wore a khaki naval officer's uniform and a great deal of braid on his shoulderboards. He was quite a pleasant character with a great sense of humor. Why did the Americans want to attack the French? he asked. I said that we were not attacking the French, but that we were going after Rommel. He smiled. 'But you are attacking the French, *mon ami.* This is French territory. How many of you are there? What do you expect?' I didn't answer that, so he changed the subject. I took the opportunity to tell him I had a cold, and I wanted to see a doctor. 'Patience, my young man,' he said. 'We are not ready at all to receive prisoners . . . we will do our best.'

"On the way back to my cell, I asked the guard who it was who had interviewed me, and he said it was Admiral Michelier. At least I had been taken to the top man. Later, I was taken into a room decorated with pictures of Laval, Pétain, and Hitler.

"Three or four French naval officers were sitting at a table with a civilian, a smartly dressed, blond, close-cropped fellow. It didn't take me one minute to realize he was a German. He began to give me the third degree in excellent English with a London accent. 'You might just as well tell me what you know,' he said. 'You will probably get a good meal if you do. We are aware of everything that has taken place. You know, of course, that your squadron has suffered very heavy losses. Your comrade Mikronis is in hospital, and most of your squadron planes have been shot down.'

"I just stood looking at him and smiling because he didn't sound real. After a while he said something in French to the others, got up and stalked out.

"I wanted to laugh, especially as the Frenchmen smiled at each other, but I said nothing and just enjoyed watching them. They certainly were glad I had not given any information to that Heinie. One of the younger officers told me that he hated the Germans and was glad to welcome the Americans. He made a gesture a little later and said, 'As long as it is not the British, we do not mind.'

"I changed the subject, and asked him if there were many Germans. 'They are everywhere,' he said. 'They have the best hotels, the best food and wine, and they have taken our women. No one can do anything about it.' I told him that things would be better now, but he was gloomy about that even. I felt sorry for the guy as I did for all these French because they didn't seem to know what it was all about."

Windy was still looking a bit tense after his experience.

"I can appreciate what he went through," continued Mac. "He looked half dead when I first saw him in the prison. He'd been running a temperature most of the time."

"Mac, you haven't told about the other boys," suggested Spanky. "I mean the American soldiers who were in the stables with us."

"They were a swell bunch," affirmed Mac. "Some men! The kind of fellows America turns out when she is not expecting war, who do a good job when war comes. You know in that prison camp I picked up one yarn that made me feel exceedingly proud. I found Spanky talking to some doughboys, at least that is what they seemed to me, even if it's an old-fashioned word. He told me that they were members of a military police group that had left their ship in three barges.

"They were supposed to land at Fedala, but because of a navigational error, they found themselves landing right under the guns of French destroyers in Casablanca Harbor in broad daylight. Seeing the hopelessness of the situation the lieutenant rushed to the bow of the boat waving a white flag of surrender. The destroyer machine-gunned them by way of reply. The barrage killed many of the men, including the lieutenant at the bow. These men were game, though. When the coxswain was shot, the engineer of the boat took over the helm.

"Sergeant Cunningham, one of the M.P.s, assumed command when his senior officer was killed. His first thought was to get the barge away from the destroyers before losing all his men. He therefore began to retreat on an erratic course, but his men were constantly being hit. When he had some distance between the boats and the guns, he decided to use the barge as a shield. He cut out the motor so the propeller would not injure anyone and coolly ordered the men over the side. The men responded to the order, all going over the side as one man.

"When Cunningham himself hit the water he remembered that some of his men were wounded and that the life belts they were using had to be inflated by the individual. Having previously ordered the three best swimmers aboard to keep the barge parallel with the destroyers, he went to look after the wounded men. Although under heavy fire all the time he inflated the life belt of each wounded man, with the help of some of the boys in better condition. He then saw to it that the group stayed together, taking great pains to pick up men in distress. All the time he kept talking to keep his men well informed of his plan and what he wanted to achieve. It was not easy to keep his thirty or more men under control with so many of them wounded, but he kept on.

"Cunningham knew it would be suicide to make a swim for it through an area where every inch of air housed a bullet, so he used the procedure of 'taking it by inches' until finally he had gotten all his men out of the range of the guns. He then warned the three swimmers propelling the barge to be sure it was kept from striking some of the wounded. Then he led the group en masse for the shore a hundred yards away. There he assembled his men, saw that his wounded were given first aid, and walked up the shore to surrender to a French Navy patrol who took them prisoners.

"I wanted to meet this Sergeant Cunningham. He came up, a quiet, shy kind of man, and meeting him, I was suddenly embarrassed. This young American had done so much. Looking at him then, I was short of words. Quite frankly all I could say was, 'Cunningham, you're a hero.'

"He replied modestly, 'Only doing my duty, sir,' and would say no more. His pals chimed in, 'The hell he was. If it hadn't been for him and his quick thinking, none of us would be here now, sir.' Another added, 'The boys in the hospital up there feel as we do about Cunningham.'

"It was getting to be late afternoon," continued Mac. "My thoughts returned to such things as food and lodging for the men for the night. A jeep arrived and I went to investigate. A U.S. Army officer told me that buses were on their way to take care of us.

"The soldiers cheered as if they were at a ball game when the buses rolled to a stop. The lieutenant in charge of the bus said we were going to Medouina.

"Spanky, who by this time felt tired of roughing it, cried, 'But where can we sleep?' The lieutenant shrugged his shoulders. We would probably have to sleep on the ground.

"I protested then and there. 'None of that for me,'" said Windy.

"Me, too," said Spanky.

"I wanted a bit of comfort myself, so I suggested they should drop us off at Cazes," said Mac. "Some of our air force units should have been out there by now. I thought I would rather chance my luck with them than on the ground at Medouina.

"'O.K., jump aboard then and let's go,' said the lieutenant."

"We missed Chuck then," Spanky interrupted. "He was nowhere in sight."

Mac laughed. "I'd forgotten something. You must understand that Chuck is quite a woman's man. He looks it, at least—which I suspect is why he brought that hat and tie. There were several very good-looking gals in the crowd. One of them was a real humdinger as gals go, with good lines and a lovely dark Latin face. She was making a very definite pass at Chuck. She really was cute enough to be American. I decided I might be of help to liven up a dull situation, so I told her quite seriously that Chuck was Clark Gable. With his beard and his mustache and his height, Chuck might have been anyone. She didn't fall for that, because I suspect Gable was her hero anyhow, but she made it quite plain that Chuck would be the next best thing. I did my stuff with good old New England French that had had some considerable dusting off during my imprisonment, and it worked wonders. She took to Chuck, and although his French was limited to *Bonjour,* they got along well, and soon she was the envy of all the other gals in the crowd.

"I could see by the way she was throwing him some soft Gallic smiles that he had registered."

Chuck, shaven and debonair, and minus his mustache, raised his voice in a good-natured pro-test. "Steady, Mac, remember you were there. She was just as interested in you, and with your French, you were setting the pace."

"Only for you, Chuck," replied Mac. "And how. But tell us what happened to you."

"Nothing much," went on Chuck. "You know what gals are. This one was pretty thrilled to see us. I suppose she got a kick out of the idea that a battle had been fought in the sky over her home town, and then she was able to talk to the fliers. I didn't see you fellows had gone, and I was doing my best. She told me her name was Marie—she wrote it down, and I told her mine. Then she wanted a souvenir. I hadn't anything much to give her. Suddenly she put out her hand, and pointed to my cap insignia. I had brought that cap as an afterthought, and there she was making soft eyes and begging me for it."

"So you gave it to her," said Spanky. "Good thing she didn't want your tie."

"She wouldn't get that," said Chuck, "you know how particular I am about ties, but honestly, I had to give her something to cement Franco–American relations. I hadn't got the heart to refuse her. She really was a cute child. And then I realized you chaps had gone, so I ran for it."

"We waited for Chuck as long as we could," said Mac, "and then set off. Presently, I heard Spanky yell that Chuck was in sight, and there he was tearing down the street like a madman. He clambered up beside Windy, breathless. As Chuck is a very particular part of our squadron—out of hours that is—we wanted to be sure that he had done the right thing. All we could get from Chuck was that things had been going along nicely when he saw that we were on the way. 'It's a good story, Chuck,' said Windy. 'But wipe that lipstick off.' Our great Chuck began to blush. This gal certainly had shot him down with her bright eyes.

"At the airport we parted company with the Army men. The field itself looked as if it had been hit by a hurricane. Nobody had bothered to clean it up. Along the ramp there were several burned-out skeletons of French fighter planes. They looked particularly pathetic, and on the south edge of the field there were other blackened remains. As we walked across, I noticed that some of the planes were partially buried in the ground. Some of the engines had dug themselves holes a little

way away from the planes. All around were
unexploded bombs, machine-gun bullets, and every
imaginable kind of junk associated with airplanes.
Windy immediately began souvenir hunting. He
collected several insignia for the squadron trophy
department. He told me we had been fighting not
only the Lafayette Escadrille but the famous Stork
squadron that had distinguished itself so much
during the last war. While we were having a look
around, a French commercial airliner arrived and
embarked a few passengers. We couldn't see who
they were, but I felt something should be done
about it."

"I felt the same," said Windy. "You see, when
I had bailed out on this airfield before, those transport planes were flying out Germans as fast as they
could. I figured they were still going, and it
seemed all wrong."

"There was quite an unfriendly atmosphere
about the whole place then," went on Mac. "We
may have been overimpressed, but as we had done
the damage, we could not help wondering how the
French would feel. A few French officers came
out to look at us, but none of them spoke. It was
obvious that we couldn't sleep there, so Windy
suggested that we might go over to the civil side
of the airport. He wanted to show us where he had
seen the German planes taking off on Sunday
morning. The civil side of the airfield was not very
active, but suddenly we were greeted by a tall
Frenchman who came running out and hailed us
as if we had been old friends. He introduced him-

self as Colonel Lasserre and told us that he, like many others, had been deprived of his commission because he had refused to fight against the Americans.

"Lasserre had an automobile stowed away in back of the hangars. 'The dirty Boches did not see it,' he said triumphantly. 'I've been keeping it for that one day I could make my escape and fight for France.'

"We drove to the American Consulate in style. Lasserre talked all the time. He was a great friend of General Giraud, and he would of course get his commission back. He told us some strange stories of the French Air Force. 'You know, my friends, the French Navy are against everyone but themselves. The French Army worship Pétain. But the Air—well, they are the best of France. They would fight for the sake of fighting, but they would not fight Americans.' He made a wide sweep of his hand, indicating the south. 'Do you know that down there were hundreds of bombers that never took to the air because the squadron commanders decided they were to stay on the ground rather than oppose a people with whom France had always been friendly? There were foolish acts, of course, and some were brave acts. The pilots of one squadron refused to take the air when the alert was given. Their old Colonel, who must have been seventy-three, told them that if they would not fly, he would go himself. He got into a fighter plane, which he probably had never flown before, and flew away to join the pilots of another squadron going into action. He was a brave man, but he wasted his life.'

"The Colonel had many stories like that. He was a typical France-loving Frenchman with only one ambition—to start fighting again and exterminate the Germans. He was emotional, and there were tears in his eyes when he said, 'And when they took my commission away, it seemed as if this was the end of life. But I remembered that it could not last long. I was only being loyal to the tradition of France, and so I found my courage and waited . . . *Le bon Dieu* would not make me wait long. I would have endured everlasting shame if I had fought against America.'

"It was good to hear that kind of thing . . . to meet a man who had not been influenced by German propaganda.

"We arrived at the American Consulate almost at the same moment as the staff who had just been released from internment. Naturally, they were all too busy to worry about a few Navy flying officers, but I found one helpful individual who suggested we go to the Army headquarters at the Villa Maas.

"We thumbed a ride in a jeep and drove through the residential section, blocks of beautiful houses, sometimes one to a block, with gardens resplendent with palm trees and bright flowers, shaven lawns, and fish pools.

"Finally, the jeep turned into a wide driveway lined with trees—our destination.

"It was fascinating to find oneself suddenly in the midst of luxury and beauty. The Villa Maas, a magnificent white two-storied building situated on the hillside facing south, had been the headquarters of a German unit and was being taken over by the Americans. The Germans had obviously left in a hurry. As I went into the white lobby with its walls covered with mirrors and paintings and in the middle of the room a beautiful glass-topped modern French table with onyx legs, I noticed that our fellows, too, had done quite a little removing. A dozen or so oil paintings of Hitler were stacked up in a corner, as well as several plaques decorated with the Swastika.

"'Don't touch anything,' warned a military policeman. 'We're looking all over for booby traps.'

"I went inside what was probably the cocktail room in better days, and there were further stacks of pictures, Pétain this time, each embellished with a motto. Pétain was everywhere—you saw his picture on calendars, banners, in little stores, and in public and private toilets.

"I wasn't long at the Villa Maas before I realized that the Germans certainly had the knack of taking the best places and that we were following their example. My main concern was to find somewhere to sleep. I was Navy and the Villa Maas was being taken over by the Army. That was a problem. After we had eaten some Army food— and that K ration is excellent when you are hungry—Colonel Waters of the Intelligence Department decided that we could be quartered at the Anfa Hotel in town, so we set off and arrived dead tired but happy at the thought of being in a bed for the first time since we had taken off from the carrier.

"A bed is a bed, though, and a bug is a bug, and those two don't mix when you want to sleep. Both Spanky and I were trying to be very polite about the whole thing and neither of us had confided our dreadful secret. I heard Spanky scratching and tossing and he probably heard me. At four in the morning I could stand it no longer, so I got up and began to walk around. Presently the telephone bell rang. The Villa Maas had been working all night and they had a message for me. This was just the excuse I wanted—to get out—so I told them not to put it on the phone, that I would come and collect it myself. It was a strange time to make a telephone call for what was a routine, but I blessed them.

"When I got back to the Villa Maas I found out that our experiences would be very welcome to the Intelligence Department, especially Windy's. Windy had collected some personal diaries from a German pilot who had been operating with the Vichy Air Force.

"When I felt that I could not reasonably devote any more time to that matter I went back to the task of trying to get somebody to listen to my story and also to take me back to the carrier. Nothing had happened up to lunch time, and so I decided that if we were going to have to stay in the area of Casablanca for any considerable period, we might just as well see what we could of the town. I was particularly anxious to see what damage the bombing had done to the *Jean Bart* and to the surrounding gun installations, and also I wanted to get a peek at the destroyers that I had strafed.

"I found an Army Air Corps colonel who was going into town in an automobile and begged a lift from him. He was trying to find a place for his head-quarters in Casablanca and I sold him the idea that my knowledge of the town would be useful.

"He drove the gang of us into Casablanca. Everything was surprisingly normal, with the French civilians and natives looking around, star-ing a little, perhaps, at the American soldiers. The French soldiers were also moving around with their hands in their pockets and cigarettes in their mouths, taking very little interest. I wanted to see the harbor so without more ado George, Chuck, and I walked past the guards at the entrance to the port. Whether they thought we were high of-ficers or whether they just didn't care is difficult to conjecture.

"The harbor had taken some battering. The bombs had done a remarkably good job. Every-where there were signs of very heavy damage. As we went on with our inspection during which I was contriving to make notes, French soldiers and sailors approached. They looked hostile and surly. I was glad they did not understand that we were Navy fliers or they might have attempted to take summary revenge. We were the only Americans in the middle of all this damage wreaked by American bombs.

"The great ship *Jean Bart* lay there at her moorings with great holes gaping in her beam. Some of her wounds were still smoking, her guns were cocked in all directions and where her plates had been ripped through, thick jagged edges of metal were exposed. It is a pathetic sight to see a huge battleship such as this after she has been well and truly bombed.

"Wherever you looked in that naval harbor you saw the result of our air attack. Deserted anti-air-craft guns—machine-guns—twisted and bent, burnt-out oil stores, empty cartridge cases and occasionally a corpse or two, lying in that grotesque attitude which comes to those whose death is sudden.

"As we walked, the French naval guards occasionally made an attempt to bar our way with their rifles and bayonets, but we walked on with very straight faces acknowledging their challenge with salutes, as if we were big shots. They stood aside. Once we encountered a group of French officers, who probably belonged to the *Jean Bart*. One of them had been wounded in the forehead, which had been hurriedly bandaged. I sensed that they had probably recognized who we were because I heard one of them say in a loud voice, 'Uh, we have no friends now. We are betrayed.' The other one answered, 'Well, at least we don't want any friends of that kind.'

"They were very bitter and they seemed to be baiting us like schoolboys challenging another gang to fight. You could understand when you saw their ship and the tragedy of its last battle in harbor.

"Windy and Tom were not content with inspecting the battleship. They thought they would like to have a look at the French Admiralty, but the guard outside that austere building had other ideas; they shaped up and yelled at us to keep out and presently, some French officers came out and lined up some Marines. We therefore decided not to pay a formal call to a building whose inhabitants at that time must have been feeling extremely bitter."

Chapter 11

"YOU KNOW how I got down," said Chuck August, looking exceedingly debonair even without the mustache. "I fell as heavily as I have fallen anywhere, even playing football. As I bailed out, my shoulder had hit the right tip of the tail plane, and I began to flat-spin in the air. How I got out of that I don't really know—but I did—thank God! I managed to get the chute open when I seemed a few yards from the ground. I was, too. The parachute had hardly opened when I struck so hard that I nearly lost consciousness. I was stunned. But I remember then trying to collapse the parachute unconsciously; also I had been trying to check the time of my fall, but contact with the plane had not only ripped off my escape gear, but also my wrist watch.

"I collected what seemed like bits and pieces of myself to find myself surrounded by a large number of male and female Arabs."

"I bet you sat up straight—when you saw the females," laughed Mac. "At least, if you were sufficiently conscious to be running to form."

"You're wrong this time," went on Chuck. "The most welcome sight was a couple of French civilians on the outside of the circle. But they moved off when I came up, and the rest of the crowd ran to my Wildcat. I could see that I ought to put in an appearance there, so I followed. The plane was smoking but not burning. I had hurt myself a bit, but I limped up and managed to push my way through the crowd and get to the plane. The right wheel had sheared off, and the inside of the nose cowling had been hit with some fairly large-caliber stuff. I felt quite ashamed when I looked at the tail of the fuselage to find it riddled with .30-caliber bullets. That Vichy pilot had certainly made a mess of me. All the radio gear had been demolished, too.

"The good old Navy routine came to my help. I can see now that I'll bless our training for the rest of my life. I went through my checklist, destroyed everything that would help the enemy. I couldn't get hold of a map on the chart board because the left wing was jammed across the cockpit, which had buckled completely. The engine had been severed from the airplane and was lying approximately four feet away from the fuselage. There was oil all over the place, and the ground was saturated with gasoline. I decided the best thing to do was to set fire to the whole show to save any further trouble. I drew my Very pistol, and immediately the French began to holler and scream. They thought I was going to attack them. The women began to put the kids' heads behind their skirts, and the men began to gabble and yell at me. I tried to calm them, and they backed away. Then I took three pot shots at the plane. I knew the gasoline would burn her if I could ignite it. She burst into flames and burned fiercely. The crowd seemed quite happy then; the bonfire calmed them.

"One of the Frenchmen noticed that I had rolled my chute and put it behind a rock. He went over, picked it up, and then signaled me to follow him. We walked about two blocks, followed by the crowd, who were pressing all around us, and at exactly ten o'clock by their time, I was sitting in his kitchen having two excellent shots of brandy. My French was not even as good as his English, but the brandy did the trick, and after considerable gesticulation, I conveyed to him that I wanted to get to Fedala as quickly as possible. He had produced a map. I suspect he was an armchair general in his spare time, and he liked to follow exactly how the war was going, because every time he put down his pencil and said, '*La*,' I said '*Oui*,' and then he said something that I thought was 'battleship,' and I said 'yes.' He was delighted. We were doing fine and had another drink on the strength of our maneuvers.

"I was afraid then that he might have taken one too many drinks to have grasped what I meant, but suddenly there appeared in the doorway a young French doctor with his wife, who incidentally was exceedingly attractive, and she knew it. She gave me a kind of soft brown-eyed welcome behind her young husband. He immediately grasped that I was an American airman, and it was only a matter of minutes for him to start examining me. The girl stood by, looking on."

"I'll bet you enjoyed that examination," ribbed Windy. "How was the mustache standing up? Did you take her telephone number?"

"I would have," said Chuck, "but you know the instructions we had about not molesting the local women, and after all, I had to presume she lived in the place. I was rather embarrassed about the whole thing. The mustache, however, was good as mustaches go.

"The little doctor," he went on, "produced a stethoscope and went over my heart, bound up my hand, and said I was all right. Presently, I heard the noise of an automobile driving up the dirt driveway. Three armed guards came in, little fellows in khaki coats much too big for them, with rifles and bayonets. They were followed by a tall, rather aristocratic young Frenchman who introduced himself as the commanding officer of the Escadrille Lafayette. That was the outfit we had shellacked so badly that morning. I'll admit I felt a bit uncomfortable about the situation, but he was extremely courteous. We saluted each other, he with much clicking of heels, and he informed me that I was a prisoner. He motioned me to come outside. We all went out, the doctor and his wife, the soldiers, and myself. The doctor and his wife were fine people and said I was to come and stay with them.

"The lieutenant smiled at that, and said we had to hurry. He helped me into the automobile, and I realized then that he had been wounded. There was a patch of gauze over his right eye. He sat up beside me very stiff and straight, the picture of military dignity. I suddenly remembered that in my gear I had put a tie and a cap. I could see the end of the tie protruding from the little bag one of the guards was carrying. I made signs to the lieutenant that I wanted a tie. He smiled and handed it to me."

"Now if that isn't just like Chuck," said Mac. "Only you would take a tie and a hat on a hop. What made you do it, Chuck?"

"Oh," said Chuck, "I feel that a Navy officer should be correctly dressed for all occasions. And I was right this time—these Vichy fliers were exceptionally well turned out.

"We soon arrived at the airport which I had been attacking. The French pilots who were on duty came hurrying out to meet me, some of them in flying gear and some in blue uniforms with gold rank bars.

"Some of them spoke a little English. They were mostly cheerful and curious about me. They wanted to know the type of plane I'd been flying, where I'd come from, and particularly how many pilots we had lost. I told them that as far as I knew I was the only one, and they looked a bit glum. Lieutenant V. was quite frank, even if I was his prisoner. He told me he had sent eighteen planes up, had seen six of them crashing, and had got four back to the airport. Eight had not been heard of again. Gosh, I thought, our Wildcats had done some job.

"It is difficult not to feel a trifle jubilant over something like that, even if you are a prisoner. I was sorry for them, though. There was something terribly human and likable about those French kids. I knew they had put up a good fight. Some of them had out-flown us, and yet they hadn't really had much chance. The main reason may have been that their combat tactics were those of World War I. But they were very chivalrous about the whole thing and couldn't have treated me better under any circumstances.

"One of them told me that Mikronis had also been shot down near Fedala. He was in the hospital with a bullet wound in the cheek. He had landed heavily but was not in a serious condition.

"One of them asked, 'Were the British helping you?' I said no, and he replied, 'Good! We hate the British.' I couldn't help smiling at him.

"'And the Germans?' I asked.

"'Yes,' he said, 'We hate the Germans,' adding dramatically, 'We love only France.'

"Then they told me I would have to go in front of the commander of the air station to be questioned. His interrogation was extremely friendly and haphazard. He asked me the usual questions: name, rank, and age, and if I were married. When I said no, he smiled. I expected him to ask where I had come from, the sea or from Gibraltar, and how many pilots had participated in the attack, but he just brushed away all those details, closed his book with a rather bored little smile, and said, 'And now, my friend, I suggest you join us for lunch.'

"We went downstairs to the mess, which had no windows and showed some signs of the bombardment. I sat at the head of the table on the commander's right. Everyone tried to be as friendly as the circumstances would allow. Native servants brought in the lunch, which consisted of two glasses of rather sour wine, one boiled egg, some sliced tomatoes, and French bread. Sometimes, when conversation sagged between us, which was only natural with my limited knowledge of the language, I heard some of the Frenchmen saying, 'This is bad. This is bad.'

"One young fellow was in tears. He had seen three of his comrades shot down, and he had landed himself with his plane full of holes. These French pilots didn't seem enthusiastic about fighting the Americans or fighting for the Vichy government, but they were hurt that they had been vanquished so quickly. One of them, an older man, clapped me on the shoulder and said, 'Well, my friend, I suppose you want to see what damage you did.' His face was a bit green and then he smiled. 'You certainly did a good job. It should be a lesson to us. Of course, we might have done the same to you if we had had the chance, if we had had the leadership, if we had had the cause.' He seemed to be cussing under his breath and there were tears in his eyes. 'Look over there,' he said. 'Look at those planes. Isn't it a tragedy?

Beautiful machines and they never flew.'

"He took me to the window, and I saw there were still several Dewoitine 520s parked on the east-to-west runway and quite a number of military planes in the two large hangars north and east and west of the runway. The military planes were Douglas A-20s, and several fighter planes were being repaired. I saw one D-520 with a flat tire. Just then, Lieutenant Maison, a pleasant young fellow who could speak passable English, attached himself to me and began to ply me with questions. They had suddenly remembered that they hadn't searched me; and they didn't know I had already been looked over by the soldiers. He said, 'Have you any concealed weapons?'

"I knew I still had my shark knife. We carry them on our legs, you know. I laughed a little as I said, 'If you mean firearms, monsieur, no.' He understood, and began searching me. When he came to the shark knife, he yanked it out and stood looking at me as if it were definitely a concealed weapon. I told him it was for *poisson*. I didn't know the French for 'shark.' He still seemed to think it was decidedly fishy. Some of the other officers saw the knife, and there was a general confab. Maison seemed to reassure them when he asked me, 'You are not intending to make an attack on us, August?' I answered, 'No, of course not.'

"As we were driving away from the airfield into Casa, Maison asked me if I was sure he could have my shark knife. He added very charmingly, As a memento of the *brave* pilot August.' I simply didn't have the heart to refuse, as if a refusal would have done any good anyway.

"When we got into Casa, where everything seemed very much as usual, Maison said, 'My friend, you are going to be turned over to the Navy for interrogation.'

"I gathered he didn't like the Navy any more than he did the French Army. The Admiralty Building in Casablanca was a typical French official headquarters, with old-fashioned, high-ceilinged corridors and dark oak doors with brass handles. Not even Maison could get me past the lobby.

"'You wait here,' he said. 'I'll find someone.'

"For an hour I waited, cooling my heels and feeling tired as hell, while Maison with my shark knife tucked in the pocket of his blouse rushed here and there, trying to find a French naval officer who would interrogate me. He came back looking very depressed. I was to be put in the naval prison across the street.

"The French Navy made it very clear that I was a prisoner of war. I was marched off with considerable clatter of rifle butts and a great show of discipline. The prison was a low-roofed building, situated behind a tall façade. Immediately I got there, I was expertly searched again, and everything was taken from me except my identification tag. I guess they took my cigarettes, pocket money, and the fifty dollars which the U.S. Navy so thoughtfully had provided us with. Also my cigarette lighter, my Eversharp pencil and fountain pen, and, of course, the 'Allah be Praised' booklet, which seemed to provide a great deal of amusement.

"Lieutenant Maison hung around with distress signals flying all over his honest face. I believe he thought they were going to ill-treat me, and it hurt him because he had assumed the responsibility of being my guardian. The entire situation was rather like a Hollywood movie. Finally, a little fellow escorted by two sailors arrived with a bunch of keys jangling at his waist. He solemnly walked along the big corridor and opened a cell with a loud, grating noise. I went in the place, which was pretty dark and miserable. I was just wondering how I could protest, when I heard a voice say, 'Sit down and make yourself at home.' It was an honest-to-goodness American voice.

"I could see a dark form on what looked like a low bench. It got up and introduced itself as Tom Dougherty. Tom had been a photographic pilot on one of our battleships. He'd been making pictures of the shellfire on various objectives at Casablanca, when he was attacked by an H-75. His rear-seat gunner had been wounded in the right leg. Tom had been able to taxi to the beach and then had been taken prisoner by the shore battery. His gunner had been taken to a hospital.

"'This is one hell of a place,' Tom said, 'but you're welcome. I hope they don't forget to give us some food. I haven't had anything to eat today.'

"I told him I had just had a good meal and was feeling fine. 'Huh,' said Tom, 'they get so excited they forget everything. Seems like we're here for the duration, so we'll have to shout if we want anything.' From the leg of his pants, he produced a package of Philip Morris cigarettes, several bars of chocolate, a can of fish, and some packages of wet chewing gum. Quite a Houdini. He told me they had searched him, but that he'd carried this stuff in a cartridge container. We had quite a feast.

"The cell was very small, for two of us, with an oak door about three inches thick, and a barred window, so heavily protected that only a few tiny rays of sunshine could get in. The bed was terrible. Just three planks, about three feet by twelve, and two of us were supposed to sleep on it, with one Army blanket. I decided I wasn't going to stand for it, so I banged on the door and finally got a guard. He just listened and said nothing. So I kept hollering and shouting until a French naval officer came down the corridor. I told him that they had no right to have taken my cigarettes, and finally, after an argument, he came back and brought me one of my Chesterfields. I figured the others had been smoked.

"They left us alone until about seven in the evening. What they called dinner was then served—a chunk of filthy, stale bread, a little beef, and a glass of water.

"The bread was so bad that one taste of it put us right off the supper. Tom Dougherty and I were comparing notes, and he told me that there was another American pilot in the building, and I gathered from the description that it must be Shields.

I went to the door of the cell and hollered, 'Windy! Windy!' The guards came along and told me I wasn't to make so much noise, but I kept on shouting, and finally the officer came. I told him as best I could that this treatment was not such as should be accorded an officer, and I insisted that we be allowed to see a doctor. Tom was in pretty bad shape. He had been in the water and had not been able to change his clothes. I gave him my flying suit and began to argue with another French officer. Finally, he allowed me to go up and see Shields. There was poor old Windy in another little cell, with a terrible cold. He looked so bad that I began to wonder if he would pull through. I finally got hold of a third Frenchman. Windy helped with his bit of French, and eventually we were given a blanket apiece.

"The Frenchmen were obviously rather tired of listening to me, and suddenly, without a word of warning, they slammed me into the cell with Windy, which meant that Tom would be alone. Windy and I had a wooden bunk three feet wide, and even if we had been doped, I don't think we could have slept. To make matters worse, the guards kept coming in every fifteen minutes to switch on the lights and look at us. What they expected to see, I don't know, but every time they came in I got more fully awake, and we kept up a barrage of what were not exactly compliments.

"At dawn the next day, and that was the ninth of November, neither Windy nor I was feeling any too good. Windy's cold had turned to a fever, and he was shivering. They brought us a poor apology for breakfast—some kind of bread, and coffee made of barley. The coffee was extremely hot and tasted very good. We both decided to start the day well by clamoring to be removed to more comfortable quarters. Torpedo heaven was heaven indeed compared with this place. For some time, no one took any notice of us. The French sailors kept shrugging their shoulders and turning their backs.

"Some time later, we heard a bit of excitement up the corridor. Apparently they were bringing in some American Army prisoners. By craning our necks we could just see the men lined up against the wall, being stripped and searched. There seemed to be quite a number of them, far too many to go into the cell chosen for them opposite ours. So the guards came and took Windy and me and put us back into the original cell I had occupied with Tom. We were worse off then than before—three of us in one tiny cell with one bed—and none of us very fit. Windy had sprained his ankle and it was swelling now. Tom had a wrenched back and was in great pain, and my thigh had turned black from the bruising I'd gotten jumping from the plane.

"After a long argument with the guard, who seemed disposed to listen because he wanted a cigarette, they brought in someone who could understand English. He just endured what we had to say, said nothing helpful, and left us.

"Sometime late in the afternoon, I was brought before a number of naval officers. An interpreter whom I had never seen before began to question me. After the usual routine queries, they began to ask me what sort of plane I flew and whether I'd come from Gibraltar. I didn't give them anything at all. Finally one of them asked, in an angry tone of voice, 'Why must the Americans attack the French and do the same as the British?' I countered by asking why they had resisted when they knew the Americans had come to help them against the Germans? He shouted something at me. I told him very quietly that they were obviously collaborating with the Nazis.

"The senior officer then delivered himself of a speech that was rather like the leading part played by an actor on the stage. When he had finished, the interpreter translated for me. 'The Commandant says that Vichy represents a form of government peculiar to the French people, and that it is not and never will be coupled with or controlled by Nazi Germany. Vichy is working for France.' Then, 'He is very angry with you because you said that Vichy is controlled by the Nazis. Every true Frenchman knows that Vichy is the soul of France.'

"There didn't seem to be any point in continuing such an argument, so I turned around and said that I was surprised that the Vichy Government and the French Navy should submit us to such discomfort, especially as we were all of us injured. The interpreter frowned some, then turned to the Commandant and rattled off something. The Commandant delivered his reply in just the same

dramatic manner. The gist of it was that everything possible was being done. How were they to
know that the Americans were attacking and that
they would be taking American prisoners? All
available quarters were occupied by men who
were defending France. We were to put up with
what we had, and sooner or later, we should be
transferred.

"I was getting mad by this time, and so I told
them as firmly as possible that I expected better
food and medical treatment. I added that I was
prepared to pay for anything that was necessary.
The French Commandant snapped again, telling
them to take me away. The guard took me, this
time to the large cell where Windy and I had been
the night before. The soldiers had been taken elsewhere.

"That afternoon, after a lunch that in no way
lived up to its name, we were all taken out of the
Bastille to the Naval Arsenal across the street.
Here we had indication for the first time that the
war was still going on. As we walked across, we
heard bursts of machine-gun fire from the docks
and presently, there was a fusillade of firing from
what seemed to be a few yards away. Immediately
that happened, all the Navy personnel were ordered to stand to. They came tumbling out of barracks and officers' quarters and shouldered their
arms, then rigged up machine-guns behind barricades.

"We were immensely cheered. This was some
indication that the invasion was going in our favor.

From our room on the ground floor, we were able to see all this activity. Occasionally a bomb exploded and shook bits of plaster from the ceiling. Shortly afterwards, a guard from the police station came to take Shields for questioning."

"They took me to see the Admiral," laughed Windy. "He asked me the usual questions, and when I didn't answer, he took me down and showed me the docks. 'I suppose you'd like to see the damage you fellows have done.' I agreed, and he showed me some of the wounds that our planes had inflicted on Casa. This fellow seemed to know his job. He was a very fine type of man with the stamp of the Navy all over him. I think he was much interested himself in the damage that had been done and wanted to have another look. He spoke to me with extreme courtesy that was a little embarrassing. He told me that it was the dive-bombers and the TBFs that had really scored the hits. 'Your fliers were extremely courageous. Our anti-aircraft fire didn't shake them a bit. I saw one of your men fly through the barrage of about twenty guns. It was magnificent.' He paused. 'I have always been an admirer of America and the Americans. I think it is a pity that we should have to fight like this.'

"We parted good friends, after I'd taken time out to tell him that we were being very poorly fed and that our lavatory conditions were awful. He shrugged and replied, 'But my young friend, we didn't expect you,' which after all was a very good argument."

"I don't know whether it was Windy's influence with the Admiral, or what," went on Chuck August, "but it wasn't long before a young man in an extremely smart uniform came along and took us all to the naval infirmary, which smelled very strongly of *medicaments* but which was reasonably clean and efficient. Here we were given a rather laconic once-over. I suppose it satisfied their consciences, but it didn't make us feel any better. They gave Windy a couple of red-coated pills for his fever and applied some iodine to our bruises. While we were there, one very big explosion shattered some windows nearby. Across the room from us, I saw the first casualty, a native soldier who was brought in with a very bad wound in his stomach. It quite turned me up, seeing how much of him was hanging outside. His eyes were very glazed, which meant that he was probably unconscious. His arrival was greeted with many explosive remarks, but nobody seemed to do anything for him. We were then taken across the road again to the Bastille, and standing there in the reception room, making quite a lot of noise, was Spanky Carter.

"We almost fell on his neck. Spanky looked tired, but he seemed pretty well, alert, and as helpful as usual—a great guy to have with you in an emergency. As Spanky was our senior, we immediately unloaded our own troubles on him, with particular stress on what they had been doing to us.

"Spanky is just the right type to handle a situation like that. He set to work, with considerable determination and angrily. Before long, he had those Vichy Navy people running around fetching one Mr. Big after another. For a time, then, we were left alone. The noncommissioned officer then decided that we were a menace, especially as the explosions were getting nearer, and ordered us back to our cells. We said we wouldn't go and insisted on going over to the Admiralty across the road to speak to the naval officers over there. The guards banged their rifle butts on the ground and flourished their bayonets generally, but we were all together, and we just stood there. The little *sous-officier* went and fetched a commander. He ordered us into the cells and then made the usual speech to the effect that as we weren't expected, no better accommodations could be had.

"There we were—Spanky, Windy, Tom, and myself, all in one cell. The only thing that we had achieved was a blanket apiece, but later a boy arrived with some mattresses. Windy asked him his name. He said it was 'Bobby,' and immediately that old American psychology of using names began to work. We started to 'Bobby' him, and produced some money. He told us he was nineteen and that he had a brother fighting for the Free French. He whispered it with pride. We asked him if he could get us some food, and he said yes. We gave him a few dollars, and he disappeared.

"We never thought he'd come back, but he did, and to our utter joy he put some tangerines and mineral water into the cell. And later he came back with some big oranges. We had quite a feast."

"Yes," said Spanky Carter. "They were very good. You know I was definitely in favor of those oranges. The first thing I had on getting ashore was an orange. When I woke up that next morning on the beach, in that slit trench I dug for myself, I wasn't feeling too comfortable, but I decided the best thing to do was to head inland. I hadn't gone very far when I met an old Frenchman, to whom I announced that I was an American officer.

"He was considerably impressed, and immediately I was invited into his house, a compact little place set in the middle of vineyards and what looked to me like fields devoted to extensive vegetable raising. His wife was in the kitchen when I came in, and within a few minutes they had made me quite at home, cooking me a meal—real coffee, beefsteak, French bread and butter. There seemed to be no shortage of anything.

"The woman had already stored away one of President Roosevelt's pamphlets and regarded it as a real treasure. I told them I wanted to get to Fedala, where I thought the American troops would have landed, and they agreed that the best thing for me to do was rest a while and they would try to find me a means of transportation.

"But we had talked too long before going up to bed. Although I had hardly been observed by anyone, two of the neighbors came in. They were Italian women. They took one look at me and went off. The old Frenchman was very worried about this. He said they would be sure to give me away to the police. His remarks were decidedly color-ful. He was right. Sure enough the two women hadn't been gone very long before a couple of guards arrived and took me off to the French Na-val Headquarters.

"Before I went, I recompensed the old Frenchman and gave him some of my less impor-tant possessions, as souvenirs. He was so broken up about the guards taking me away that he nearly cried. His wife made up a little parcel of food for me, which later I lost, and so I arrived at the prison in very much the same condition as the others."

"So we were all together that night," went on August, "and it was some night. One good thing did happen. Spanky had learned just enough French to impress the guard, and I added my little bit. We told those fellows that if they dared flash that light on us in the night, their fate would be worse than anything they could imagine, and it wouldn't be very long, either. They must have believed us because they kept the lights out, and so each of us got some sleep—in turn—although the accommodation wasn't so good.

"The next morning, we were really having a good time. We not only had coffee and bread for breakfast, but Bobby turned up and volunteered to get more oranges. To these he added some er-satz soap, with which we were allowed to go to the washroom one at a time.

"The high spot was when the U.S. Navy planes started bombing the *Jean Bart*. We heard those terrific crashes, and some tiny pieces of the ceiling began to fall on us. Most satisfying! Later, a bomb fell about a hundred yards from our jail, and we heard the windows shattering all around! That shook the French Navy men. They didn't like it a bit. We could hear them talking excitedly and scurrying here and there. Outside machine-guns were popping off, although the planes were miles away, and occasionally anti-aircraft guns would bark.

"Presently, someone came and told us that we were to be transferred to better quarters. This was cheering. They brought in lunch. It was so bad, especially the meat, that we didn't bother with it. After lunch, the guard took us out into the grounds for an airing. The place was packed with mechanical equipment, automobiles, trucks, and other light vehicles. Most of them had been imported from the United States. Ford trucks, Chevrolets, and Goodrich tires were very much in evidence. All of this equipment looked as if it had not been used for some time.

"We could hear explosions in the distance, and once some photographic planes came over, escorted by fighters. Their appearance was a sign that our promenade was at an end, and we were hurried back into our cell. The guard had hardly closed the door when Bobby came in to say that it was quite evident we were going somewhere else. He was followed by an officer who told us to pack our things. We asked for the things that had been removed from us. No one seemed to know anything about them.

"We had just got ourselves outside in the fresh air, which smelled remarkably good after the stuffiness of the prison, when a section of Wildcats and scout bombers appeared, and made a strafing attack on the docks. We were immediately hurried inside again as the gunners manned their machine-guns. Half an hour later, they ushered us into a bus, which seemed to have taken quite a lot of punishment. The driver told us that it had been strafed six times. All the glass had been shattered, and there were bullet holes in the roof and seats. None of them could have been incendiaries, as there was no sign of burning.

"When we got to the Hippodrome, a French major came to meet us. He apologized for the accommodations, but said, as usual, that we were not expected. He went on at length to explain the unfortunate necessity of subjecting American officers to such conditions, adding that sooner or later he hoped to find us something better.

"That Hippodrome, as Mac said, was certainly a crumby place. They put me in a stall that must have been built for a very thin horse. I tried lying down lengthwise, because I couldn't sit comfortably. My legs got in the way of everything. Lying down on that straw was some ordeal, too. I soon began scratching, and I went on scratching until after we were released, and got to the Anfa Hotel with all its great luxury, glittering lobby, a cocktail bar, tea lounge, modern baths and bellhops."

"You should tell about your champagne bath," reminded Mac.

"That was something," said Chuck. "Windy and I were in one room, and I soon found I was covered with lice and bugs that were biting me all over. Even though I'd had a bath, nothing seemed to remove them. It occurred to me that alcohol might do the trick, or at least put them to sleep, so I went downstairs and bought two or three bottles of champagne at about seventy-five cents a bottle. Upstairs I stripped and got in the bathtub, while Windy was howling with laughter. I rubbed myself all over with the champagne. It didn't work very well, and within a few hours they were biting again. They didn't appreciate good champagne. Those animals were quite the worst of the whole show."

Chapter 12

"NEXT MORNING we were at the hotel you know," said Mac. "I got busy again, trying to make arrangements for us to be taken back, but it was always the same story. Everyone was too busy, and few people knew exactly what was going on anyway. We were all still being troubled with bed-bugs. Windy had a most interesting story to tell, because the room he had been staying in had just been occupied by German pilots. They had left their diaries, photographs and magazines, various souvenirs of their prowess in action over France, Greece, and Russia. They had apparently got out of Casablanca in a great hurry, because they had taken nothing."

"Those Germans certainly had been looking after themselves," joined in Windy. "When I opened the closet, I found it filled with preserved foods, jam, canned meat, fruit, and real coffee. They had canned butter, all kinds of candy, and some packages of women's stockings and underwear, and piles of German magazines, mostly dealing with the movies and full of glamour pictures. The only difference between our idea and their idea of glamour was that while we go in for legs, they concentrate on nudity in general. One of the magazines dealt with the adventures of German aces, and another seemed to be devoted to the Strength through Joy, with healthy-looking wenches on skis in the snow. In the bathroom, I found several bottles of red wine, some olive oil, and some lettuce and tomatoes which were going to be a salad before their departure."

"The best thing that happened to us that day," came in Mac, "was a dinner at the Villa Maas. It consisted mostly of Army rations provided for us by the infantry. The cook had supplemented these with a few French vegetables. It was a real feast. Over the table, one of the Army officers started telling the story about a French plane that had strafed them at Fedala. Apparently it had only been over once or twice and had done very little damage, although when I got back to the ship I heard a lot about the Phantom Raider. On the other hand, the officer was probably on the beach for a short while only as his unit advanced inland.

"Tom Dougherty and I decided to go and have a look at our planes. Tom's looked pretty bad. It was a wonder that he had managed to get down, because he had taken lead all over, and the machine was definitely lost. Later we went to have a look at the destroyers, the *Albatross* and the *Milan*. I was particularly interested in them as they had shot down my plane when I attacked them. I came away quite satisfied that our .50-caliber bullets had done a good job. Those destroyers were not modern, of course, but the numerous attacks from our planes had literally filled them full of holes. The smokestacks, decks and fittings had all been severely damaged.

"Later I learned that the French report stated that the sixteen planes which attacked the destroyers had left them in a very battered condition. The cruisers had also been damaged so severely that they were not able to undertake an offensive mission during that day. The first attack on the destroyers had killed everyone on deck except the men in the turrets. The two destroyers had had to be beached because of the holes made by the .50-caliber bullets. The bridge of one of them had been, completely burned away, and there were bullet holes from one side clear through to the other.

"Back at the Anfa Hotel, we got good news. We were to be taken aboard the U.S. ship at Pier 3. This sounded wonderful.

"Immediately we got aboard the first thing we did, naturally, was to be deloused, a really satisfying process. Everyone came out feeling remarkably well, ready for anything. The next luxury was a real American dinner in the wardroom, served with napkins, which seemed to us quite remarkable. I then remembered that I should see a doctor. I went in and he gave me anti-tetanus, because my wound was looking very bad indeed. The inoculation was exceedingly painful, and when I went to bed that night my teeth began to chatter, and I was in such pain that someone had to bring the doctor again. I really felt I was slipping a bit, and I asked for some morphine. They gave me something else, but I couldn't sleep. I just lay awake and thought how lucky I was to be still alive and to be on board ship rather than in Vichy hands. Whatever would have happened to me if I had been given that same injection and had had to sleep in the stables of the Hippodrome I couldn't imagine. Compared with the other fellows, though, I had come out pretty well.

"Next morning, there was some excitement when a destroyer came in to land some survivors of a vessel that had been torpedoed.

"We were told that we might be leaving for home that day, and we decided to finish off our stay in North Africa by going to say good-bye to our friends who had been so decent during our ordeal.

"Spanky, Windy, Chuck, and myself engaged in a shopping tour. I bought some candy and cigarettes and champagne and carried them over to the Fourth Bureau where I had spent so much time. The office was still open, and people were working, but they were very depressed.

"'It's been awful since you left,' said Jean. 'So many of our friends have been killed in this unnecessary fighting. One of my cousins has been wounded, and many of my good friends are missing. It is a terrible thing that so many lives have been lost when we didn't really want to fight you. None of the Frenchmen did. It was just that our leaders were stubborn and would not understand.' I advised him not to say too much about that, as he was still serving, and tried to cheer him up by saying that things would be better. Then I handed out the candy and cigarettes to the men and clerks. One of the girls came up and asked if she could kiss me. I couldn't see a good reason why she should or why she shouldn't, so I acquiesced. Everybody laughed and the atmosphere was cheery again.

"My friend Courvilliers came in then. He was all smiles. He greeted me profusely. 'If you can wait a minute, I would like you to meet a friend of mine,' he said. I said I would be there for awhile and filled in the time making a request for the return of my pistol and other gear. I met with complete failure. Although the stuff was supposed to have been brought to headquarters, there was no trace of it. I decided to go to the cavalry camp after it.

"Courvilliers arrived with a very pretty girl. 'I want you to meet *mon amie,*' he said, a little shyly. 'She has heard so much about you that I would not want you to leave without meeting her.' Courvilliers was still being helpful. He found an automobile and drove me over to the cavalry camp. There I ran up against the usual obstacle. The officers who were supposed to have been responsible for my kit were not there. My friend, the little corporal, was there, however, and he greeted me like an old friend. I gave him a package of cigarettes and a bar of chocolate. He was delighted.

"We drove to the wine shop next, where I took leave of the two old people who had been so kind. They seemed profoundly relieved that I was safe.

When I thanked the old man, he kept saying, 'It is nothing, it is nothing.'

"Then we went on to see the young doctor and his wife who had attended to Chuck, and we finally wound up our tour with the best laugh of the trip.

"Spanky, who is very serious about everything he does, started to walk up the driveway of the little farm where he'd been looked after. The door opened and the old lady came running out, shrieking with surprise and delight. She threw her arms around him and kissed him on each cheek, exclaiming, 'Oh, my baby, my baby, I am so glad to see my baby safe!' Was Spanky's face red as he ducked that one! It took him quite a time to disengage himself and when he stood there smiling and protesting, the old man came and kissed him and the old lady kissed him again, and it wasn't until we had begun to run interference for him that we could rescue him."

Chuck laughed. "It seemed that Spanky had done some good work in his short time! The doctor's wife didn't even offer to kiss me." Spanky got very red as Mac recounted this little episode. "I don't know what I'd done to deserve that, except that perhaps to her I represented America and President Roosevelt. Her dearest possession was a picture of the president and that proclamation. She knew it by heart. Of course, I had to hear the story about the Italian women, then, and how they had been a thorn in the flesh of the old couple for years anyway."

"After that," said Mac, "we went aboard the ship

and prepared to leave. Then we heard that we were not to go until the next day, so I decided to fill in the time finding out as much as possible about the pilots from our various squadrons who were missing.

"From the French I got a diagram with the position of the grave of Lieutenant Trumpeter of Fighting Blues, who had been shot down on that first Sunday.

"The French had buried him with military honors. His plane had hit the ground so hard that there had been very little left of it. Later in the day, I received a report from the captain of a French Air Force unit, which I think gives a good example of the chivalry and respect with which the French Air Force treated their opponents. The captain, I learned later, was one of those who had not wished to fight. The squadron had been at Medouina on the morning of the ninth, when they were attacked by Fighting Blues. He wrote:

> I have the honor here to give you an account of the death of Lt. Edward Micka. While our planes were on the ground, early on Monday, they were machine-gunned by your Grumman fighters. The pilots came down with complete disregard for the fire from our guns. While one of the planes was burning, the Lieutenant began a new attack. He had just finished his run and was only a few feet above the ground, when one of our bombers, loaded with bombs, exploded. Lieutenant Micka's plane was severely damaged. One of its wings

was broken off, and he crashed into the ground about five hundred yards away.

I instructed our men to retrieve the body, which had been severely burned—death being instantaneous. We buried him on the spot with full military honors. Over the grave, we put a white cross, to which we affixed the identification tag of the brave flier.

For your information, the grave is located about six hundred yards north of the northern border of the airfield at Medouina, and about four hundred yards to the east of Ber Rechid-Medouina-Casablanca highway.

"I then decided," continued Mac, "that if I had a few hours to spare, I might just as well see if I could take my plane back to America. We went over to the Army headquarters and to a hotel that had been used by the Germans, to see if there was any kind of transportation. I got a jeep and was soon inspecting the plane. It was good to see it again, and it gave me the queerest feeling to see the plane in which I had spent so many hours, and which was like an old friend. I felt it should be salvaged. Nothing had been touched, as far as I could see, except for one or two small items. After a few hours, we got it hitched to the jeep and onto the highway where I folded the wings back and drained the gas.

"We had a bit of trouble getting it along the road. There was always the danger of turning over at the banked curves, which are a feature of the

French coastal roads. I had to get some men to hold the tail in the center of the road, so that it would not slide to the wrong side and to turn the plane at right angles when the road curved—quite a complicated job on the whole. Then the tail wheel started to sieze up, and I had to keep stopping and applying the grease gun.

"I certainly was doing a lot of traveling in Africa. I had flown over a little bit, of course, and then I had walked a lot and done some riding. I thought of that trip on the rump of the horse. It seemed damn ridiculous and was still a painful memory. Now I was alternately riding and walking behind a jeep, taking my plane home.

"As night fell, our problems increased. The greatest danger was from Army trucks, which went speeding along in the blackout, very dangerously. I got a sentry to walk aft with a flashlight and secured another jeep to act as an escort in front.

"I will admit to feeling very happy as we neared Casablanca. I was rescuing an old friend. Earlier in the trip, I kept walking around the plane making an inspection, and I could see that with very little work it would be ready to fly again. The engine was in perfect condition, although it hadn't been touched for a week.

"Just outside the city, one of the Army trucks nearly put an end to our journey. The driver missed us by an inch. At first, I was angry, but then I saw the funny side—we had no lights—and the driver was probably a bit startled to see this plane with the wings folded back trundling along the road. It was midnight before I arrived at the pier and secured the plane for the night. I turned in at one o'clock and at 0530 I was up again, getting men to help me get the plane aboard. They told me the transfer must be completed by 0800. Even then there were a lot of problems. I got an assault boat to tow the lighter. Then I had to get another boat to lower the plane from the dock to the lighter, by means of a forward boom. The lighter took off and I relaxed.

"And then someone came along to say that we couldn't take the plane aboard. I was terribly disappointed. I went ashore at once and asked the captain of one of the ships if it wasn't possible in some way. He said that it was, but that someone else had decided against it. While we were talking, there was a visual signal from the ship, calling me aboard. I went, of course, and discussed the whole matter with the air officer. It was finally decided that I was to turn the plane over to one of the other squadrons. I might just as well do a good job, I thought, and I gave them the new tail wheel, which I'd been carrying around, as well as some plugs and various parts I'd collected to get it back in shape. In spite of the excitement of going home, I was very let down. I was worried, too, because I had not been able to get in touch with home to tell Ruth and the family I was safe. She would have gotten the usual telegrams and letters. I had time to think of all this now. And I hadn't been able to get any news of Mikronis as I would have liked."

Chapter 13

"THE BOYS tell me that the ship made the pier almost to the minute," said Mac. "Without me of course. Spanky, Chuck, and Windy were late too.

"I had been busy on the way over writing reports, and setting down my experiences so that they would be useful to the squadron. Going back was a great experience. I found myself getting excited as each day passed. At the advanced base I went ashore to see if there was any news of anyone. I half hoped that Tag might have turned up. I learned that Mikronis was being sent back on a hospital ship. At odd moments, I could not help thinking of Ruth and the children, and of my mother. They would be worrying. It seemed wrong that I should be safe and have no means of telling them. As far as I knew, my messages to the ship had not gone through. Never have I so urgently wanted a trip to end.

"The ship couldn't go fast enough for me. A storm that hit us in mid-Atlantic didn't help matters. We suddenly ran into a gale, a real Atlantic howler. The waves began to wash over the flight deck, carrying away catwalks and generally doing heavy damage. The carrier began bouncing like a cork, and was taking the most alarming nose dives. I wasn't seasick but I felt bad inside. Frankly, I was awed by the might of the ocean. I had learned to respect the sea during my service as a ship officer but having been released from the responsibilities of being a sailor had dimmed that. I began to realize it again, but increasingly so as I viewed the heavy breakers once again from the sailor's aspect. The storm lasted at full fury for two days, and then lapsed into rough weather that made it generally a tough trip.

"To touch dry land was more than welcome even if it had not been that I was returning from a period of action.

"On shore, I ran to a phone booth. Waiting for the connection to my home was a minute of agony. Ruth answered. 'Hello, Mac—I've been expecting you to turn up today. I just got a letter from Mr. Knox about you this morning. Yes, it was to say you were missing. It will do for Steve's autograph album. . . . Of course I was worried at first, but I knew you would come. Tommy phoned, and Hubie and the others told me you must be all right. I'll get some dinner, dear.' In a matter of half an hour, I was home.

"Relaxing in that familiar room, it did not seem possible that I had ever been away. Casablanca was a million miles off. Ruth said, 'I knew nothing could happen to you. The telegram scared me a bit, so did the letter, but I just wouldn't think anything else except that you would phone as you did. I was going to a bridge party tonight, but I thought I might as well wait in. I didn't go to meet the ship, of course. I decided that this was my home base. You would telephone here, and I wouldn't like to be out when you did.' Ruth has the right angle for a Navy flier's wife, which is a kind of religion: always to expect good news and keep calm if you don't. It has to be that way. Yes, home seemed very good just then. That evening we realized that nothing had upset our plans for life, nothing ever could. It is salubrious to feel that way. I spent a long time that evening phoning Mother and relatives, for although Tommy had sent a message I had been reported missing. It was a pleasant enough task except that it entailed patience waiting to get the long-distance calls and answering so many questions.

"The social life of the squadron soon resumed. There were bridge parties and cocktail parties, and the swapping of such reminiscences as were not military secrets.

"Two days after I got back a telegram arrived to say I was safe. I took it in myself—another souvenir.

"We had news that Mikronis was on the way. All we lacked was news of Tag Grell. That he would arrive one day was a sure thing.

"The first shore evening I had, I turned up the squadron history," said Mac. "It had more than an interest now seeing that the Red Rippers had blooded their tusks. There's a scrapbook at squadron office which is Chuck August's special care. Chuck is by way of being a draftsman, you know, as well as a letter writer to the widely dispersed female population of the U.S.A.

"Our squadron had the *Lexington* as its first carrier and knocked up an astonishing record of making two thousand landings on her flight deck without a single fatality or major injury to personnel. Afterwards, it was attached to the *Saratoga* and the *Langley*. Some painstaking diarist recorded that over eight thousand hours were flown in two years with the loss of only one pilot and that the squadron had flown twenty-five thousand miles, or once around the earth—not such bad going it seemed.

"The squadron has numbered some well-known Navy fliers in its history. One was Rittenhouse, the Navy pilot who won the Schneider Cup Race at Cowes, England, in 1923, and then there were Lt. 'Mary' Gardner and Lt. F. M. Trapnell, who were known far and wide as members of the famous Navy stunt team that succeeded the 'Sea Hawks.' As for gunnery trophies, the Red Rippers have managed to keep up a constant high record on this score. They won the Efficiency Pennant in Gunnery for 1929–1930. As I sat in the office reading all the dope, Chuck and Ed and Windy came in and we began to talk about squadron insignia. Each plane has one painted on its side. Every pilot who joins the squadron is given a wooden shield with the insignia in colors. We keep these shields in a steel box in the squadron office and it is presented to a pilot when he leaves. These shields are quite a tradition.

"The moment seemed appropriate to read up on the history of the insignia. It consists of a shield of royal blue crossed by a bolt of red and containing two red circular quarterings. The crest is the head of a wild boar surmounted by a length of braid. The truth of the insignia is that it was designed by some of the younger pilots when the squadron was formed, and its story was not intended for publication, being esoteric and semi-Rabelaisian. Whether the boar's tusks or the bolt of red lightning suggested the title 'Red Rippers' is not clear, but there it is. We sincerely hope that it will become the terror of the enemy be he German or Jap.

"Some anonymous scribe had gone to work with the record to give his idea of the meaning of our emblem: 'The wild boar is the ugliest-snouted, worst-tempered, fastest-moving creature in the whole Noah's Ark of nature. He is as full of tricks as a thirteen-spade bridge hand. At a mile he can outrun many horses and most horses raise a lather overtaking him in three. When he can run no longer he turns on his pursuers, lowers his massive head and joyously gores horses, dogs, and men with scimitar-like tusks, hooked and murderous ivories, often a foot long. His humped shoulders and muscle-sheathed neck rank him just below the bull in sheer weight-lifting strength. An angry boar can break a heavy barred gate by ramming it with his skull. A boar takes no nonsense from anything in jungle, field and forest. He is the only animal that dares to drink at the same pool as the tiger. Add to his strength and savagery that he is the most guileful of animals, and you get an idea of his worth. The boar is no fat and indolent creature. He is as shifty as a pickerel in eelgrass. He thinks as he gallops, and he has no intention of letting you stab him in the rump.'

"No wonder the Red Rippers have a good record. All the fellows should read this history, especially as we have a few scalps to our credit— even if a few of us did get some bullets in our rumps."

"Which, thanks to Mr. Grumman's armoring, never quite got there," joined in Chuck. "Gosh, I'll never forget the fright I had when those Vichy boys were peppering me, and I could hear the bullets smacking against the armor plate—a decidedly unsalubrious experience."

"Might have saved you writer's cramp," ribbed Ed. "Tell me, Chuck, what do you find to say in all those letters?"

"Be yourself, Ed," protested the exceedingly genial and elegant six feet of Chuck. "I just say what you would say to those willowy blondes you dream of and meet in Gotham, only I write it kind of casually and fill in with news. I've got to go back to civilian life you know, so I have to keep in touch. Besides I write to my kid brothers, too."

"Get married, Chuck . . . think of the postage you'll save. You'll be able to mail three letters in one envelope," advised Windy. "I suppose you'll be sending air mail to Casablanca Marie, now."

"Thanks for reminding me, Windy. I've a letter to write," laughed Chuck. "If Mac'll put it into French for me."

"Everything was the same," continued Mac. "The Red Rippers had got their tails up.

"After that we had a squadron reunion.

"No one said anything about having been worried about us two boys. Just let it be understood. Once we were together again, we were all cooking with gas and felt ready for anything. The superstition about that photograph had not worked on us, at least."

"I was one of the late ones," contributed Mikronis, "and I landed in a hospital here, a hospital which was a great deal up on the Vichy naval one where I was temporarily stored. When I finally got back, I felt quite a stranger in the squadron—had to pinch myself a bit to see if everything was real. Everything was going on normally—training hops, furlough, a few new automobiles, a few new cars. Mac was in charge of the squadron, and Tommy Booth was moving up somewhere else. There were changes of course. Chuck had lost his mustache, the jukebox had some new records, which was a change, and they were breaking in some new pilots. Otherwise, it was the same old squadron. There were moments, I admit, when I never thought I would see it again."

Mikronis is short, square, quiet and easy going. Ed says you see him best when he is beside Bus, who's the robust man's man type, always looking for trouble, and a born fighter. "Nick the

Greek," as the squadron calls Mikronis, is a thinker and watcher, just the type that completes a fighting team.

"Will Nick give?" urged Ed. "Tell us the story, Nick."

"But there isn't a story really," said Nick quietly, "and it's so late, months away."

"So," laughed Hubie, "the romantic Greek boy gets shot down, wakes up in the arms of a nice-looking gal, and it's no story. Come on, Nick, give."

Nick gave. "It all started when I got separated from my section in that first dive on the eighth. I had just strafed two Douglas bombers on the ground, when a Curtiss Hawk came at me. He started to give the bursts but missed. I was climbing in a turn, but I managed to get above him, and I think I hit him—I was feeling good, too. . . . Then a chunk of flak or some bullets hit my motor. It cut out immediately. Hell, I thought, this is it. I turned south to land on the airport. I was much too low to jump, and the plane was quite air-worthy. The Vichyman immediately got on my tail, began to fire. I think he gave me five bursts. The bullets were clattering all over the place, which scared me first, then made me angry. I went into a glide. Then I realized I was bleeding. I had been hit either by shrapnel or by fragments of my plane. I saw the Vichy pilot flying beside me, almost wing tip to wing tip. He was smiling and waving his hand. I was losing speed, so I put down the nose hard and opened the flaps. Then I passed out."

"Good magazine stuff, Nick," someone chipped in. "Continue. Tell us how you felt in your momentary stress."

"I can't remember, honestly," went on Mikronis, in that quiet voice of his. "All I remember is coming to on the ground—not on the airfield, but leaning up against the wall of a farmhouse with a French farmer in a blue smock talking to me. I could see the plane about 150 yards away in a field. It hadn't even nosed over. From where I saw it, it didn't look damaged in any way except for the cowling. When I tried to move towards it, however, the farmer produced a rifle and stuck it in my stomach. I had to stay where I was.

"All kinds of people were beginning to arrive. The farmer must have been a World War veteran or a bandit. He frisked me in appropriate style, taking everything, including my shark knife and all my flying gear. I was feeling weak and dizzy so I sat on the ground. All at once I heard a dogfight going on overhead. Machine-guns were tipping off and engines buzzing. I looked up and saw three Vichy planes come crashing down, one burning, another spinning very fast. A Wildcat was dogfighting with a Dewoitine. I don't know who the pilot was, but he did a good job. . . . He got on the Vichy plane's tail and the pilot parachuted with his overalls burning, but the wind carried him out of sight, so I don't know what happened. That Wildcat certainly hit the Vichyman good and hard. The Dewoitine rolled over on its back and burst into flames.

"The French were watching all the time. Some were cheering. They did not seem to realize they were seeing their own planes shot down. I sat there watching and feeling quite cheered about it, until I suddenly felt very faint and nearly passed out again. The farmer's wife came out, and I remember being taken inside and put to bed. Later some Red Cross volunteers arrived, but they had no kit. I told them I wanted to get back to the plane, but they wouldn't let me. I asked them to go and get my first-aid kit. One of them did. She applied one dressing to the wound on my face. I never saw the kit again.

"On the way to Cazes in the ambulance, I had quite a view of what was going on. I saw a number of Dewoitines dispersed in the trees and what looked like a plane burning fiercely in a field. Soldiers were running all over the place, and there was a lot of machine-gun fire from all directions. The first stop was the dressing station on the airfield, where a doctor started to patch me up. Then they took me to a big building near the docks called the Marine Nationale.

"Those armed guards who went with me were very friendly indeed. I think they were French Air Force men. They were all grinning and smiling and seemed highly pleased with everything. When I got to the Naval Station, two French officers started questioning me. Later, a German came in, and took charge of the interview. He spoke perfect English. He was quite brusque with the French—they were obviously impressed by his authority.

"His being there put me on my mettle. He asked me my name and rank, where I'd come from, where I lived, had the convoy come from Gibraltar, and how many planes, ships, and troops were involved. He also wanted to know what type of plane I had flown. I just told him that I was not permitted to tell him. He burst into German, then spoke in French to the officers. I wonder now if he had suddenly made up his mind to take the next plane out. He immediately ordered all my personal gear to be brought in and went through it like a weasel looking for a rabbit. Two things caught his attention more than anything else. One was my fountain pen and the other two packages of Life Savers. Those Life Savers were some problem to him. I figure he thought they were incendiary pellets. He was sure they were connected in some way with the fountain pen. When he started to take the pen to pieces, I told him it was just a fountain pen. He snorted and went on till he got his fingers nicely inked up. Then he took one of the Life Savers and looked through the hole, first one way and then another. He then put a pencil point through it, sniffed it, but didn't taste it. 'What are these?' he asked. This was the right moment to say I was not permitted to tell him. He got really mad then and put them aside as if they were very dangerous. I was dying to have one myself but I refrained.

"The German then went into a low-voiced huddle with the two French officers. Presently, he told me that I was going to be taken back. My guards were waiting for me, and we started off. The automobile broke down before we'd gone two blocks. While the driver was trying to get it to work, I had a good chance to see what had been happening. Everywhere was chaos. There were bomb holes all around us. The railway tracks had several craters, and there were several cars which had been blown over on their sides. I didn't see a window intact in any of the buildings. Gangs of workmen were busy patching up the shell holes in the street. There were no civilians about as far as I could see. I gathered that a big fire was in progress somewhere, as fire trucks went by us twice.

"When I got to the hospital, it was crowded. Hundreds of French wounded—some of them looked as if they had been hit badly—were waiting in the lobby. I could hear them groaning and yelling as the doctors applied treatment. They put me to bed in a private room and left me. Late in the afternoon, I woke up feeling very painful. My bandages had got too dirty, and I thought it would be a good idea to change them. I rang the bell, called. No one came. I knocked on the door and called. There was no answer, so I walked around the hospital and made a tour of inspection. It was obvious the place was working under severe stress. The staff must have been short of medicines, bandages, and doctors, because many of the soldiers I had seen when I came in were still there untreated. There were guards only at the gate.

"After a while I found a civilian nurse who brought me some wine, coffee and tea, which seemed very good—but no food. I went back to bed and slept most of the night.

"I woke up about ten Monday morning and as no one came near me, I walked around some more. In one of the wards I found an American seaman, Clyde Etheridge, who had been shot down in a photographic plane. Etheridge wasn't hurt badly and was cheerful.

"I was very hungry, but I couldn't find anything to eat anywhere. Some of the hospital attendants were friendly, particularly the Arabs.

"Clyde Etheridge was particularly popular with the Arabs because he was wearing his hair cut short. They took that as a sign he had been a prisoner of the Germans, whom they hated. . . . They had been put to forced labor by the Nazis, who had cut off their hair. Etheridge was being treated like a god because of his haircut. This didn't get us any food, however.

"Later I found a French Marine, who could speak a little English, a swell chunky kind of guy. He said he was going to find somebody to help me, and hobbled off—he'd been wounded in the ankle—leaving me to talk with his friends. They were all fine fellows, these French Marines, all of them very anti-German, and all wanted to fight with the Allies. 'We'll fight with the British, the Americans, with anyone who will let us get at the Boches,' one of them said. 'To hell with the Nazis!' Some of them had relatives in German labor camps. They were all fine physical types— typical Marines. Marines seem to be the same in any language. I enjoyed their company. They wanted to share everything with me—cigarettes, candy, dates.

"When the other Marine came back, he was trailing a hospital orderly with some food. It was terrible—some mush made from split peas, hard and very dry, and heavy brown bread, a stew with meat in it, and some kind of broth, with coffee and wine, all so bad I couldn't eat it.

"On noticing this, one of the Marines went out into the yard and came back with some small tangerines which he had filched for me. I was very glad of them. Then I went back to my room where I found an orderly waiting for me, smoking a cigarette. He took me to a sick bay where a doctor looked me over. They cut the hair away from my wound and put on a clean bandage and left me.

"The rest of the day was my own. I walked around as much as I could and found a few American soldiers and sailors. They and a few British officers who had been torpedoed two months before were the most cheerful people in the hospital. French morale was very bad. Our fellows and the British seemed to be much tougher and better able to put up with the discomforts, and with considerable humor. The British sense of humor is something to see in a spot like this. These guys had a joke about everything and they soon had me laughing so much that I forgot my little worries. I think the French thought they were a bit mad.

"When we heard of the capitulation, I made a round of the hospital followed by my faithful

Marine. I started to get a list of all the Americans
in the hospital, which I turned over to an American officer who had arrived. I spent the night in
the hospital, because there was no place else to
go. On Thursday morning, there came to me a re-
minder that war is a grim affair, and how very
lucky I was to be alive. From the hospital morgue
were brought the bodies of twenty-six American
soldiers and two sailors. They were buried with
full military honors rendered by the French, who
had provided coffins, crosses, and burial parties.
It was a somber and dignified funeral. I noticed
that some of the French volunteer nurses were
standing behind us, weeping. On the graves were
placed wreaths from British and American con-
suls, and the French buglers sounded taps. Each
grave was tagged and numbered.

"About lunch time, I decided to leave. There
was no one to stop me any more. I hopped into an
Army truck that was going to Casablanca. There
I got quite a reception. The French civilians were
in the streets, waving and throwing flowers and
what looked like sprigs of orange branches at the
Americans. They seemed to be very happy that
everything was over. I saw quite a few broken-
down trucks and barricades that had been hastily
put aside. The truck driver stopped suddenly and
said he couldn't go any farther and put me down.
I did not know where I was. I noticed a French
pilot on the sidewalk, so I asked him to direct me
to Fedala. He was a tall amiable guy . . . and he
seemed very amused at this. He took me into a

cafe and pressed an *aperitif* on me. Between his
English and my French we got along quite well.

"'Fedala,' he said, *'mon Dieu,* you have already been there! You Americans have wiped up
all our beautiful planes.'

"He didn't seem to bear any grudge. When I
told him that I was wounded and not feeling well,
he became very concerned and went to the telephone. He came back and took me to an American medical center, where I got a jeep to take me
to an Army evacuation center, where I had some
broth.

"After treatment by a U.S. Army doctor and
drawing some toilet articles to replace the ones
I'd lost, I was put to bed on board a ship. I had
not been there long before the general alarm
sounded. I dressed as fast as I could and hurried
out on deck. I got there just in time to see three
nearby ships being torpedoed. One burned and
sank instantly, another exploded, and the third
didn't explode but it began to settle in the water.
The ship I was on then headed into Casablanca
and tied up. I was feeling pretty sick by this time,
but I managed to get a walk around the deck and
observe the astonishing destruction our bombing
and shelling had done. There seemed to be hardly
an enemy ship that had not been sunk. The moles
had been badly damaged, and the guns were
twisted and distorted.

"I had been trying very hard to get into communication with my own ship and was hoping I
could make the return trip on her with the squadron

but nothing doing. That evening I felt worse. The doctor said I had contracted a fever and put me to bed again. All I remember about the journey home is that we ran into one hell of a storm—the worst I've ever experienced. That's about all."

"Quite an adventure for one so young, Nick," said Mac. "I'm sorry I couldn't locate you. We had the same storm over here.

"Christmas came and passed, and we were well into January when our lost sheep, Lt. T. A. Grell, Tag to you, arrived," continued Mac. "We had news that he had been picked up but no further details. Tag got in, phoned his wife, and then called Tommy after supper. Tommy called me, and we got together. The Red Rippers were now complete and it called for a little celebration."

"I haven't really very much to tell," said Grell, "except that the journey home was terrific." Tag didn't report to the squadron until February seventh. "I guess it never took anyone that long to cross the Atlantic. I seemed to be always traveling in the wrong direction.

"You know what happened. During the second hop on Dog-day, I was in Tommy Booth's section, strafing the airfield at Port Lyautey. I had just made my second run when I discovered that my machine had been taking more than I'd anticipated. I'd heard a rattling noise going on, but at times like that you don't worry very much because you have a feeling of bored immunity to such trifles. You only see the bullets that go past you. All at once I noticed there was a strange smell in the cockpit, which I took to be oil. Then I saw that my wing had been ripped up, just as if a Gremlin had been at work with a can opener. But the engine was still giving good revolutions. I told Tommy I thought I could make the carrier, and set off out to sea.

"I got about twenty-two miles away from Casablanca when my engine cut out completely. I told Harris, the Short Man, what had happened, and that I was going down. He asked me if I was sure I couldn't make it. I told him only by swimming. He began to circle around, and I made what wasn't a bad water landing. I had no time to use my rubber boat, because the plane keeled over nose down and sank instantly. I inflated my Mae West and started swimming. I could see Harris looking around for me, and flying over to a pair of fishing boats, to show me help was near. He kept flying around them, but they did not change their course and went on in a northeasterly direction. I cussed them a bit and began to swim towards them, but they turned away. I cussed again and then I figured the only thing to do was get back to Africa.

"Swimming in the sea with a Mae West is very different from the kind of swim you take for pleasure. You are so low in the water that you can hardly see anything, and even the South Atlantic was cold and overwhelmingly vast. I'd been swimming for about an hour and a half and was feeling cold and depressed when I saw two more fishing boats heading for the spot where my plane had gone down. I began to swim like mad in their direction. I was so nervous then that I thought I'd never get to them. Then all at once I was seized by a nauseating fear—I thought I saw a shark or barracuda quite near. It may have been a porpoise. I took out my shark knife. Whatever it was shark or barracuda, I'd make a fight for it. It was surely the most terrible feeling anyone can have—to have swum so far and be so tired and then be faced by a new and unexpected danger like that.

"I began to understand why they had given us those shark knives. They certainly would not have done this unless they knew that there were unpleasant fish in these waters. Nothing materialized, so I swam on, and presently—it was about an hour later—the fishing boats came quite close. I could see they were going to pick me up and was feeling good. The crew launched a small boat and within a few minutes they had hauled me on board."

"And that about completes our story of a carrier mission," concluded Mac. "There is one thing that stands out of it all—that it was a successful campaign, and it proves above everything else that carrier-based aircraft are ideal for supporting invasion troops.

It may be a kind of shape of things to come—the third front I mean. If it is, we hope we Red Rippers will be there to do some more—with our Wildcats, our jukebox, and the crewmen who helped us to do our job. We'd like to have the Padre along with us too—the same gang doing a bigger and better job!"

"And here's to all Red Rippers, past, present and future," said Tommy Booth somberly. "I'm sorry that I am in the past at the moment, but I've a feeling the old squadron will get along swell with Mac."

"And here's to Mr. Grumman and his Wildcats," came in Ed. "If he ever makes a better fighter plane, may we fly it."

About the Authors

MALCOLM T. WORDELL was born in Dartmouth, Massachusetts, in 1911. He graduated from the U.S. Naval Academy and was commissioned an ensign in 1935. He was designated a naval aviator in 1939. Assigned to VF-41, he served in the North African campaign, leading a flight of Wildcat fighters during the first mission of Operation Torch. Wordell was shot down and imprisoned but was soon repatriated. Given command of VF-44, Wordell served in the Pacific, where he became an ace, eventually scoring nine kills. He retired from active service in 1946 with the rank of captain. After a life in private industry, he died in 1996.

EDWIN N. SEILER was born in New York in 1918. He graduated from Princeton University with majors in English and music. He enlisted in the Navy in 1940 and was designated a naval aviator in 1941. Assigned to VF-41, he participated in the North African campaign. Later assigned to VF-44, he went to the Pacific and participated in several campaigns until he was killed in action in January 1945 while strafing enemy targets on Okinawa. Recommended for the Medal of Honor for his last mission, Seiler received a posthumous Silver Star.

KEITH AYLING was born in England in 1898. A prolific writer, he produced several accounts of aerial action involving Royal Air Force and American aviators during World War II.